THE FIFTH STAR

THE

FIFTH STAR

★ ★ ★ ★ ★

HIGH COMMAND
IN AN ERA OF
GLOBAL WAR

George M. Hall

PRAEGER

Westport, Connecticut
London

Library of Congress Cataloging-in-Publication Data

Hall, George M. (George Morgan).
  The fifth star : high command in an era of global war / George M. Hall.
    p.   cm.
  Includes bibliographical references and index.
  ISBN 0-275-94802-1
    1. Generals—United States—Biography.   2. Admirals—United States—
Biography.   3. United States—History, Military—20th century.   4. United States—
History, Naval—20th century.   5. Command of troops.   I. Title.
E745.H35   1994
355'.0092'273—dc20
[B]   93-32765

British Library Cataloguing in Publication Data is available.

Library of Congress Catalog Card Number: 93-32765
ISBN: 0-275-94802-1

First published in 1994

Praeger Publishers, 88 Post Road West, Westport, CT 06881
An imprint of Greenwood Publishing Group, Inc.

Printed in the United States of America

The paper used in this book complies with the
Permanent Paper Standard issued by the National
Information Standards Organization (Z39.48-1984).

10 9 8 7 6 5 4 3 2 1

In memory of the thousands of American and British servicemen who perished at the hands of their captors or who died afterward as a result of mistreatment in prisoner of war camps.

CONTENTS

ILLUSTRATIONS

PHOTOGRAPHS

FIGURES

PREFACE

This book started as a collection of biographical sketches with little more cohesion than that each principal had worn, or had the authority to wear, five stars. Underlying the idea was the hope that it might encourage better understanding among the services as the importance of joint operations grows. This purpose is still valid; but in the process of the research, I realized there was a larger story to be told. The period of 1890–1953—for Anglo-Saxons if not the world—was a modern *Iliad;* and the principals in this book, along with both Roosevelts and Sir Winston Churchill, had developed into something of a mortal parallel of an extended Olympian family.

The motivation for writing it arose from three sources. The first occurred growing up as a navy brat. At the time I assumed all admirals were crusty and austere. Then I noticed some effusive comments Fleet Admiral Nimitz had written to my father, a navy commander, on a photograph of the surrender ceremony. In part, Nimitz wrote, "From one *Skipjack* skipper to another." My father served on that submarine before and during World War I. But as he had been an enlisted petty officer at the time, I asked him what Nimitz meant by "skipper." He told me that the admiral himself had once commanded the *Skipjack* and later moved up to division (flotilla) commander. Then one day, my father decided to take it out for a short cruise on his own initiative. As he returned to dock, Lieutenant Nimitz was standing there and said: "That's very good seamanship, Mr. Hall. You're confined to quarters for thirty days." Thus, while Admiral Nimitz was a stickler for most regulations, he also appreciated initiative in subordinates; he could remember casual events many years afterward and have a little fun. In the process, he endeared himself to millions of sailors.

The second event was less auspicious. While at the preparatory school for the Military Academy, I noticed a poster in the supply room that read "Stairway to the Stars." On the first riser was "West Point," on the next

"Second Lieutenant," and so forth until, near the top, five stars blazed like a royal diadem. The year was 1953, and some wag had inked in "President" over the stars, obviously referring to Eisenhower. Not to be outdone, another wag added "God" above that, apparently referring to MacArthur. I still laugh at this because there is a grain of truth to most philosophical humor. MacArthur was not immortal, but he was one of those rare military figures that will be remembered and written about for millennia.

The third was an assignment to the general officer management function about twelve years ago. I had a number of photographic portraits of some historic general officers framed and displayed on the wall, each with an appropriate quotation. Unwittingly, that display proved to be an outline of sorts for the manuscript.

Those portraits were placed in order of date of rank, a rule that carries here with two exceptions, primarily for editorial reasons. The first shifts the chapter on Arnold to just after Marshall and King, because Arnold served as a member of the joint chiefs. The second shifts the chapter on Halsey to follow those on MacArthur and Nimitz. This places the three principals who served in the Pacific theater in sequence, followed by the two associated with the European theater, namely Eisenhower and Bradley.

One last point. As this book went to press, the British government revealed that on December 4, 1941, British military intelligence intercepted a message to the Japanese ambassador in Washington, D.C., instructing him to destroy all codes. Because Churchill did *not* inform Roosevelt of this message, the speculation is that had he done so, Pearl Harbor might have been avoided and the course of World War II changed. That was not likely. Japan had already decided to declare war against the United States. The only thing that *might* have happened would have been to direct a higher state of alert at Pearl Harbor.

But as it was imperative for the Japanese to disable the American fleet at the outset, there was no way they would have been deterred. Moreover, the Japanese invasion fleet was only two days sailing away from its launch point, and Admiral Nagumo had orders to proceed with the attack unless detected by December 5th. Now it would have taken at least two days for the intelligence from Great Britain to translate into action twelve thousand miles away. At that, Halsey's two-carrier task force would have had to search for Nagumo in the dark of night, December 6–7, find him, and sink at least three of the six Japanese carriers without a declaration of war. That is truly wishful thinking.

In any event, writing this book took twice the time anticipated, but the compensation was an extension of the period in which I had the privilege of sharing the company of so illustrious a group. On the other hand, when musing on great men as these, it is always depressing to realize how badly one comes up short.

ACKNOWLEDGMENTS

I wish to thank the following individuals for information that was not readily available in published form to support the book, and for their assistance in providing photographs: the late General James A. Van Fleet, U.S. Army, retired, a classmate of generals Eisenhower and Bradley; Mary Beth Straight and Dorothy Sappington at the U.S. Naval Institute, Annapolis, Maryland; and Alice K. Juda at the library of the Naval War College, Newport, Rhode Island. There must be a special place in heaven reserved for librarians. They are the most unselfish and helpful of all the professions, and it is always a humbling experience to work with them.

My thanks to Karen Stewart at the Naval Academy Alumni Association, Annapolis, Maryland; Jane H. Price, archivist at the U.S. Naval Academy, Annapolis, Maryland; John Slonaker, Louise A. Arnold-Friend, and Michael J. Winey of the U.S. Army Military History Institute, Carlisle Barracks, Pennsylvania; and Edward J. Drea at the U.S. Army Center for Military History, Washington, D.C.

My thanks also to Robert Ellis at the National Archives Trust Fund Board; Randall W. Becker of the Grand Encampment of Knights Templer and Bob Proudly of the Masonic Service Organization; Rita Gonzalaz and Joe Brewer at the government reference section of the University of Arizona library; and Dr. Stephen Grove in the Historian's Office and Suzanne Christoff, Archivist, at the U.S. Military Academy, West Point, New York. Mrs. Christoff went the second mile on several occasions.

At the Greenwood Publishing Group, Dan Eades was the individual who passed the manuscript through the "in print" gate, Penny Sippel did the honors of production, and Vincent Peciulis labored over the manuscript with high diligence.

THE
FIFTH
STAR

PART I

THE PRINCIPALS

In the United States, the use of the five-star insignia of rank is unique to the period 1944–1981, but the authority for it goes back to March 3, 1799. In that year, Congress authorized the grade of *General of the Armies of the United States* on a one-time basis for a single individual in lieu of the then senior rank of lieutenant general. The intent was to honor General Washington. After the Civil War, this title was revived to honor General Ulysses Grant.[1] A similar act was passed for two distinguished admirals, David G. Farragut and David C. Porter, who were each designated *Admiral of the Navy*. In 1899, following the Spanish-American War, this title was also bestowed on Commodore George Dewey.

Twenty years later, on September 3, 1919, Congress gave the president authority to promote General John J. Pershing to *General of the Armies of the United States,* the same rank that had been given to Washington, except that in practice it was shortened to *General of the Armies.* And because another provision of law authorized recipients of these special ranks to designate their own insignia, this meant that Pershing could choose any number of stars to wear. He chose the four he already had, but the authority to wear five was permanent. The effect of this act also granted Pershing full pay and allowances for life.

Then in World War II, the odd protocol of American four-star officers commanding five-star equivalents in the British armed services more or less forced the United States to reinstitute these higher ranks on a more formal basis.[2] The new titles were *General of the Army* and *Fleet Admiral.*[3] The process of obtaining this legislation took more than a year; and in the end, eight billets were authorized: four for the army (including the army air force) and four for the navy. Seven promotions were made immediately, with the following dates of rank:

Fleet Admiral William D. Leahy	December 15, 1944
General of the Army George C. Marshall	December 16, 1944
Fleet Admiral Ernest J. King	December 17, 1944
General of the Army Douglas MacArthur	December 18, 1944
Fleet Admiral Chester W. Nimitz	December 19, 1944
General of the Army Dwight D. Eisenhower	December 20, 1944
General of the Army Henry H. Arnold	December 21, 1944

The fourth navy billet was given to Admiral William F. Halsey, Jr., several months after World War II ended, specifically on December 11, 1945. In 1946, the act was amended to permit all of the incumbents to receive full pay and allowances for life, whether or not they were serving in duty assignments. In 1947, General Arnold's rank was redesignated *General of the Air Force,* concurrent with creation of the air force as a separate armed service.

The last of the five-star promotions was granted shortly after the Korean conflict began. General Omar N. Bradley, then serving as the first formal chairman of the Joint Chiefs of Staff, was promoted to *General of the Army* on September 20, 1950. This was a private, not a public, bill and stated explicitly that it was in recognition of Bradley's services, not because he was chairman of the joint chiefs. This was the government's way of avoiding a precedent and, at the same time, placing the chairman on a par with MacArthur who was in command in the Far East.

Several other points on senior rank are germane to this book. First, admirals are called *flag officers,* whereas generals are called *general officers.* Aides for flag officers are called *flag lieutenants* and *flag secretaries.* For generals, the titles are *aide-de-camp* and *secretary of the general staff.*

Second, the senior officer of the navy has the title of *Chief of Naval Operations;* of the army (and the air force), *Chief of Staff.* The latter is confusing because senior commanders in all the services usually have a subordinate primary staff officer with the same title.

Third, until well into this century two-star rank was normally the highest permanent grade to which an officer could be promoted. Any rank above this was considered temporary and usually went with a specific job. Upon leaving that job or retiring, the individual reverted to his two-star rank.[4] Think of it as a statutory yo-yo.

Fourth, until recent times the navy did not have a one-star admiral. When a captain was promoted to flag rank, he immediately put on two stars. Rear admirals were then divided into "lower half" and "upper half" for administration, but this distinction was of little consequence in practical matters.[5] Today, lower-half rear admirals wear only one star; upper half, two stars, and the pay is different. If all of this sounds entangling, it is.

Unfortunately, there's more. A flag officer is so called because that officer displays his flag on a ship but does not command it. The flag officer commands a fleet or flotilla of ships for operations, while captains command each ship therein. Hence, while an admiral gives mission-type orders, the admiral does not tell captains how to run their ships. However, a ship's captain may have flag command of more than one ship, in which case the captain runs his own ship *and* gives mission-type orders to the others under his command. The navy calls his ship a flagship but does not fly a flag on it because the captain is not an admiral and therefore doesn't have one to fly. Furthermore, the captain of a ship can hold any rank from ensign to captain; but regardless of rank, he is *always* addressed by his officers and men as "Captain," even though he signs written orders with his actual rank. All four admirals in this tale commanded ships long before they reached the rank of captain and had flagships before reaching admiral.

The reason for this muddle is simple. In land operations, higher headquarters are easily separated from fighting units; any old farmhouse, trailer truck, tent, or chateau will suffice. This is not true for the navy. At sea, headquarters are superimposed on fighting ships and therefore must be maintained separately and so identified in order to prevent undue interference in the operation of the host.[6]

This leaves only the confusion that results from army versus navy ranks, which are also called grades. They are:

Army	*Navy*
Second Lieutenant	Ensign
First Lieutenant	Lieutenant Junior Grade
Captain	Lieutenant
Major	Lieutenant Commander
Lieutenant Colonel	Commander
Colonel	Captain

The term *lieutenant* is also used informally to designate the chief subordinates of a senior officer, as in Russell F. Weigley's *Eisenhower's Lieutenants*. This book is the story of a nation's lieutenants in an era of great crisis—the ten men who, from among the ten thousand who have worn stars in this century, were given the privilege of wearing five.

1

GLOBAL OLYMPUS

States are as their men are;
they grow out of human character.

—Plato

Arguably, the *Iliad* retains its fascination because of the interplay between gods and mortals in time of war and because it focuses sharply on the character of these players. The warriors were fearsome, but the gods could beam themselves to any location instantly and influence the outcome of a battle. They were somewhat prescient yet argued among themselves incessantly even when their purposes were similar. Thus, despite their immortal attributes, the denizens of Olympus acted more like humans than theological entities.

The first half of this century witnessed a conflict similar in some ways to the *Iliad*. Homer's original spanned ten continuous years of fighting; the modern revival, roughly ten discontinuous years, at least for the United States. The original was fought for a considerably less significant objective, namely, to retrieve Helen; but this must be recognized as a literary device. There really was a Troy, and the Athenian empire invaded it on at least one occasion. As Troy was located at the crossroads of the known world at the time, it's a safe bet that the war was fought to secure a strategic outpost, not to rescue a lady, no matter how beautiful she may have been. It was no different eight centuries later when Athens, under Pericles' leadership, took on Sparta and her allies in what became known as the Peloponnesian War, a conflict aptly chronicled by Thucydides.

On the other hand, the poet Robert Graves once speculated that Troy might have abducted Helen and thus gave Greece the excuse she needed to mount the invasion. Interestingly, when the United States was looking for a reason of state to depose Manuel Noriega from the dictatorship of Panama, the critical moment in the political decision making process occurred when the Panamanian Defense Forces abducted a naval officer and his wife for questioning. The officer was repeatedly kicked in the groin, but his wife was only threatened. Yet as argued persuasively by Bob Woodward in *The Commanders,* it was the plight of the wife that turned political heads.[1]

More importantly, while the main players in this modern Iliad may have lacked the immortality of their ancient forebears, they did wage war to preserve something that was immortal: the right of nations and individuals to self determination, in a word, justice. Justice is represented by another and equally mythical lady, this one holding a balance scale. Moreover, the navy still uses feminine terms to refer informally to the ships that protected this ideal, most notably the carrier *Lady Lexington.* Admiral King, who normally detested any hint of sentimentality, admitted that he came to love her. Finally, the shield of the Military Academy has for more than a century bourn the likeness of Pallas Athena, the goddess of war and a key player in the *Iliad.*

But should legends, even of this caliber, be cited in historical writing? At least one historian of note, who was also a major player in the global wars of this century, seems to think so. In telling about the early history of England and the Arthurian legend, Sir Winston Churchill said:

> If we could see exactly what happened we should find ourselves in the presence of a theme as well founded, as inspired, and as inalienable from the inheritance of mankind as the *Odyssey* or the Old Testament. It is all true, or ought to be; and more or better besides. And whenever men are fighting against barbarism, tyranny, and massacre, for freedom, law, and honour, let them remember that the fame of their deeds, even though they themselves be exterminated, may perhaps be celebrated as long as the world rolls round.[2]

To restate the case, then, when the issue is ideological and thus transcends mortality, the gods and mankind are on common ground. In ancient times, this took the form of myths. Today, historiography has displaced myth as the parameter of literature, but even that cannot gainsay the story to be told when very great men rise to the challenge of Armageddon.

Furthermore, technology gave man at least some of the powers once reserved for the gods. First, many of the principals operated from their capitals and were seldom exposed to fire. Second, if they could not relocate instantly, the airplane reduced the time required to a day or two, and the radio transmitted decisions at the speed of light. Third, the lethality and scope of modern weapons, culminating in the nuclear arsenal, gave the incumbents of high command more influence than Zeus ever dreamed of. Finally, one of the principals—General Douglas MacArthur—put himself in the line of fire so many times without incurring so much as a scratch, that he became not "a fugitive from the law of averages" but exempt from them.[3]

Carrying the analogy further, the conduct of war during this era was something of an extended family affair. Cousins Theodore Roosevelt, Franklin Delano Roosevelt, Sir Winston Churchill, and Douglas MacArthur were all descended from the same woman—Sarah Barney Belcher of Taunton, Massachusetts.[4] They in turn "adopted" their favorite military protégés, who in turn "adopted" their own lieutenants to the point where all ten of the five-star generals and admirals were part of the same family in the Olympian sense.

A single incident illustrates how closely they came to operate like their ancient forebears. In the late summer of 1944, Admiral Halsey discovered that the central Philippines were less well defended than assumed and radioed MacArthur to suggest moving up the invasion date by two months. MacArthur agreed and signaled the joint chiefs—Leahy, Marshall, King, and Arnold. The latter, who were at dinner during the second Quebec conference, discussed it briefly and nodded approval within the hour.

Who, then, played the role of latter-day Zeus? It was probably Theodore Roosevelt, an individual with multifarious talents, the youngest President ever, a prolific author with eighteen thousand pages to his credit, a bully Jefferson, a prime mover and a fighter, and the progenitor of nearly every child's favorite stuffed animal. He died in 1919, but his work and his decisions cast a long shadow, especially his championship of what became the modern navy and his mentorship of General Pershing. His ghost or spirit, as the case may be, permeates Washington more than any other president, with the possible exception of Abraham Lincoln. While President, he admitted to that exception, and in his Nobel laureate acceptance speech, he said:

> We must ever bear in mind that the great end in view is righteousness, justice as between man and man, nation and nation, the chance to lead our lives on a somewhat higher level, with a broader spirit of brotherly love for one another. Peace is generally good in itself, but it is never the highest good unless it comes as the handmaiden of righteousness; and it becomes a very evil thing if it serves merely as a mask for cowardice and sloth, or as an instrument to further the ends of despotism or anarchy.[5]

Inherent in this analogy is a preference for the great-man theory over its great-events counterpart. The great-events argument holds that mankind is more or less a prisoner of fate, although a handful of forceful individuals can sometimes nudge events slightly left or right. By contrast, the great-man viewpoint posits that a few decisive individuals sculpt history. Perhaps the answer is that during peacetime, the collective exercise of individual freedom operates with a kind of statistical determinacy, typically ignoring the consequences of excessive idealism, naiveté, mounting debt, and other assorted maladies, until the force of the consequences generates a crisis. At that point the bleating Cassandras metamorphose into purposeful leaders—Churchill is the classic example—upon whom the fate of nations rests.

This modern Iliad unfolded in three acts, culminating respectively in World War I, World War II, and the Korean conflict. Act I began in 1890. In that year, Frederick Jackson Turner wrote that the American frontier no longer existed. The Indian wars ended with the massacre at Wounded Knee, to which Pershing was a bystander, and left the army with little to do. Concurrently, Alfred Thayer Mahan published *The Influence of Sea Power Upon History, 1660–1783*.[6] The British Admiralty immediately recognized the significance of that book, which in turn whetted the U.S. appetite and gave Americans a substitute at sea for the decaying army. In short, the spirit of manifest destiny yearned for a new outlet.

Thus when the battleship *Maine* blew up in Havana harbor, William Randolph Hearst cabled his correspondent on site: "You supply the pictures; I'll supply the war."[7] The growing navy flexed its muscles against a second-rate competitor and what was left of the army mobilized for deployment overseas.

The war itself was brief and the casualties minor. The significance was the acquisition of the Philippines and the concurrent annexation of Hawaii, which served as a shuttle base to maintain military influence in the Pacific basin. Then within a few years, the United States also gained suzerainty over the Canal Zone in Panama.[8] Of these new possessions, the Philippines were prominent; and as a harbinger, the military commander Arthur MacArthur, father of Douglas MacArthur, bickered endlessly with the civil commissioner William Howard Taft. For his troubles, the elder Mac-Arthur was sacked. Taft's explanation stretches to cover the younger Mac-Arthur's fate fifty years later:

> An officer who has exercised both civil and military power and who is called upon to surrender a portion of his power to another cannot, unless he is free from the ordinary characteristics of human nature, altogether divorce himself from the habit of exercising civil power and the tendency to look with disfavor upon what seems to be a curtailing of his power.[9]

This modest U.S. empire was not without its problems. The United States inherited the Moro insurrectionists, who had railed against the former Spanish rulers and now took aim at their new host. In the process, Pershing, Douglas MacArthur, Marshall, and Arnold would serve early tours there. Pershing, in particular, established his reputation by almost single-handedly doing what hundreds of thousands of Americans would fail to do in Vietnam sixty years later. His performance inspired Theodore Roosevelt to promote him directly to brigadier general three years later, whereupon he went back and again demonstrated his prowess on a larger scale.

In time, the insurrection abated, and the military outlook turned to defense against potential external threats, primarily Japan. In 1915, this refocus allowed First Lieutenant "Hap" Arnold to observe First Lieutenant George C. Marshall direct a defending "army"—as its acting chief of staff—in a war game. The scene was the Bataan peninsula and Corregidor island, one that replayed with deadly consequences a quarter-century later. The import of the moment, however, was that Arnold instantly surmised he had just met a future Chief of Staff, telling his wife, but not the object, of his discovery. Arnold and Marshall became fast friends and fellow hunters. When Marshall did become Chief of Staff he returned the unspoken compliment in spades, making Arnold the first air force Chief of Staff.[10]

Meanwhile, the navy expanded from what was the globe's sixth largest fleet in 1900 to the second largest by 1909, trailing only Great Britain. Part of this spurt was heralded by Roosevelt's "Great White Fleet." This impressive armada of battleships—capital ships were painted white in those days—sailed around the world to give credence to Mahan's thesis, although of the future fleet admirals only Halsey sailed with it.

This expansion gave junior navy officers a leg up on the army because promotions were doled out at a faster pace. The result was that the four navy principals progressed steadily through the various grades of rank and gained significant experience as flag officers before global war erupted. By contrast, all but one of the generals languished in lower grades, except for brief temporary promotions during World War I. They would leap to senior rank only at the end. Accordingly, it took the army more time to organize its clout in World War II.

Concurrent with this manifest destiny for the global warrior were the early attempts to manage it more effectively. Before this era, the army and the navy were each run by entrenched bureaus. The army had a commanding general, but in practice the incumbent commanded nothing but a desk. Theodore Roosevelt's Secretary of War Elihu Root superimposed a general staff system over the army bureaus and changed the title of "Commanding General" to "Chief of Staff." The reform was moderately effective in some ways but would not be fully implemented until Marshall was struck with lightning a few days after Pearl Harbor.

In parallel, the navy had a commander of the U.S. fleet, who did command ships but was at sea and beholden to the bureau chiefs for everything he needed except sea water. Ten years after Root's reforms, Taft's Secretary of the Navy George von Lengerke Meyer tried the same tack by creating the post of Chief of Naval Operations (CNO) and four division chiefs; but his successor, Josephus Daniels, let the billets atrophy except for the CNO, which Daniels emasculated. Hence, these bureaucracies would exacerbate unpreparedness, stymie war planning, and in general make the job later performed by the principals all the more difficult, although on the navy side Leahy and King as bureau chiefs helped perpetuate it.

Unfortunately, the United States was not alone in flexing its new muscle. In 1905, the Japanese under Admiral Heilachrino Togo, in his flagship *Mikasa,* sank most of the Russian fleet in the battle of Tsushima. Nimitz was nearby on observer duty—as were Pershing and MacArthur—and came to have a lifelong respect for Togo and the Japanese, though he did not hesitate to wage war against them ruthlessly when it came to that. The same dual mind-set was true for MacArthur, as evinced by his benevolence and magnanimity while serving as proconsul of occupied Japan forty years later. By contrast, Leahy, King, and Halsey each developed an antipathy toward their future enemy early in the century.

Meanwhile on the other side of the globe, Kaiser Wilhelm II and his lieutenants, especially Count Alfred Schlieffen and, later, Helmuth von Moltke (the younger), were planning the conquest of western Europe and Russia, a plot unleashed in 1914 following the assassination of Archduke Ferdinand in Sarajevo. The ensuing mêlée consumed millions of lives well before the United States entered it, and that entry came by way of events in Mexico.

In 1916, Pancho Villa and his followers murdered eighteen Americans on a train within his own country and later raided Columbus, New Mexico, where they killed another fifteen before escaping across the border. This led to the famed, if ineffective, punitive expedition into Mexico under General Pershing. It was ineffective because Pershing's hands were tied. The United States did not want war with Mexico, and the Mexican government's tolerance of the American military presence was limited. Nevertheless, the general turned in a sterling performance under the circumstances, gained experience mobilizing and commanding a comparatively large body of men, and won the respect of President Woodrow Wilson for not trespassing into political prerogatives.

Then came the Zimmermann telegram. The German foreign minister sent a wire to his ambassador in Mexico, authorizing the latter to negotiate with Mexico to join with Germany in a war against the United States. He dangled the return of "lost" territories, primarily Texas, as payment in kind. The telegram was intercepted by British intelligence and in light of the unrestricted submarine warfare then commenced by Germany, the declaration of war followed in train.

Pershing was selected as the commanding general of the American Expeditionary Force (AEF). MacArthur, serving as a major on the army general staff in Washington, was influential in that decision and proposed a "rainbow" division (the 42nd), comprising various national guard units from many states, for immediate deployment. In the process, he was promoted to temporary colonel and made the division's chief of staff.

The bloodiness of World War I was due largely to technology and the commendable trait of most military leaders to persevere, combined with a regrettable tendency to do so with little ingenuity in battle or concern for vast casualties. During the Civil War, this technology favored the offensive, namely, railroads to shift troops and the telegraph to control widespread operations. By the time of World War I, the machine gun, which made its appearance in the Civil War, and heavy artillery came to favor the defensive. The tank and the airplane were too embryonic to offset this imbalance, although twenty years later those two weapons would reverse the picture again by reinvigorating mobile warfare.

Within that intensity, MacArthur—he looms large throughout the era—became the most decorated soldier in American history, winning two Distinguished Service Crosses, seven Silver Stars, a Distinguished Service Medal, and a cache of other awards, in all, seven rows of ribbons on his tunic. This collection would nearly double in World War II, at which point he stopped wearing any of them. He was promoted to brigadier general and later given command of the entire division. The nomination for the second star fell only to the unexpected early armistice.

Elsewhere, Marshall served as Pershing's operations officer in the grade of temporary colonel, barely missing *his* first star because of the armistice. Arnold, Eisenhower, and Bradley tried to get overseas, but each remained tethered to stateside assignments. The navy also saw action, mainly in convoy and antisubmarine warfare; but of the four admirals only Halsey saw much action. Of more significance was the friendship that developed between Commander Leahy, then serving as a staff officer in Main Navy, and the Assistant Secretary of the Navy Franklin D. Roosevelt, who also struck up a friendship with Commander Halsey.

The armistice marked the end of act I but as countless historians have pointed out, negotiating that armistice just before the German army could have been defeated decisively, and then imposing massive reparations, merely set the stage for act II. That next war would claim sixty million lives and engulf nearly the entire globe. Unfortunately, the United States developed a naive idea of what it takes to win a major conflict. Most

Official U.S. Army photograph. Courtesy U.S. Army Military History Institute.

1. Pershing presenting the Distinguished Service Cross to MacArthur. Colonel George C. Marshall may have been standing off to the side, and down in an adjacent division was an artillery captain named Harry S Truman. They would later come to see larger issues from different perspectives.

Americans believed that Pershing simply marched in with the AEF and won a war that France and Great Britain were on the verge of losing.

That simply was not the case. It was a war of attrition, meaning the allied powers outlasted Germany and her remaining allies from the former Triple Alliance. The addition of American forces may have tipped the balance on the scales, but the combat actions of those units were comparatively minor and were fought only during the closing months of a war that rivaled hell for more than four years.

In any event, the United States "returned to normalcy," and most of the temporary wartime promotions were rescinded. MacArthur kept his star by virtue of becoming Superintendent of the Military Academy; but Marshall, Arnold, Eisenhower, and Bradley all reverted to captain or major, so that they could tread anew the somnolent path to senior rank. Pershing served as Chief of Staff of the Army from 1921 through 1924, with Marshall as his aide. Afterward he became the military's elder statesman, initially as director of the American Battle Monuments Commission. In that capacity, Eisenhower replaced Marshall as the general's assistant, then went on to serve under MacArthur for nine years. And Bradley would serve under Marshall when the latter was Assistant Commandant of the Infantry School at Fort Benning, Georgia. The paths of these officers crossed and recrossed many times during this formative period.

Needless to say, the country assumed there would be no further need for Pershing or any successor. Wilson's moral argument for entering the war—to make the world safe for democracy—seemed to prevail. America signed several multinational arms limitation agreements, notwithstanding that the United States neither ratified the peace treaty nor became a member of the League of Nations. Accordingly, the strength of the armed services decayed, the army more so than the navy, with the Great Depression only making things worse.

In the interim, MacArthur—completing his term as Chief of Staff of the Army and wearing four stars—marched into President Franklin Roosevelt's office and, after expressing his concern over inadequate military funding in vain, railed, "When we lose the next war, and an American boy with an enemy bayonet through his belly and an enemy foot on his dying throat spits out his last curse, I want that name not to be MacArthur, but Roosevelt."[11] Roosevelt, for once truly stung, pleaded, "You must not talk that way to the President." MacArthur apologized and in the process wrung out a few more dollars for the army. Shortly afterward, Roosevelt extended MacArthur's term as chief of staff for a fifth year.

MacArthur wasn't the only officer who knew how to employ dramatics to advance the affairs of state, although very few moderns have ever been able to outdo Douglas in this regard. Once during a Congressional hearing on army air-corps funding, Arnold arranged to have a squadron of planes fly directly over the capital at low altitude. When a senator asked the reason for this impudence, Arnold replied, "Gentlemen, what you just heard was the entire air force of this country."

Unfortunately, the military leaders of Germany and Japan encountered no such difficulties. Their countries willingly paid for new technology as a means of gaining empire on the quick. Germany, it seems, had a streak of conquest in her ethos and was bent on avenging the humiliation she suffered at the end of World War I. Hitler would demand that the degrading armistice with Vichy France be signed in the same railroad car that witnessed the German surrender in 1918. In the other hemisphere, Japan's ambitions, perhaps more economic than militaristic, also grew out of control; but she suffered from geographical dwarfism in matters of land and raw resources. Military conquests—under the euphemism *Greater East Asia Coprosperity Sphere*—were to be the means to rectify that scarcity. Japan invaded Manchuria in 1931 and took on China proper in 1937.

Meanwhile, Italy tried her luck in Africa, and Germany struck Poland on September 1, 1939. That same day George C. Marshall assumed his duties as Chief of Staff. He would hold that job for more than six years, the only senior-ranked individual in World War II, American or British, to keep the same job from beginning to end. But Pearl Harbor was twenty-seven months away, and in that interim no man ever worked harder or more diligently than Marshall to prepare his country for a war that the majority of its citizens presumed would never materialize.

And so Armageddon came. Yet it should be recognized that in terms of the battlefield, the United States and Great Britain played only secondary roles. America did supply roughly half of the implements of war used by the Allied powers, but the brunt of the fighting was borne by the Soviet Union and China. The majority of the German and Japanese forces were immersed on those fronts and for a much longer period of time than was spent resisting the Anglo-Saxons. A few statistics prove the point, and these do not include the thirty million deaths incurred in the Stalinist purges and the Holocaust: [12]

	Military Fatalities	Civilian Fatalities	Total Fatalities	Percent
United States	292,000	6,000	298,000	1.0%
British Com.	373,000	93,000	466,000	1.6%
China	1,310,000	650,000	1,960,000	19.5%
U.S.S.R.	11,000,000	7,000,000	18,000,000	60.7%
Other	852,000	8,141,000	8,993,000	17.2%
Total	13,827,000	15,890,000	29,717,000	100.0%

To a man risking his life on the field of battle, these numbers are meaningless. To men directing the efforts of a nation in the context of a global
situation, they cannot be ignored. Churchill realized this from the beginning and was convinced that on the basis of comparative national power
alone, the Allies would eventually overwhelm the German and Japanese
upstarts. Years later, Hollywood dramatized this abstraction in *Battle of
the Bulge*. In that film the German commander of the assault force admits
his country will lose the war, pointing to a piece of birthday cake found
on a captured American soldier. He surmises that if the Allied forces could
ship that luxury with the same priority as ammunition, there was no way
Germany could resist indefinitely.

Still, the here and now of national interests, not global abstractions, are
what occupy the minds of statesmen and generals. Thus British and
American histories concentrate on the battlefronts the Allies shared and on
how they fought over priorities, not only the importance of the European
and Pacific theaters but also the strategy for defeating Germany first. Great
Britain and the American generals—MacArthur excepted—regarded the
Pacific as a distant lake. Not so the admirals. That was the theater where
they did most of their fighting.

Actually, the principals spent most of their time fighting each other. In
coalition warfare, heads of state and senior military commanders scrim-
mage about nine hours in ten. Their wartime diaries and journals attest to
this, as do the minutes from the many wartime conferences. Still, there
was a war to be fought. As mentioned, Marshall groomed Arnold as his
nearly coequal air Chief of Staff. MacArthur, retired by 1937 and on the
payroll of the Philippines, was recalled to active duty to command all
forces in the Southwest Pacific. And Eisenhower emerged from obscurity
to become the Supreme Allied Commander in the European theater, finding in Bradley a dependable senior field leader.

On the navy side, Admiral King, who had been banished to a limbo
assignment because he antagonized too many colleagues (Leahy included),
was pronounced rehabilitated and made Commander in Chief of the U.S.
Fleet. A few months later Roosevelt added Chief of Naval Operations to
King's job description, whereby King held the most powerful military
position ever created in the United States. Independent of that, Nimitz
was pulled from his desk in Main Navy and sent to the Pacific with literal
instructions to stay there until the war was won. He in turn came to rely
on Admiral Halsey as his chief fighter, although Admiral Raymond
Spruance later proved to be Halsey's equal.

The three service chiefs—Marshall, King, and Arnold—then formed
themselves into the first edition of the Joint Chiefs of Staff.[13] Shortly afterward, they created a partnership of sorts with their British counterparts in
what became known as the Combined Chiefs of Staff.[14] But because the
joint chiefs adopted a rule of unanimity to support decisions, they bickered

endlessly in defense of their respective services. Roosevelt, who was not inclined to manage military consortiums on a daily basis, recalled Admiral Leahy to active duty from the latter's ambassadorship to Vichy France, to serve as his personal chief of staff and also as informal chairman of the joint chiefs. Fortunately, Leahy was the most patient among the principals and, in the process, worked a few near miracles largely forgotten today, although Harry Hopkins engineered a great deal of the groundwork, in this respect, before Leahy came on board.

In spite of the often bitter comments they wrote down about each other in their diaries and journals, the principals and their colleagues kept up a banter that would have made the boys on Mount Olympus envious. Arnold pulled outrageous practical jokes on Marshall, initially causing him to rage and then break down in laughter.[15] Next, when Leahy was on a trip with the president to Canada, the train stopped by a lake to let the passengers do a little fishing. The admiral was photographed with rod and reel in dress blue uniform. Afterwards, he faced interrogation on how he got the fish to recognize his rank; none of them had ever had any luck with that tack.

And then there was the time a shipment of 420 planes had been sent to the South Pacific minus solenoids. Without solenoids, the guns were inoperative. The screaming radiograms so hounded Arnold that he sent three replacement sets by three different routes. Before the sets arrived, however, the radio traffic bellowed even louder, causing the aging but competent Secretary of War Henry Stimson to get involved personally. When Stimson became confused and called the solenoids "hemorrhoids," the ground-huggers immediately endorsed the War Department's acknowledgment that the air force could be a pain in the rear at times.

Some unusual friendships developed, too. The most notable cropped up between MacArthur and Halsey, notwithstanding that the admiral more than once set the general straight in front of his own staff. After the surrender ceremony on board the *Missouri*—Halsey's flagship—MacArthur turned to him and said, "Bill, when you leave, the Pacific will become just another ocean." Among courageous fighters, there is but one language.

Friendships and banter aside, two insidious problems arose among the growing body of admirals and generals and their British counterparts. First, seniority was nearly obliterated. One four-star admiral (Halsey) reported to another four-star (Nimitz) who reported to a third four-star (King) who occasionally came under the thumb of yet a fourth four-star (Leahy). Second, as mentioned in the prologue, four-star American generals and admirals were placed in command over British field marshals and the equivalents in the navy and air force, all of whom were considered to have five-star rank. Thus began the comic relief scene of World War II.

Roosevelt first proposed promoting Leahy to five-star rank, but the admiral demurred unless the same or equivalent promotions were also given

Official Department of Defense photograph. Courtesy National Archives.

2. The Allied "Board of Directors" at the Second Quebec Conference. Shortly after this photo-graph was taken, the Combined Chiefs of Staff toured the Plains of Abraham, where General Wolfe defeated the French in 1759. Some years later, MacArthur said that this battle was the inspiration for his strategy at Inchon.

to his fellow members on the Joint Chiefs of Staff. Roosevelt agreed, but then Marshall demurred. He was beholden to General of the Armies Pershing, who still cast a long shadow from his apartment at Walter Reed Army Hospital. Marshall therefore wanted nothing to detract from the status of his distinguished mentor. Roosevelt dropped the matter for a while, at least officially, but strangely enough the press did not. Various titles were bandied about, including the British "field marshal" and "admiral of the fleet." General Marshall balked again; he did not want to be called Field Marshal Marshall. Then Leahy was proposed for six-star rank, which he found abhorrent. Still, the protocol problem with the British got nastier, especially the internecine squabbles between Field Marshal Montgomery and General Eisenhower. Out of exasperation, Roosevelt reentered the fray (officially) and persuaded Congress to create eight five-star billets.

The army needed four: two for Marshall and Arnold on the Joint Chiefs of Staff, and two for Eisenhower and MacArthur as theater commanders. Thus after Leahy and King, this left two for the navy. Nimitz in the Pacific was an obvious candidate, but the Atlantic theater did not exist as a single entity; and moreover, by late 1944 antisubmarine warfare had been reduced to a science. Hence, King had to look one level down from Nimitz, meaning either Halsey or Spruance. The problem was that Halsey had blundered at Leyte Gulf and then twice unnecessarily sailed his fleet through typhoons, incurring much damage. Consequently, King and Nimitz agreed to hold the choice in abeyance until after the war. Then just before King turned the office over to Nimitz, Halsey got the nod. In compensation, Congress eventually granted Spruance permanent four-star rank with full pay and allowances for life.[16]

Of course, by the time these promotions were made, the war was winding down. President Roosevelt died four months later, three weeks before Germany surrendered. Vice President Truman succeeded to the office to find that the only significant military decision left was whether to invade Japan or to blockade, and then whether to bomb her into submission. The four admirals favored the blockade option, whereas the generals preferred invasion. And while they all knew about the atomic bomb, there was no assurance prior to mid-July 1945 that the bomb would work. Truman opted for invasion; and then after the successful test, elected to use the bomb in order to persuade Japan to surrender and thus avoid millions of casualties on both sides. He had the concurrence of the army but apparently did not consult with naval commanders, except perhaps with Admiral Leahy.

In quantitative terms, the atomic bomb was not especially significant. The arsenal held just two of them, each of which could inflict only a fraction of the devastation wrought by a single massive firebomb raid. On the other hand, the tremendous destructive power shoehorned into a small package made the weapon fearsome. Furthermore, the Japanese had no idea how many existed at the time. They surrendered, and so began act III.

In this act, the former sleeping giants—the United States and the Soviet Union—had come of age and wielded huge armed forces. No nation would ever challenge either of them directly, while the closest they came to war between themselves was the Cuban Missile Crisis in 1962. The problem was that the former ally had become a cold war adversary, using the *perceived* threat of communism as a global poison of sorts to do what the Axis powers had failed to do with pure military force. Against that backdrop, Pershing passed away in 1948 at the age of eighty-eight. Arnold died early in 1950, the victim of one heart attack too many. King had a stroke in 1947 and was hospitalized for most of his remaining nine years. Halsey and Nimitz retired in 1947. And although Leahy lingered as Truman's military chief of staff until 1949, it was more out of friendship than need.

It was a different story for the remaining four. Eisenhower served as Chief of Staff, president of Columbia University, the first Supreme Commander of NATO, and then on to the White House for eight years. MacArthur was appointed Supreme Commander of Allied Forces Pacific (SCAP) in occupied Japan. Bradley served two years as chief of the Veterans Administration, followed Eisenhower as Chief of Staff, then was appointed the first formal chairman of the Joint Chiefs of Staff. And Marshall served as ambassador to China, then Secretary of State, and finally—after a break of several years for medical reasons—as Secretary of Defense. As such, the outbreak of the Korean war in late June 1950 returned these four principals to the fore of international conflict.

The year before, the United States had dismissed Korea as of strategic interest. That was the theory. The ensuing invasion of South Korea by North Korean forces, commonly believed to be proxies of either Communist China or the Soviet Union (or both), put the superintending policy of containment to a practical test. The following were the governing factors: (1) the attack was unprovoked and without a declaration of war; (2) neither the Chinese nor the Russians were then engaged in active combat in Korea; and (3) Korea had been under U.S. protection until 1948, when, because of the Soviet refusal to agree to the disposition of that country, the temporary line of demarcation for the occupying forces became the boundary of two new countries. Furthermore, Truman was a decisive individual.

Within a few weeks, American and other troops were committed to the defense of South Korea, albeit under a United Nations aegis rather than a U.S. declaration of war. At first, these forces were pushed into a defensive perimeter around Pusan. MacArthur's envelopment at Inchon then forced the North Koreans to retreat from South Korea. This brilliant success posed the question whether to continue the war north of the 38th parallel.

The answer depended on the risk of China or the Soviet Union entering the war. The prevailing opinion was that they would not; and even when evidence pointed to the contrary, the offensive continued. But once the Chinese counteroffensive began in earnest, the United States realized that it would take more resources to win than it was willing to expend. As such, the bet was hedged. MacArthur wanted to pursue the war into China, at least with bombing runs; the government in Washington increasingly favored a draw.

Washington prevailed. It almost always does. It did not want a prolonged war on the Asian mainland against an enemy with five times the U.S. population and with whom it had few fundamental quarrels beyond ideology. Still, as the conflict congealed into a wobbly version of trench warfare, both sides sought the bargaining table. That, too, bogged down; hence, when Eisenhower was elected president in 1952, he promised to go to Korea in order to bring the war to an end. Ike chose to end it by telling the North Koreans to get serious about the negotiations or expect nuclear bombardment. The import of that message easily penetrated the sometimes inscrutable oriental mind; and accordingly, the North Koreans signed a permanent truce in July 1953.

From that point forward, America went into comparative decline. Its absolute power increased, but that of other nations increased at a faster rate. Moreover, it failed to recognize the overwhelming advantage in national power controlled by the Allied forces in World War II and the clear-cut moral and ethical distinctions between themselves and the Axis powers. Arguably this naiveté led to Vietnam, a debacle that goes beyond the scope of this book.

The United States had better luck on the lightly defended Caribbean island of Grenada and later in a two-day raid in Panama City; yet given the preponderance of U.S. forces committed to these small nearby areas, the outcomes were never in doubt. A more significant outcome was secured in the Persian Gulf conflict, but even that magnificent victory must take into account three factors: (1) twenty-eight nations were aligned against one; (2) the allies had six months to build up their forces on site without any hostile counteraction; and (3) the conflict ultimately was over access to oil, which made success imperative.[17]

Thus by September 1950, except for the brief reprise in the Persian Gulf forty years later, the golden age of Anglo-Saxon military force—deployed against unmistakably unwarranted aggression—passed into history. An unusual number of great men, political and military, had ascended to power to render a performance that was remarkable and comparatively free of the human failings that normally permeate affairs of state.

The balance of this part of the book offers a biographical sketch of each principal. Part 2 then compares the principals, with the understanding that it takes a benchmark of some kind to do so. The central theme of that benchmark, which is implied through the biographical sketches before being formalized, considers the leadership ability of each vis-à-vis the different levels of perspective that operate within armed conflicts.

Success in battle does not always portend a similar outcome in war. Therefore, it often takes a different kind of leadership to prevail against an opponent all the way to the surrender table than it does to defeat him on the battlefield. On the eve of his retreat from Moscow, Napoleon wryly admitted, "I beat the Russians every time, but that gets me nowhere."[18] Much later, in the aftermath of Vietnam, an American army colonel who was conversing with a North Vietnamese counterpart said, "You know, you never defeated us on the battlefield." The latter weighed this for a moment, and then replied, "That may be so, but it is also irrelevant."[19]

To put the case in another light, as the level of perspective rises from the heat of battle to the encompassing space and duration of a war, a nation's logistical and geographical leverage begin to supplant the heroism and the artillery of its captains. This perhaps explains why so few leaders do equally well at different tasks. They do not seem able to shift perspective readily; and even if they could, a different level will likely demand a mix of attributes different from that which their experience has honed.

Almost beyond question, General Douglas MacArthur was the most well endowed among these senior officers, and yet he was the one who fell the hardest—what the ancient Greek writers called a tragedy. If so, there must be reasons. The perspective developed in the second part of this book attempts to explain why. But first, let us recall the principals to center stage.

2

JOHN JOSEPH PERSHING

So the vital strength of his spirit won through, and he made his way beyond the walls of his country and ranged over the measureless whole, both in mind and spirit.
—Lucretius

General Pershing was a martinet. There's no disputing that point, but he was a martinet with many offsetting qualities, not the least of which was demonstrated in a sidelight of World War I. When the local requisitions program for the American Expeditionary Force bogged down, he arranged for his colorful friend Charles G. Dawes to be commissioned directly as a colonel to head the General Purchasing Board. Now Dawes did not understand much about soldiering, and he was a little too old by that point to learn it. Accordingly, Pershing knew enough not to force the issue. So when Dawes, newly promoted to brigadier general, finally rendered a passable salute, Pershing whispered, "Charlie, that's not a bad imitation, but next time move the cigar over to the other side."

Secretary of War Newton Baker was also puzzled. At the end of the war he gave up trying to understand how the same man could be such a brilliant strategist and at the same time have so much concern for unbuttoned buttons. Actually, Pershing was not that great a strategist, but he was a master of organization and operations and always kept the higher-level perspectives clearly in mind. His frequent attention to petty detail was part of a much larger view. Disciplined troops fought better and had fewer casualties. In short, he could see the forest, the trees—and, at times, nearly every leaf on those trees.

Perhaps this depth of perception explains why a single individual stands out prominently in a crisis. Events become focused, hence mandating that

Official U.S. Army photograph. Courtesy U.S. Army Military History Institute.
3. General of the Armies John J. Pershing. By Act of Congress, Pershing's fifth star was only a quick call away to a local silversmith. Pershing never made that call, but he retained the option until the day he passed away twenty-nine years later.

decision making should follow suit. Into this focal point steps a leader who must either sort out the complexities and make the momentous decisions or be labeled by history as mediocre at best. Few individuals seek that kind of responsibility; fewer yet can handle it. Of the latter, only a rare person of character can survive the exercise of that much power without succumbing to the ever-present leech of corruption. But General Pershing was one of those rare individuals.

The oldest of nine children, John Joseph Pershing was born in Laclede, Missouri, on January 13, 1860, to John and Elizabeth Pershing.[1] Like most rural children of the era, he learned farming and self-reliance at an early age. After graduating from high school, he turned to teaching because that line of work did not require a college degree in those days. He taught in both white and black schools, and in the process developed an open mind toward different races and cultures. But he also proved his backbone by quickly establishing his authority over roughneck boys his own size and a few years younger. Then he paid his way through two semesters of what was called normal school in Kirksville, Missouri, thus becoming a certified teacher. This awakened an intellect that at first aimed for the law. He sought an appointment to West Point as the educational means to that end. The four years at the academy changed that focus, although he would later earn a law degree and toy with going into practice.

As a cadet, Pershing seems to have been inspired by the superintendent, Colonel Wesley Merritt (later Major General), whom he took for a role model. Merritt was a strict disciplinarian who also invited Mark Twain to lecture to the cadets. Apparently, the role model took root, perhaps a bit rigid at first. Plebes spent their first three weeks in what was called "beast barracks." At the end of that apprenticeship, they moved to summer camp across the Plain, by which time they had been trained to act rather mechanically. Upperclassmen took advantage of the situation to pull pranks on the unsuspecting plebes. One night after taps, when Pershing was walking guard, one of the upperclassmen dressed up as a ghost and approached. "Who goes there?" Pershing asked. No answer. Again, "Who goes there?" This time the "ghost" opened a folding chair and sat down. Pershing asked, "Who sits there?"

Pershing's academic performance was so-so, and even his otherwise clean disciplinary record was riddled with demerits for being late to formations. Yet on the leadership side, he earned the highest cadet rank each year: the ranking corporal; next, the ranking first sergeant; and in his first class (senior) year, he won the coveted position of First Captain.[2] He also formed a large number of friendships and was elected class president each year, and for life at graduation.

He would serve with many of those friends again. In World War I, fourteen of the forty-two division commanders were classmates, and another sixteen graduated from the other six classes in attendance at some time during his cadet days. Additionally, both army commanders, all of the corps commanders, all but a few of the remaining division commanders, and most of the senior officers on his staff were also West Pointers; yet this was not parochialism. The explanation is far simpler. First, since the end of the Civil War the army had remained small; hence, the academy was able to supply eighty to ninety percent of the career officers it needed. Second, the length of service of the graduates from the classes of 1883 through 1889 made them the most eligible for general officer rank.

Pershing's first assignment was with Troop L of the 6th Cavalry, initially stationed at Fort Bayard, New Mexico. He charged into his duties with a little too much enthusiasm, nearly losing his life owing to carelessness in an Indian skirmish. He learned to play poker so well that he came to regret taking so much money, and thereafter played only for nominal stakes. He was something of a minor rake; and with respect to parties he wryly admitted years afterward, "It would have been more pleasant had some of the boys not gotten a little too full, one of whom I am which." At the same time he further developed his unusual ability to work well with other cultures. When not warring against Indians, he sought their friendship and would even engage in foot races with them, taking his share of the honors.

Later, he was given command of a company of Sioux Indian scouts, winning their respect so deeply that, unknown to him, they took turns acting as his bodyguards. This assignment brought him to the scene of the massacre at Wounded Knee; but it was the cavalry troopers, not his scouts, who were responsible for the carnage. Things might have been different had he been in command. Except for matters that required specialized training, Pershing never asked his men to do anything he could not do himself, nor would he tolerate any serious misconduct.

In all, his early service on the Plains lasted five years, after which he was appointed professor of military science at the University of Nebraska, one of the early Reserve Officer Training Corps (ROTC) programs. He quickly discovered that the few students in the program were at best indifferent. Within a year he turned them into a disciplined lot and created a drill team, then known as the Varsity Rifles, and later the Pershing Rifles. One student, George L. Sheldon, became governor of the state and remembered the future general for his strength of character. Pershing also taught math classes in a university-run preparatory school, where his students included Willa Cather and Dorothy Canfield Fisher. They came to admire him but said he was too much of a martinet to teach math effectively. And within the first two years, he fulfilled his early ambition by completing the law school program on campus. As a result he began his lifelong friendship with the affable Lincoln attorney Charles G. Dawes.[3]

Still, Pershing remained a lieutenant owing to the rigid and slow promotion system then in effect. Because a lieutenant had few places to go
other than the Plains, there he returned, this time with Troop D of the
10th Cavalry at Fort Assiniboine, Montana. These were black troops,
known affectionately as "buffalo soldiers." Once again, Pershing's open
mind almost immediately won the respect of these black soldiers; but regardless of race, creed, or religion, he would not tolerate shirkers. When
he saw one soldier goldbricking on shore while his buddies were pushing
a wagon across a ford, Pershing told the goldbricker to pitch in. When
the soldier didn't move, Pershing decked him with a single punch. That
might warrant a court-martial today, but at the time it only increased the
respect his men had for him. In retirement, the surviving veterans gathered in Washington to serenade him on each of his birthdays. The human
soul may plea for love, but it needs character even more. It's just that it
often takes years to recognize that need and to express thanks to someone
who helped instill it.

The assignment at Fort Assiniboine also provided the turning point of
Pershing's career. The army Commanding General, Nelson A. Miles, visited Fort Assiniboine and was impressed with Pershing. In 1896, Miles
ordered Pershing to join his staff in Washington and then sent him to
observe a military presentation in Madison Square Garden in New York.
On that occasion, Pershing sat with his classmate Avery Andrews, who
had left the army and had started a new career in politics and law. Theodore Roosevelt, who had been commissioner of police in New York and
then Assistant Secretary of the Navy under President McKinley, joined
them. Roosevelt was also impressed with the thirty-six-year-old rough-
riding veteran of the Plains, and from that day forward Roosevelt became
Pershing's mentor. Still, the benefits of that relationship lay in the future.
Pershing wanted to return to West Point as a tactical officer and persuaded
General Miles to send him there.

It has always been the practice of West Point to select the most promising candidates to serve as tactical officers; and while some of them subsequently fail, a substantial percentage rise to general officer rank.[4] Pershing
was the exception. He failed miserably as a tactical officer but went on to
become the most renown general officer of his generation. The prime
cause of this failure was his attempt to shame the cadets by comparing
their supposedly poor performance with his beloved buffalo soldiers. The
cadets responded by giving him the nickname "Black Jack," except that
the original version used a word other than "Black."

That nickname may have later gained a more positive connotation, but
at the time it marked the low point in his career. The academy, especially
in that period, was regimented to the hilt. Enforcing the regulations up to
a point was to be expected. But an officer who went beyond that point

met only hatred. Against those they hated the most, cadets inflicted the ignominy of "silencing," a fate from which Pershing became the only victim to salvage his career.[5]

To do that, Pershing first needed to get away from the academy. When the Spanish-American War broke out a few months later, Pershing pulled every string that he could to get into it, finally accepting a regimental quartermaster billet. Notwithstanding that, he met up with his mentor, saw some action, was decorated with the Silver Star, and then ordered back to the War Department, where he organized the Board of Insular Affairs to oversee new territorial possessions. From there, he went to the Philippines and for the first two years was the adjutant for the commanding general. In practice, this made him the chief administrative officer. Eventually he tired of being a high-level lackey and with promotion to captain sought the field to prove himself. What followed marked him so indelibly that President Theodore Roosevelt commended him by name in his State of the Union address a year later.

Briefly, the Moro insurrectionists were resolved to drive out their new masters, while Pershing was just as determined to stay. During his campaign, he took on one recalcitrant tribal village after the next, culminating with his famed march around Lake Lanao. Afterward, just as he had during his days on the Plains, he set out to win over his adversaries. He succeeded to the point where they made "Cap-teen Perr-sing" an honorary member of their tribes. He relished the moment.

Pershing returned to the states in 1903, where he met and courted Helen Frances Warren. She was the daughter of Senator Frances E. Warren, who was the chairman of the Military Affairs Committee. Then, after a brief assignment as military observer to the Russo-Japanese War (where he met Douglas MacArthur on similar duty), he and Frances were married at an elaborate ceremony with Theodore Roosevelt heading up the guest list. Concurrently, his personal generosity and sense of honor was tested. He was supporting his widowed mother and had just lent his brother most of his savings to salvage the latter's business. It failed anyway; but when his new bride offered to reimburse him with her personal savings, Pershing declined.

Shortly afterwards, Roosevelt promoted Pershing from captain directly to brigadier general, jumping over 862 more senior officers. Although similar promotions had been made at least three times previously, the circumstances surrounding this one raised a howl.[6] On the other hand, Roosevelt had been stymied in his attempts to promote Pershing to the rank of major ahead of the strict seniority rules laid down by Congress. An officer progressed from second lieutenant to colonel by standing in line for about thirty-six years within his branch of service. The only permissible accelerated promotion was a star.

Then it was back to the Philippines for seven years (with one short break), where Pershing again demonstrated his tactical skill against other insurrectionist camps. In the battle of Mount Bagsak, Pershing's own men sent affidavits to the War Department recommending him for the Medal of Honor; but when he heard about this action, he dispatched a letter to the Adjutant General. In part, he wrote, "I do not consider that my action on that occasion was such as to entitle me to be decorated with the Medal of Honor. I went to that part of the line because my presence there was necessary."[7]

On the domestic side, he and Frances had four children—three girls and a boy—in what seems to have been a truly idyllic marriage. The only sour note arose from officers jealous of his promotion. They instigated rumors that he was the father of several illegitimate Filipino children. He worked hard to put these unfounded rumors to rest; but when he was tentatively selected for the superintendency at West Point, they resurfaced in New York papers. This time he took the newspapers to court and won—but it was too late.[8]

When he did return to the states in late 1913, it was to command the 8th Infantry Brigade, headquartered at the Presidio of San Francisco, from which he was often detached for duty along the troubled border with Mexico. While away, a fire swept through their quarters and claimed the lives of his wife and three of their four children. He never recovered from the loss, and the only way he survived was to throw himself totally into his work. The next three years gave him more opportunity than he bargained for.

Troubles along the border grew worse, especially with Pancho Villa, who was a revolutionary operating within a civil war and who at one time had been favored by the United States. When the United States leaned in another direction, Villa felt betrayed and, as mentioned in the first chapter, took revenge by murdering eighteen Americans aboard a Mexican train and later killing fifteen more in a raid on Columbus, New Mexico.

The United States, still cocky from its success against Indians in the previous century and from Pershing's more recent victories in the Philippines, tried to isolate Villa's "army" as a guerrilla band apart from the larger context of the civil war. Unfortunately, the mechanics of the Mexican battlefield were different, and, therefore, "Black Jack" would fail. The number of troops engaged in actual reconnaissance and fighting per unit of area was much lower, time was limited, lines of supply were long and tenuous, and the tactical options were politically restricted.

Nevertheless, the expedition did provide Pershing with experience that proved essential to his later success in France. First, he had command of nearly eleven thousand men. Second, he experimented with air reconnaissance. The eight "Jennies" of the First Aero Squadron did not live up to their billing; but that was a matter of technology, not concept. Third, he learned something about keeping columns an optimum distance apart: far enough to enhance screening yet close enough to concentrate if the situation called for it. Fourth, and this was probably the most important, he learned just how dependent he was on logistical support. Logistical considerations influenced almost every major decision that he would later make in France.

Pershing also grew in command stature. Admittedly, he chaffed under the restrictions imposed by President Wilson, but he did not exceed the limits of his authority or mission. The result was that Wilson trusted him and did not hesitate to approve of his promotion to major general. Only once did he falter, and this occurred when the local power broker in Chihuahua, General Carrizal, interposed his forces between the Americans and the border. Pershing overreacted to the point where Robert Dunn, correspondent for *The New York Tribune,* proposed a tongue-in-cheek communique: "ARMY IN FULL RETREAT TO SALT LAKE CITY. PERSHING DECLARES ALLEGHENY MOUNTAINS MUST BE DEFENDED AT ANY COST." Pershing was not amused and went on to recommend a general military occupation of northern Mexico. Fortunately, cooler heads prevailed including, after a spell, his own.

At any rate, Pershing's command of the punitive expedition made him the natural choice to lead the American Expeditionary Force, once the two more senior contenders were ruled out. Major General Leonard Wood, the Chief of Staff, had lambasted Wilson publicly. The other, Major General Frederick Funston, died suddenly.

Pershing arrived in France in June 1917, well in advance of any significant American troops. The story of his decisions over the next eighteen months is high drama and is discussed more fully in chapter 14. He spent more than ninety percent of his time dueling with the allied high command and, by correspondence, with Chief of Staff Peyton March in Washington. The reason was that the allies wanted to use American troops as fillers for their own units, whereas Pershing was intent on making a *distinct* and, hopefully, decisive American contribution to the prosecution of the war.

The adjective *distinct* was no ego trip. The tactics of trench warfare had devolved into a genocidal meat grinder, into which Pershing had no intention of feeding Americans even if it would have meant eventual victory by pure attrition. Instead, he advocated maneuver warfare. The problem was that he had first to prove that U.S. soldiers could fight effectively against massed troops supported by murderous machine-gun fire and backed by relentless heavy artillery. Only a Don Quixote would dream of prevailing against those odds. Pershing needed a battlefield that offered at least some temporary room for maneuver. The opportunity arose during the Aisne-Marne offensive, especially at Cantigny, Reims, and Belleau Wood.

Cantigny, a German artillery observation post, came first. The Americans took it and held it against repeated counterattacks, suffering heavy casualties in the process. Reims was equally significant. It was the spear-head of a major German offensive that was heading for Paris and had already caused many Parisians—not to mention allied troops—to flee southward. Pershing interposed his forces on the road from Paris and drew the line, as it were. Some historians have subsequently concluded that after six days of advancing, the Germans had overreached themselves. They had shot their bolt, and therefore the American counterattack was not quite what the press made it out to be. Perhaps so, but there was no disputing the outcome. From that point forward Pershing was able to give more time to the mission at hand.

The main American contribution to the war came at the St. Mihiel salient and in the final offensive. As the objective of a limited but self-sustained offensive, the salient was just about the right size. The problem was that by the time Pershing planned to kick off the operation, the allies were ready to launch their general, broad-front final push against the Germans, with the Americans assigned to the Meuse-Argonne sector. Thus, the reduction of the salient became a sideshow in the larger perspective; moreover, Germany had already planned to withdraw from it. Pershing knew he could proceed only if the battle went well and if he could then redeploy his forces quickly for the main offensive. Aerial reconnaissance took care of the first by confirming the start of the German withdrawal. And Colonel George C. Marshall, Pershing's operations staff officer, took care of the rapid redeployment.

Needless to say, the general offensive was successful; and although the American contribution was only a third of the total allied effort at best, it still meant the difference between victory and prolonged trench warfare. Hence, Pershing returned home to great honor and adulation. Congress revived the special rank of General of the Armies for him, while friends encouraged the general to try politics. Unfortunately, that swamp was not for him; he sunk in up to his neck when the water was only knee deep. He stayed with the army; and when Peyton March's term expired in 1921, moved up to Chief of Staff.

Understandably, Pershing's years in that office have not been especially noted by history. His main task was to preside over a demobilized army that Congress further depleted each year. At the end of his four years, Pershing accepted the directorship of the American Battle Monuments Commission. During that period, he compiled his war memoir, *My Experiences in the World War,* which was published in two volumes in 1931 and won the Pulitzer prize in history the following year. He lived until 1948, albeit in a state of increasing physical debilitation from 1941 forward.

Happily, much of his character rubbed off on his surviving son Warren. When Pershing offered to visit his son at college and walk around the campus, Warren demurred on the grounds that it would be "too swank."

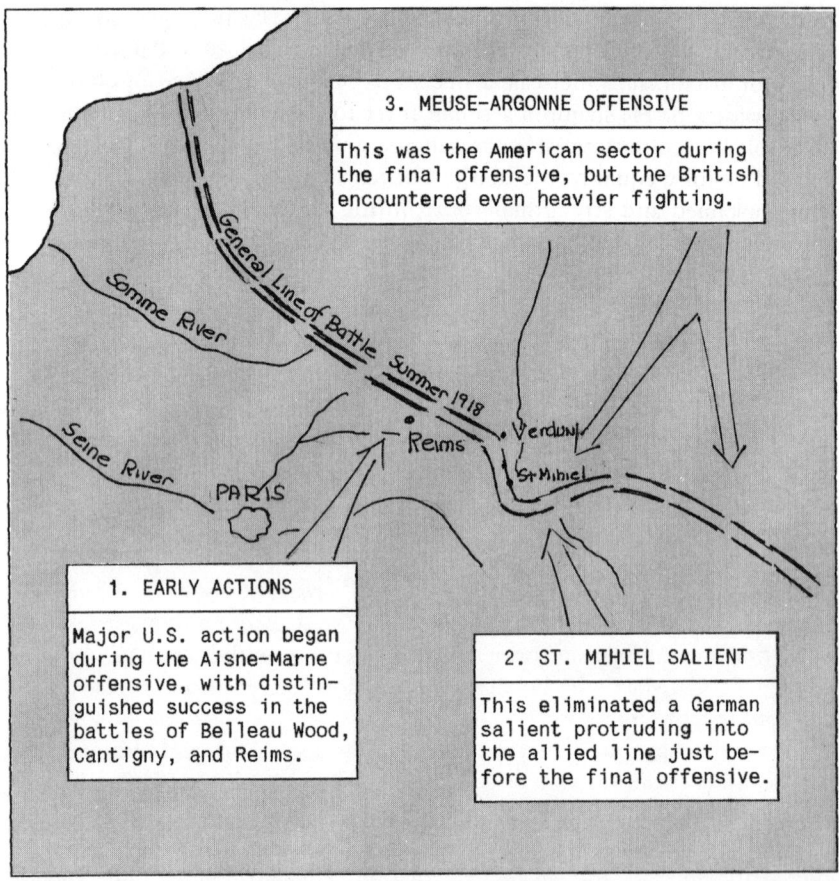

3. MEUSE-ARGONNE OFFENSIVE

This was the American sector during the final offensive, but the British encountered even heavier fighting.

Somme River

General Line of Battle Summer 1918

Seine River

PARIS

Reims

Verdun

St Mihiel

1. EARLY ACTIONS

Major U.S. action began during the Aisne-Marne offensive, with distinguished success in the battles of Belleau Wood, Cantigny, and Reims.

2. ST. MIHIEL SALIENT

This eliminated a German salient protruding into the allied line just before the final offensive.

Figure 1. American Initiatives in World War I. Pershing's most enduring accomplishment was to ensure a distinct American contribution to the successful prosecution of World War I, notwithstanding enormous pressures and cabals operating to the contrary.

When World War II came, Warren enlisted in the army, went to officers candidate school, and fought in Europe, making his father quite proud.

Looking back, it may be said that Theodore Roosevelt, by way of Pershing, passed the torch of Zeus, so to speak, to his distant cousin Franklin D. Roosevelt. The general stood for everything that both Roosevelts believed in when they were at their best. General MacArthur, who had been the chief competition for that role of torchbearer, put the matter this way:

General Pershing's fame rests largely upon his personal character. He was not a genius at strategy and his tactical experience was limited, but in his indomitable will for victory, in his implacable belief in the American soldier, in his invincible resistance to all attempts to exploit or patronize American arms, he rose to the highest flights of his profession. He inspired a self-respect for our national forces and a foreign recognition of our military might which has properly placed us fully equal to the best of the human race. My memories of him sustained and strengthened me during many a lonely and bitter moment of the Pacific and Korean Wars.[9]

3

WILLIAM DANIEL LEAHY

Do what is necessary, and only as the reason requires. For this brings not only tranquility which comes from doing things well, but also that which comes from doing fewer things.

—Marcus Aurelius

The cruiser *St. Louis* stood at anchor off Constantinople. She was on a semidiplomatic mission as part of a multinational fleet overseeing various parochial interests during the Greco-Turkish War in 1921. The British counterpart was the battleship *Iron Duke,* which had a bear for a mascot. Apparently bored, the bear went AWOL, swam over to the *St. Louis,* clamored aboard the gangway, and took up residence in the crew's quarters. The bear's masters soon came to fetch him; and, later, the British admiral sent his flag lieutenant over to apologize for the bear's conduct as unbecoming a member of the crew of one of His Majesty's ships.

Captain Leahy asked the lieutenant to convey his respects to the admiral, adding "there had been at one time in the distant past some serious question about the propriety of permitting the search of American warships for refugees from foreign services" but that "this appeared to be a special case between friends in which I am very much pleased to be of assistance." That whimsical humor exemplified the imperturbability and good judgment of the navy's ranking admiral during World War II. When not on duty, Leahy was known to doze peacefully during gunnery practice; and he nearly slept through the San Francisco earthquake in 1906. It was an attribute that served him well throughout his fifty-six years of active service, fifty-three of them in uniform. By the same token, he was not a memorable character. When Leahy wrote *I Was There*—a compilation from his wartime journal—he resisted the publisher's entreaties to include anecdotes to enliven the book. He was a steady rider, utterly dependable but leaving the color to others.

4. Fleet Admiral William D. Leahy. He was the most imperturbable of the ten principals, nearly sleeping through the San Francisco earthquake in 1906. This trait served him well when he became Chief of Staff to President Roosevelt in World War II.

William Leahy was the first of eight children born to Michael Arthur and Rose Hamilton Leahy in the small town of Hampton, Iowa. His father was a Civil War veteran and an accomplished attorney. In order for Leahy's father to pursue the law profession, the family moved to Warsau, Wisconsin, and later to Ashland in the same state, which Leahy adopted as his hometown and visited on numerous occasions throughout his life. Interestingly, three of the four fleet admirals came from nonservice families living in small inland towns (Halsey was the exception), as did five of the six generals. These hamlets may have lacked sophistication, but they offered something better. The future admiral remarked that "pride of ancestry has been and is of value to us in that it makes repugnant any deviation from traditional ideals and gives strength with which to resist temptation to drift into the lower orders of human society."

In high school, Leahy's parents and teachers urged him to go to law school, but young William had decided on a military career and tried to obtain an appointment to West Point. His congressman did not have one available, offering Annapolis instead. So in the year 1893, Leahy became a naval cadet. The term *midshipman* would not be adopted for another six years. He spent his summers on cruises, one of them aboard the wooden frigate *Constellation,* commanded by Admiral Halsey's father. At graduation, he was thirty-fifth in a class of forty-seven and did not hold any cadet officer rank. Yet his classmate Admiral Thomas C. Hart remarked that although Leahy was somewhat lazy, whenever there was a serious problem his classmates took it to him for resolution: "He had more common sense than all of us."

After graduation, like all cadets at the time, Leahy spent two additional years as a "passed midshipman" before commissioning as an ensign (a practice that continued until 1912). His first assignment was aboard the battleship *Oregon* under the command of Captain Charles E. Clark, whom Leahy felt was an ideal commander. This was during the time of the Spanish-American War; and on July 3, 1898, Leahy experienced his first and only day in combat.

The small U.S. fleet had bottled up the Spanish in Havana harbor. When the latter made a run for it, the future admiral was commanding one of the 13-inch naval gun turrets. That put an end to the Spanish ship *Colon.* Afterward, Leahy leaped with glee, as did most of his shipmates; but when the bodies of the army wounded were brought on board for transport back to the states he wrote: "There is glory enough for those of us who return safely or who are killed in the discharge of hazardous duty, but to the wreck of a man lying in a hospital tent, and to his mother, there is little glory in war."

He next served on a number of other ships in quick succession, among them the *Philadelphia,* the *Newark,* the *Oregon* again, and the *Castine.* Later, his duties brought him to the Philippines, where he became distraught upon learning that a native priest was tortured to death by American captors and that a fifteen-year-old boy was summarily shot as a spy. These reactions imbued him with a certain leniency that offset his strong tendency to judge others somewhat harshly—including Harry Hopkins—before he got to know them.[1] The saving grace was that upon realizing he was wrong, he admitted to it and made the appropriate amends if called for.

Every serious officer of the line yearns for his first command at sea, and Leahy's came on the small gunboat *Mariveles*. The boat had a crew of one passed midshipmen and twenty-three enlisted personnel. It also had a bad engine and had to be scrapped shortly after he took the helm. Leahy then took command of the supply ship *Glacier:* this was not his favorite tour, but it was offset by his enduring marriage to Louise Tennent Harrington in San Francisco in 1904. This marriage produced one son, William Harrington Leahy, who graduated from Annapolis in the class of 1927 and retired as a rear admiral.

Leahy was next assigned as an instructor in physics and chemistry at Annapolis. However, he never cared for formal schooling on either side of an instructor's desk and registered his discontent by declining to make any entries in his journal—the only period in his career that he did not do so. Later, he would avoid the Naval War College, becoming one of the few officers who skipped it in peacetime and still made it to the top. Yet he did not lack curiosity or the ability to learn. Far from it, whenever the opportunity presented itself he went out of his way to explore a community rather than party. And he would often travel and explore by way of taking scenic routes between changes of assignments. This itinerary included the Inca ruins near Cimbote, Peru, where he wondered how a relatively few Spaniards could so thoroughly destroy an ancient civilization with its advanced engineering. By the outbreak of World War II, he had been to almost every place on the globe.

The next step in his progression was as a gunnery officer aboard the armored cruiser *California* under Captain Henry T. Mayo, who had been a mentor and role model for a number of naval officers, including Ernest King. At first, Leahy chaffed at this duty but later recognized it as a key assignment that was intended by Mayo to prepare Leahy for higher command. In turn, Leahy realized the importance of training subordinates, writing: "If a man knows how to operate the ship's guns, I can make him do it better whether he wants to or not, but if he does not know, personal bravery will be of no value." And while on this tour, Leahy pulled a temporary stint as a naval aide to the visiting President Howard Taft, commenting afterward that four days of it was about all he could stand. Little did Leahy know that he would cap his career with seven years in that role.

At any rate, Leahy's shipboard gunnery duty was followed by the job of *fleet* gunnery officer under Rear Admiral Chauncey Thomas, commander of the Pacific fleet. This gave Leahy the opportunity to learn something about higher command from the vantage point of a staff officer. Then came his first major shore duty, again serving under Mayo, now a rear admiral, in the latter's capacity as the navy's director of personnel. Unfortunately, this was not quite the assignment it appeared to be. As discussed in the first chapter, Secretary of the Navy Meyer imposed a naval general staff over the encrusted bureau structure, of which Mayo was one of four incumbents. But Meyer's successor (Daniels) had no intention of continuing them; so Mayo was a lame duck.

Yet two advantages accrued to Commander Leahy. First, when Mayo left, Leahy found himself doing an admiral's job. This is in marked contrast to today's modus operandi whereby some admirals do commanders' jobs. Or less. Second, he met Assistant Secretary of the Navy Franklin D. Roosevelt. The two developed a close working relationship; and even when Secretary Daniels scrubbed a good sea command for Leahy and instead assigned him to pilot his dispatch vessel *Dolphin,* most of the cruises were with Franklin Roosevelt on board.

Still, a desk is no substitute for a ship; and Leahy tried to get to sea in time for action in World War I. He wrangled the executive officer's billet on the battleship *Nevada,* but mechanical trouble once again thwarted his opportunity. The result was that he was sent back to Washington, this time as director of gunnery and engineering exercises. Fortunately, he was immediately detailed to Europe where he met up with Vice Admiral William S. Sims. As a younger man, Sims had spoken out against the poor state of naval gunnery and was nearly cashiered. Instead, Theodore Roosevelt heard him out and advanced him in rank and authority, similar to Truman's promotion of Rickover in another generation.

After the war, Leahy was promoted to captain and assigned to the cruiser *St. Louis* for, as mentioned, semidiplomatic duties during the Greco-Turkish War. He learned diplomacy and contributed to a humanitarian agreement covering Greek women and children. This agreement was put to the test when a fourteen-year-old Greek boy swam to his ship seeking asylum. Leahy had to choose between concealing the boy and risking nullification of the agreement or turning the boy over to Turkish authorities, who would inevitably execute him as a spy. Recalling his earlier experience in the Philippines, he opted for the former.

After this, Leahy was given his first independent command—Mine Squadron One with the *Shawmut* as a flagship. One of his duties was to form a picket line with his ships under the route of a squadron of navy sea planes. Because few of the aircraft reached their destination, he grew leery of naval aviation and became the last of the four admirals to appreciate the value of airpower. That's a polite way of saying that he was among the so-called battleship admirals. Then it was back to Washington as a detail officer in the Bureau of Navigation (later renamed the Bureau of Personnel).

This assignment was considered a definite stepping stone in those days; for by that point in his career, Leahy's reputation was solid. In the opinion of his biographer Henry H. Adams, Leahy had proved himself utterly reliable, gave all his working hours to duty whether he cared for it or not, freely praised and inspired his men but was intolerant of ineptitude, and could write clearly and forcefully. At the conclusion of this tour as detail officer, Leahy knew his next assignment would foreshadow the rest of his career. This was the navy's way of telling a newer captain what it thought of him. The navy thought well, as evidenced by giving Leahy command of the battleship *New Mexico,* the flagship of the Combat Battleship Division under Admiral Jehu Chase.

In this command, Leahy won the navy's annual Engineering Trophy, pushing his luck out of character to do it. Toward the end of the twenty-four-hour full-power run, one of the propellers bent, causing bone-jarring vibrations throughout the ship. A prudent captain would have thrown the towel in. The luck of the Irish stayed with him, though, and continued into his next assignment as chief of the Bureau of Ordnance, one of two key bureaus in the navy (the other being the Bureau of Navigation). This meant temporary promotion to rear admiral and with it entry into the innermost circle of Main Navy.

Unfortunately, the Chief of Naval Operations had just changed hands from Admiral Charles F. Hughes to William V. Pratt. The latter had vigorously supported the Hoover administration regarding the Naval Conference on Disarmament, while most other navy officers—Leahy included—failed to see the wisdom of it. The ensuing squabbles nearly did Leahy in. When Admiral Chase, by now commander of the U.S. fleet, requested Leahy for his chief of staff, Pratt instead handed Leahy the billet of Commander, Destroyers Scouting Force. This was not an especially promising assignment, although Leahy was later given the concurrent job of Commander, Destroyers Battle Fleet. This made Leahy what the navy sometimes calls a *Pooh-Bah,* an officer who reports to himself.[2]

Yet sayeth the philosopher, "This too shall come to pass." Pratt went his way, and Leahy returned to Main Navy as chief of the Bureau of Navigation, a post second in importance only to Chief of Naval Operations. In this role, Leahy advanced the careers of the most promising senior officers, among them Nimitz and Halsey. He also began to comment more fully on world events in his journal. When the Japanese invaded Manchuria, Secretary of State Henry Stimson said that the United States would not recognize the new Japanese puppet state of Manchoukuo.[3] Leahy was aghast and believed this attitude might lead the U.S. into a major war. But six years later, when he was Chief of Naval Operations and the Japanese sunk the American gunboat *Panay,* Leahy was ready to threaten Japan with an immediate declaration of war unless fulsome reparations were made. His old friend Franklin Roosevelt, by then president, disagreed and sought a more diplomatic solution.[4]

Leahy and Rear Admiral Ernest King, then chief of the Bureau of Aeronautics, were also assigned to a board considering changes to navy organization. The board was headed by Henry Latrobe Roosevelt, a classmate of Admiral King's and a distant cousin of Franklin Roosevelt. The hidden agenda was to continue the existing bureau structure, but at this point Admiral William H. Standley became Chief of Naval Operations. Standley wanted a stronger measure of authority over the bureau heads. Predictably, the board concluded otherwise.

This infuriated Standley, who then tried to wreck the careers of both Leahy and King. This was the third time through the wringer for Leahy, and it raises the question of just how much luck is involved when it comes to career advancement, considering the frequent personality conflicts that stand in the way. Undoubtedly luck plays a role; but it was undeniable competence that put men like Leahy back on track. In this particular case, Roosevelt overruled Standley; but it should be remembered that this long-standing friendship between admiral and president was based on mutual respect, not clubiness.

With that endorsement, Leahy moved on to Commander, Battleship Divisions, Battle Force, with the rank of vice admiral, and later took command of the entire battle force, adding a fourth star. Then, after slightly more than a year, he returned once more to Main Navy, this time as Chief of Naval Operations. He remained in that post for three years until mandatory retirement at age sixty-four in 1939. During his tour, he arm wrestled with Roosevelt on a number of issues, for example, the use of 16-inch, rather than 14-inch, guns on new battleships. The smaller guns meant smaller, lighter, less expensive ships, and that appealed to Roosevelt's plan to rearm the country in a period dominated by isolationists. Leahy countered that other countries were sticking with the larger guns, and indeed the Japanese were equipping two battleships with 18.1-inch guns.

Leahy won without Roosevelt holding a grudge. On the contrary, at times the President had Leahy sit in on cabinet meetings in the absence of the Secretary of the Navy and invited him to join fishing trips with the White House inner circle. Furthermore, Roosevelt was on the verge of appointing Leahy Secretary of Navy when, for bipartisan reasons, he selected W. Franklin Knox, a Republican. However, Roosevelt did mention that if war broke out he intended to bring Leahy back to chair a four-man committee with the Secretaries of State, War, and Navy as members.

That chairmanship did not quite come to pass. To do so would have abrogated the president's responsibilities in time of war, but there were moments when Leahy's role as presidential chief of staff would come close to that abrogation. In the interim, Roosevelt appointed Leahy governor of Puerto Rico. This post had been a sinecure for retired senior officers; but because war clouds were forming and the first priority of U.S. defense policy was to protect the western hemisphere, the importance of the job increased. Among other items, the United States acquired British bases in the Caribbean in trade for fifty aging destroyers.

While governor of Puerto Rico, Leahy took on the local power structure represented by Puerto Rican Senator Rafael Martinez Nadal and held the conflict to a draw until the latter died. Then Leahy ensured free elections, notwithstanding that the winner—Luis Muños Maríno—was a far-left liberal at odds with Leahy's conservative bent. Leahy also pleaded with Congress to make an exception to the minimum-wage act (then twenty-five cents an hour) because it was ruining the local economy. He had the full support of the local population, but Congress would not listen. This stubbornness led to an impoverishment that took many decades to overcome.

Still, the governorship was a welcome assignment that both he and Mrs. Leahy thoroughly enjoyed, and, therefore, it didn't last long. By 1940 Germany had overrun most of France, permitting the rest of France to exist only as a quasi–puppet state with its capital at Vichy under Field Marshal Henri Philippe Pétain. The situation was this: (1) Hitler wanted to keep Vichy France as a buffer while negotiating a possible settlement with the United Kingdom; (2) the United States did not want what remained of the French army, the French fleet, or the French African colonies to fall into the hands of the Nazis; (3) the British and the French were contentious adversaries; and (4) diplomatic relations with France had always been prickly. In the Vichy arrangement, maintenance of these unwritten protocols became nearly impossible. The one lever Leahy had was France's desperate need for U.S. medical and food supplies.

Furthermore, Germany steadily increased the pressure for greater cooperation, often by shooting hostages in occupied France. Moreover, although Pétain had a few residual leanings toward the Allies, his senior cabinet members, Admiral Jean Darlan and Pierre Laval, were more than willing to cast their lot with Germany. Thus, it is impossible to measure either the extent to which Leahy changed the growing French proclivity for things Nazi or what longer-term effect his diplomacy had on dealing with the French during the invasion of North Africa in late 1942. However, it is safe to conclude that he accomplished some good and did no wrong in a very difficult assignment.

The ambassadorship became all the more difficult, if not unbearable, when Leahy's beloved wife Louise died suddenly from complications after surgery. In the face of this bereavement and the crumbling diplomatic situation, Roosevelt ordered Leahy home with a new assignment in mind.[5] That assignment came with two hats: the first as chief of staff to the Com-

Official U.S. Navy photograph. Courtesy U.S. Naval Institute.
5. Leahy as the Chairman of the Joint Chiefs of Staff. In this role, his accomplishments were diffuse and subtle yet as significant as any of his fellow travelers on the joint chiefs.

mander in Chief; the second, to chair the Joint Chiefs of Staff. In this role, Leahy would have to address numerous conflicts, including those among the army, air force, and navy; between British and American objectives; between the military and state departments; between the Allies and U.S. armed services for resources; and within the United States, between the civil sector and the military for resources.

Moreover, the Axis powers were still on the offensive everywhere. The British had been in the thick of fighting for more than two years; whereas the United States, with four times the population and industrial base, had only recently closed with the enemy, and then only in a few pitched naval battles. Further, Roosevelt had virtually excluded the State Department from the decision-making process regarding World War II, as evidenced by Secretary of State Cordell Hull's attendance at only one Allied conference (and that was a meeting of foreign ministers in Moscow).

To say the least, it takes a quiet, competent individual to prevail in that kind of oleum. But Leahy measured up. When Admiral King got too rancid, he waited patiently until another of the joint chiefs stood up to him. When General Marshall occasionally jumped to an insupportable conclusion, Leahy would say, "Now, George, I am just a simple sailor, so if you would explain your position to me step by step, it would help." Marshall would always comply and then back off when he discovered the gap in his own logic. When members of the press railed at him—which was seldom—Leahy simply ignored them with equanimity. Finally, to overcome the de facto isolation of the State Department, Leahy established a liaison office there headed by Charles E. Bohlen. His long-term secretary Dorothy Renquist remarked how uncluttered Leahy's mind was. As a result, there seldom were any loose ends lying about his office or any need to work overtime.

When Roosevelt died in April 1945, Leahy was faced with the additional task of bringing Harry Truman up to speed. Roosevelt had kept Truman out of the picture almost entirely. Fortunately, because Leahy kept his relationship with Roosevelt more professional than personal, he was able to make the transition and serve his new boss equally well. In time, Truman developed an immense respect for Leahy and kept him on as chief of staff until 1949. By then, the Department of Defense had been organized and the formal chairmanship of the Joint Chiefs of Staff established. This made Leahy's job ceremonial, and at the age of 74, he was beginning to develop medical problems.

By mutual agreement he retired from active service, although Truman frequently invited him to join his inner circle for social occasions and vacations. At a farewell dinner, when the president invited forty-two of his closest associates to break bread one last time, Leahy sat in the place of honor. It was the social reprise of Truman's earlier remarks that went with the admiral's third Distinguished Service Medal. In part Truman's remarks read:

> His supreme loyalty to his country and his appreciation of its place in world affairs supplemented by his fundamental concern in the welfare of humanity as a whole transcended his already vast knowledge of military affairs to culminate in statesmanship beyond that required of any naval officer in our history.

Leahy lived for another ten years, much of the time in ill health, passing away on July 20, 1959. His accomplishments during the war are now all but forgotten.

4

GEORGE CATLETT MARSHALL

Remember, Roman, that you shall rule the nations by your authority, for this is your skill: to make peace the custom, to spare the conquered, and to wage war until the haughty are brought low.

—Virgil

In 1905, Lieutenant George C. Marshall was tasked to survey part of southwestern Texas. At the time, the only place in that area where provisions could be purchased was Langtry, a typical western town with the added distinction of its having been the home of Judge Roy Bean.[1] Unfortunately, Roy had passed away about two years earlier; so it is pure speculation to consider how far the future general might have gone in his career had he obtained the benefit of even a brief tutelage under "the law west of the Pecos." Fate having declared otherwise, Marshall had to settle for a reputation as the most distinguished American soldier-statesman in this century.

Born on the last day of 1880, the youngest of three children, Marshall grew up in Uniontown, Pennsylvania. One of his strongest traits was his intolerance of being ridiculed. As a young boy, he once plied a rowboat to ferry passengers across a local creek and "sold" tickets for the service. When two girls refused to surrender their tickets, he stopped rowing and pulled the plug at the bottom of his boat. Because the creek ran barely a foot of water, there was no danger of sinking or drowning; but his frustration went much deeper. Later, that capacity for frustration boiled over into rage when he overheard his older brother Stuart beg their mother not to let George go to Virginia Military Institute (VMI) because his performance was bound to disgrace the family name. Now rage can destroy most men, but in a few it becomes a crucible. George C. Marshall was one of those few.

At VMI, he majored in civil engineering and stood in the upper third of his class academically. In military leadership he was first. Like Pershing at West Point fifteen years earlier, Marshall earned the highest cadet rank each year, which meant that at the end he was First Captain. He played football as a tackle but did not form close friendships. In sum, it could be said that Marshall was something of a decisive, approachable loner who won the respect, if not the affection, of almost everyone with whom he came in contact.

He made one exception on the matter of affection. While walking down a street in adjacent Lexington, he heard the sound of lilting piano music. He lingered outside until he was invited in, whereupon the stone wall of his character more or less crumbled as he met and fell in love with Elizabeth Carter Coles. Lily, as she was always called, returned the feelings; and they were married in the winter after George's graduation. By all accounts their relationship grew into an idyllic one. The one troubling aspect of their relationship, however, was Lily's congenital heart defect. They could not risk having children on that account, and it would claim her life twenty-five years later, throwing George into a despair that went beyond grief. Greatness of Marshall's caliber does not spring from ordinary emotional depth.

Marriage, however, did not necessarily mean that Lily would become an army wife. In those days commissions as second lieutenants were automatic only for graduates of West Point. To obtain his, Marshall had to troop the halls of Congress and finally edge his way into President McKinley's office without an appointment. The President was impressed with Marshall's record at VMI and with his obvious military bearing, and thus the general's career began on a note of quiet audacity.

The first step in Marshall's military career landed him in the Philippines, to which he was scheduled to depart alone the day after his wedding. A kindly adjutant delayed the departure for a week. That first assignment was with troops at an isolated post on the southern coast of Mindanao, where he was the only officer. He humbled himself to his task and let a few good noncommissioned officers take him under wing for transformation from parade-ground cadet to field soldier, all without shirking his responsibilities. Once when crossing a ford, Marshall's men thought they spied a crocodile and fled in every direction. Marshall calmly assembled his men and marched the formation back and forth across the ford until they regained their confidence.

Marshall returned to the states after a few years with an assignment to Fort Reno, Oklahoma, from where he was detached for survey duties in Texas. His first real break came with selection for the school at Fort Leavenworth.[2] This was the last year that lieutenants would be able to attend; thereafter, the rank of captain was required, which would have taken many years to attain. Marshall wasn't as brilliant as some of the other

Official U.S. Army photograph. Courtesy U.S. Army Military History Institute.
6. General of the Army George C. Marshall. General Robert E. Lee was one of Marshall's role models; Benjamin Franklin was the other. The former amplified his austere but dignified bearing in official matters, while the latter exemplified his warmth and simplicity in private life.

student officers, but he persevered and like Eisenhower twenty years later, finished first in his class. This led to a second year of study, followed by an additional two years as an instructor.

Marshall enlivened his courses by encouraging his students—all of whom outranked him—to think for themselves, modeling himself after another instructor there, Major John F. Morrison (later Major General). Morrison, it seems, was so gifted that Marshall considered him as a standard that he was never able to match, no matter how hard he tried. And it was here that Marshall first met Douglas MacArthur, then commanding a company of troops on that post. They did not take well to each other.

At the end of four years Marshall took an extended tour of Europe, after which he had a number of miscellaneous assignments, including one as inspector-instructor for the Massachusetts National Guard and another with the 4th Infantry at Fort Logan Roots, Arkansas. At the latter, he volunteered for officer of the day for three days running so that he could sign out the miscreants in the post stockade for the purpose of organizing a Christmas party for the children living on the post. Those were difficult times, and the families of enlisted men struggled against the odds. Marshall would dote on children all of his life.

Then it was back to the Philippines, this time with Lily. As mentioned in the first chapter, it was here Marshall demonstrated his ability at running large units, notwithstanding that he was still a lieutenant. Thus, by the time the United States entered World War I, Marshall's record had gained sufficient mass to channel him quickly to General Pershing's staff, coupled with three temporary promotions until he reached the grade of colonel. His most significant achievement was shifting troops and guns from the scene of the St. Mihiel battle to the line of departure for the Meuse-Argonne offensive in a span of days over bad roads clogged with traffic. It is little wonder that Pershing came to admire him and tried to advance Marshall's career by making him chief of operations at First Army and then chief of staff for VIII Corps, a general officer position.

Pershing was also impressed for another reason. As commanding general of the American Expeditionary Force, Pershing did not always command his own temper. Consequently, when he inspected units and uncovered a serious problem, he often cursed the officer responsible in front of his staff. On one such occasion, when Pershing was clearly off the mark, Marshall tore into him with so much rage that neither he nor Pershing could remember what had been said. Nonetheless, the senior officer got the message.

Afterward, Marshall could afford to be more diplomatic. His chief was continually at odds with his nemesis in Washington, General Peyton C. March. Pershing had drafted a nasty letter to March and gave it to Marshall for editing. Three times Colonel Marshall toned it down, and three times Pershing rejected the diplomacy. Finally, Marshall said to him, "Now, General, just because you hate the guts of General March, you're setting yourself up to do something you know damn well is wrong." Pershing backed off and perhaps at that point decided to make Marshall his aide-de-camp and executive officer when, as expected, he took over March's job in 1921. Marshall would revert to his permanent rank of major, but it was some consolation to occupy quarters #3 in what is now general's row at Fort Myer, Virginia.

Upon Pershing's retirement, Marshall was assigned as executive officer of the 15th Infantry, which was on extraterritorial police duty to guard American interests in China. The commander of the brigade, Colonel Isaac Newell, was inclined to take life easy and let his new executive run the brigade for him; and from this circumstance, it is said, originated the expression, "Let George do it." In this regard, Marshall spent a great deal of time instructing small groups of men a variety of tasks and skills. Some of his peers could not understand how he found satisfaction in this mundane work after having served with Pershing in the stratosphere of Washington; but that was Marshall's nature.

Marshall then returned to Washington as an instructor at the Army War College, and it was here that his beloved Lily died. The grief combined with the boredom of being a seminar leader in a laid-back institution motivated him to seek something more active. When the Assistant Commandant's position at Fort Benning, Georgia, opened, Marshall grabbed it. There he tore into his work with a relish, reminiscent of his tour at Leavenworth. Within a year, he put together a team of instructors who would go on to serve as senior general officers in World War II, among them Omar Bradley, "Vinegar Joe" Stilwell, and Walter Bedell Smith. Marshall also insisted that instructors teach without notes so that they would project themselves onto the class rather than intone a lecture. And it was probably here that he began keeping his famous "black book" on the officers who held promise and those who didn't.

Still, he was demanding of his subordinates. The same thing happened to Pershing after the tragic death of his wife and children, but fate was kinder to Marshall. One evening in 1928 Marshall met the widow Katherine Tupper Brown. They were taken with each other immediately but waited a few years to marry, when Katherine's three children came to accept Marshall as a father. The evening that they met, he volunteered to drive her to the home where she was staying because, he said, he knew the streets of Columbus better than anyone. When after an hour the car finally pulled up to the house, Katherine chided George for his braggadocio. "Not so," he replied, "Had I not known those streets so well, there is no way I could have spent an hour driving you home without crossing your street earlier."

Marshall's next tour of duty brought him and his wife to Fort Screven on the Georgia coast. Shortly afterward, concurrent with his promotion to colonel, he was placed in command of the 8th Infantry at Fort Moultrie, South Carolina. Here he established camps for the Civilian Conservation Corps and gained firsthand knowledge of what would be required for mass mobilization. As the times grew even harder economically, he arranged for the commissaries to sell surplus goods at nominal prices to enlisted families. And because relationships with the adjacent community had soured, Marshall made a point of improving them by intense personal effort.

Then came the low point of his career. The problem was time, or rather a lack of it. Marshall was fifty-four years old. In order to have a chance at high command, he had to make brigadier general soon; and to do that he needed—or at least he thought he needed—an important assignment as a colonel. MacArthur was the Chief of Staff and made Marshall the senior instructor for the Illinois National Guard. That was the end of the line for Regular Army officers. Marshall asked MacArthur to reconsider, but it was to no avail. He and Katherine then moved to Chicago, where she later said that he turned ashen for several months. Out of desperation Marshall wrote to General Pershing and asked him to intercede, the first and only time in his career that he ever sought influence on his own behalf. Still, Marshall specified that any assignment would have to be based on his record.[3]

Pershing went to work, but as it turned out his influence accelerated the natural course of events by only a month. MacArthur may have been vindictive, but the rest of the senior echelon of the army comprised Marshall's friends and admirers. When Marshall's name came up for consideration, the vote of the promotion board was unanimous, whereupon he took command of the 5th Infantry Brigade, Vancouver Barracks, Washington. He enjoyed that tour immensely, and it gave him the strength to forbear the eight-year ordeal that was handed to him less than two years later.

The Chief of Staff, General Malin Craig, had a deputy and several principal staff officers, each of whom bore the title Assistant Chief of Staff. Upon reassignment from the 5th Infantry to Washington, Marshall drew Assistant Chief of Staff for War Plans. In that capacity he laid the groundwork for mobilization that would expand army personnel strength from under two hundred thousand men to at least a million, nine million as it turned out. It also meant wrestling with various contingency plans that were labeled *Rainbow One* through *Rainbow Five*.[4] Still, until Hitler invaded Poland most Americans did not believe war would come. Hence, Marshall concentrated on developing solid relationships with Congress and the president instead of acting the prophet. As a result, his outward

Official Department of Defense photograph. Courtesy National Archives.
7. General Marshall Aboard a Carrier with Admiral King. Though King was at first critical of Marshall, the admiral eventually came to respect him deeply. Among the reasons was the general's willingness to learn about naval aviation in order to better understand warfare in the Pacific.

austerity set in even harder, breaking down only once. That happened as chief of a brief military mission to Brazil. It seems that the local military band knew only one American tune—*Anchors Aweigh*. They played it over and over and over again until Marshall could no longer keep a straight face.

His subsequent elevation to Chief of Staff, by way of brief tenure as deputy, was a contest between himself, as a new major general, and Hugh Drum, a lieutenant general of long standing. Once more, he need not have concerned himself. His competition was so self-serving that Roosevelt lamented, "Drum, Drum, I wish he would stop beating his own drum." Marshall got the nod and assumed his new duties on the first of September 1939. The president, notwithstanding his consummate politics, understood that when the wolf came to the door, he would need better men around than the usual minions that percolate to the top in a freewheeling democracy.

Marshall's first two years in the War Department may or may not have prepared him for the six that followed, for now his duties demanded that he keep the national interests foremost in mind while convincing future battle commanders and the common soldier that he understood their perspective as well. To that end, he emphasized four priorities. First, he further honed his relationships with the president, Congress, the secretary of war, and the press to near perfection. Second, he decentralized authority to an extraordinary degree. Third, he throttled his piques to the point of magnanimity. Fourth, he never lost the common touch, making it a point to visit every major post as often as circumstances would permit. During the war itself, he extended the last item to include every theater of operations.

As for working relationships, Marshall quietly but forcefully stood up to Roosevelt and to Congress whenever he believed them mistaken. "No, Mr. President, I believe you are entirely wrong," was heard more than once. When a senator criticized the mistakes made by a major unit during maneuvers, Marshall replied, "My God, Senator, that's the reason I do it. I want the mistake made down in Louisiana, not over in Europe, and the only way to do this is to try it out and if it doesn't work, find out what we need to make it work." When King criticized him for not understanding the navy, Marshall arranged to have the admiral take him on a two-day cruise on a carrier so that he would better understand naval aviation and its role in the Pacific theater. Finally, the door between his office and the adjacent office of Secretary of War Stimson was always open.

With respect to delegating authority, Marshall railed against any officer who came to him for answers. "What I want are officers who can carry out their own decisions and tell me afterwards what they did and why." On those occasions when the decision was his alone to make, the presentation had better include a single recommendation, not a list of options. The one thing that did stymie him was the entrenched army bureaucracy. He waited patiently until war broke out, whereupon he struck with a healthy vengeance, afterward informing Congress why he did so. The members of Congress were in too much shock over Pearl Harbor to overrule him.

When it came to keeping animosities in check, there is no better case than the way he dealt with MacArthur. Marshall had developed an aversion to the man who had nearly wrecked his career without cause; but this was wartime. He recalled MacArthur to active duty in the summer of 1941 and did everything humanly possible to resupply him once war broke out. When it became obvious that the Philippines would be lost, he ordered MacArthur out in the name of the President and awarded him the Medal of Honor to offset any allegations of cowardice.[5] He also brought Eisenhower to the War Department five days after Pearl Harbor to take the Pacific desk in operations. Eisenhower had served under MacArthur for nine years and knew him better than any officer in the army. When Eisenhower was not generous enough, Marshall upped the ante.

As for the common touch, Marshall would send casualty data to the White House and to Congress weekly, using vivid graphs and colors "because you get hardened to these things and you have to be very careful to keep them always in the forefront of your mind." He declined to ride in his official limousine except when calling on the president, using a plain staff car instead and often giving rides to soldiers and workers. Then there was the time the eight-year-old son of Edward R. Stettinius, then chairman of the War Resources Board, wrote a letter to General Marshall stating that he was ready for duty, would bring his pony, and asked for further instructions. The letter arrived a few minutes before Marshall departed for one of the Allied conferences. He sat down at his desk and replied:

Orders for Joey Stettinius.
Button up your coat. Put your hat on straight. Wipe the smile off your face. Draw rations of beans instead of jam. After you have done all this I will tell you what next to do.
George C. Marshall
Chief of Staff

In all of this, Marshall permitted himself one luxury—if it can be called that. He paced himself by returning to his quarters for lunch whenever he was in Washington and avoided all but the most obligatory evening social engagements. And every few Sundays he and Katherine drove out to their home in Leesburg, Virginia, thirty-five miles distant, to do a little gardening.

The regimen was successful. He looked as healthy at the end of the war as he did at the beginning, and the upshot was that General Marshall became the indispensable man. When it came time to appoint the Supreme Commander for the counterinvasion of Europe, Roosevelt could not bring himself to let him go, nor could his fellow members on the Joint Chiefs of Staff. "Why break up a winning team?" asked Admiral King. Eisenhower got the job instead.

This was perhaps Marshall's greatest disappointment, although the President tried to soothe matters. It seems that a newspaper article claimed that Roosevelt himself intended to run the army and therefore was keeping Marshall in Washington as his lackey. Marshall sent the clipping to Harry Hopkins, who passed it on to Roosevelt, who sent it back, annotated, "True, but this means *you* are now the President."

This is not to say that General Marshall was without his faults. First, he often jumped to untenable conclusions. Second, his icy manner sometimes evoked fear in his junior subordinates. Third, he tried—just once—to pull the plug in the FDR rowboat. That episode arose from Marshall's single-minded desire to prevail in Europe by way of a direct cross-channel invasion. When it appeared that Roosevelt had succumbed to Churchill's Mediterranean alternative, Marshall changed his position radically and threw his weight behind Admiral King and General MacArthur to shift the priority of strategic effort to the Pacific theater. Roosevelt called his bluff immediately—in a gentlemanly way—by asking for detailed plans, production schedules, casualty estimates, and the like. Marshall replaced the plug.[6]

Still, those are barely visible loose threads in the rich tapestry of Marshall's legacy. He was free with praise for others but disliked it when he was the recipient. Accordingly, Secretary of War Stimson held his tongue until the end of the war in Europe, at which point he summoned Marshall to his office and in the presence of fourteen senior officers let him have it both barrels. Among the choice comments:

> I have seen a great many soldiers in my lifetime and you, Sir, are the finest soldier I have ever known. It is fortunate for this country that we have you in this position because this war cuts deeper into the eternal verities than any other.

Hard-boiled generals shed tears, and Marshall himself was strangely silent. When he went home that evening, Katherine felt a sense of foreboding that lingered until Stimson's aide brought over a copy of the remarks the following morning.

Marshall stayed on as Chief of Staff until the war in the Pacific was over and the stand-down had begun in earnest. Then he formally retired from the army; and with his wife Katherine, he left quarters #1 at Fort Myer for the last time and drove to their home in Leesburg. In this briefest of all retirements, he actually got inside the door before the phone rang. It was Truman, who asked him to accept the ambassadorship to China to try to keep events there from boiling over.

In this task of diplomacy, Marshall did not succeed; but it was not due to any lack of ability. He just was not a miracle worker. Truman realized this and afterward appointed him Secretary of State, giving him full credit for what became known as the Marshall Plan. That led to the only Nobel prize in history awarded to a professional military officer. Unfortunately, age forced Marshall's retirement from this role, and except for the first year of the Korean war, when he agreed to serve as Secretary of Defense, Marshall sought the solace of home and family after a long life of service.

Tributes to Marshall would fill a small library. His biographer Forrest C. Pogue relates that the one most commonly heard tribute by those who knew him best was to quote Jefferson's letter describing General Washington. In part, this letter reads:

He was in his mass perfect, in nothing wrong, in few points indifferent; and it may truly be said, that never did nature and fortune combine more perfectly to make a man great, and to place him in the same constellation with whatever worthies have merited from man an everlasting remembrance.[7]

Enough said.

ERNEST JOSEPH KING

I found Rome brick; I leave it marble.

—Augustus

Early in World War II, Captain George C. Dyer served on Admiral King's staff and estimated that his headquarters would require a staff of four hundred people. King blew up and said that since he got by with fourteen while a flag officer at sea, fifty would be the maximum he would tolerate on land. Dyer subsequently went to the Pacific, was severely wounded there, and was sent to Bethesda Naval Hospital to recover. While Dyer was in the area, King invited him to stop by his office; and when he came in, King handed him a paper that reported current staffing at 416. It was King's way of admitting he was wrong.

Admiral King was noted for his caustic personality, although for the most part it seems to have existed apart from his underlying character. It must have been; few sarcastic individuals rise to the top in the military profession—or stay there if they do—especially when the job includes tangling with the President on a frequent basis. Hence, King's abilities must have outweighed his style by several orders of magnitude. Moreover, many officers who served with him for any length of time came to regard him with an affection and respect that belied his personality.

Ernest King was born on November 23, 1878 in Lorain, Ohio, to James and Elizabeth King, who were immigrants from the British Isles. Ernest was the second of six children, two of whom died in infancy. He showed early promise by graduating as valedictorian in high school and gave as his address "The Uses of Adversity." It would stand him in good stead, for he had decided on a naval career, gaining entrance by competing for an appointment from his congressman. At Annapolis, class of 1901, he nearly failed plebe mathematics in the first semester, yet went on to graduate fourth among sixty-seven and in his last year held the Naval Academy equivalent of First Captain.[1] The tribute in the yearbook *Lucky Bag* read: "A man so various that he seems to be not one, but all mankind's epitome."

Some of that variety caused him to veer from the path of his promising career. His first three years of service were marred by no less than four "black marks" written into his efficiency reports. Although the last one was petty, he thereafter made it a point of turning in sterling performances.[2] Perhaps when an officer is endowed with a surfeit of high attributes, it takes longer for him to get his act together. At any rate, Ensign King displayed his initiative early by persuading the navy to adapt mechanical signaling devices employed by the British and the French. And like Leahy, he took every opportunity to explore the countries where his ships called.

In 1905 he married Martha Rankin Egerton, whom he had dated at Annapolis. They had six daughters and one son in that order, their son also graduating from the Naval Academy. Interestingly, Ernest and Mattie, as King's wife was always called, were married in the cadet chapel at West Point. King had formed a friendship with his bride's brother-in-law Lieutenant William D. Smith (later Brigadier General). The two of them would discuss and explore Civil War battlefields. In that way King came to master the principles of war. Admiral Nimitz had the same interest, explaining in part why the two future admirals—who were exact opposites in style and who strongly disagreed with each other on specifics— could nevertheless work out their differences with only one impasse; they used the same ground rules.

Unfortunately, King's marriage turned sour. His towering intelligence—tinged if not dyed with arrogance—grew to resent Mattie's apparent lack of it; and she in turn lost all interest in her husband's career. By the time of World War II, King lived alone on his small flagship *Dauntless* at the Washington Naval Yard, visiting his family (who lived in the official residence at the Naval Observatory) on Sunday afternoons. Yet, if he did not choose to live with them—he claimed the tension was too great—he cared for them in every other way and always saw to their needs.

For solace, King turned to other women. His bedroom athletics were common knowledge. In fact, it was so well known that Leahy made one exception to excluding anecdotes from his *I Was There*. In reference to accommodations at the Yalta conference, he said: "Admiral King took a lot of kidding from the rest of us . . . because he occupied the room that formerly was the boudoir of the Czarina." One the other hand, he never touched the three feminine confidantes in his life. Of these three, Charlotte

Official U.S. Navy photograph. Courtesy U.S. Naval Institute.

8. Fleet Admiral Ernest J. King. The corner of the handkerchief protruding from his pocket was an affectation. Everything else was all business, as the entire Japanese fleet and German submarine force were to learn the hard way.

Phil, wife of one his senior staff officers, was the most important. During the war King often went to the Phils' summer home in the Shenandoah Valley to unload. The other two confidantes, Abby Dunlap and Betsy Matter, were also navy wives, but much younger and sisters to boot. King doted on them as if they were his own daughters and they in turn rallied him with cheerfulness.

After his wedding, King spent the next five years at sea and then returned to the Naval Academy to teach ordnance and gunnery and also to serve as tactical officer for one of the two battalions of midshipmen. During one class session, he asked a midshipman to describe Sir William Thompson's sounding machine, a device used to gauge the depth of water in harbors and channels. Instead, the midshipman described an invention of his own that accomplished the same purpose better. After gaining departmental approval, King awarded him the maximum grade for the recitation, even though most of the faculty believed a zero would have been more appropriate. This illustrates the tendency of many if not most great men to tolerate, if not encourage, deviation from the straight and narrow, especially when the tack holds promise. As such, it is another instance suggesting that although different in style, King and Marshall were cut from the same cloth.

King also took time to further increase his already voracious reading habits, especially Mahan and similar treatises. He had practical ideas, too, winning in 1909 the $500 essay prize for an article in the *United States Naval Institute Proceedings* entitled "Some Ideas of Organization on Board Ship." This essay advocated a streamlined approach to shipboard organizational structure that placed more initiative on subordinates and freed the executive officer from minute supervisory details. King, however, would not always live up to his ideas, at least not before he rose to the rank of vice admiral and found himself cursing a young officer (on watch on his flagship) who had not taken sufficient initiative on a minor item. Thereafter, King changed his ways and inundated his fleet with homilies on the necessity to delegate authority.

In subsequent duties, King served under maverick Commander William S. Sims aboard the battleship *Minnesota*.[3] King was then appointed as the chief engineer aboard the *New Hampshire*, next as flag secretary to Rear Admiral Hugo Osterhaus, Commander-in-Chief of the Atlantic Fleet, and then as executive officer of the engineering research and development station at Annapolis. He was also elected secretary-treasurer of the U.S. Naval Institute and served as editor of the *Proceedings*. As editor he came to question the validity of rigid formation tactics at sea.

King's first command at sea was the destroyer *Terry*, which came with command of the flotilla of which it was a part. Later he transferred to the

Cassin. Harold Stark (whom he would succeed as Chief of Naval Operations) and Halsey were fellow captains. Concurrently, he was designated aide to Admiral Sims, but he eventually rejected Sim's black-and-white approach to issues. The impasse arose over improvement of escort destroyers versus design modification of an existing small ship known as a flivver. King argued that by the time the weight of the improvements was tallied, the escort ship's displacement would equal that of the destroyer, so why bother.

The next string of assignments brought King under Vice-Admiral Henry T. Mayo (Commander in Chief, Atlantic Fleets), as staff engineering officer. Mayo, who had also been Leahy's mentor, was intent on making officers more independent. King said of him that he had "hard sense and dry humor that confounded the pompous." At any rate, in this staff role King established a "machinery history"—analogous to medical records—for each ship, which greatly improved maintenance. He was also engaged in laying the complex minefield across the North Sea for the purpose of bottling up the German fleet in World War I.

After this assignment at sea, King returned to the academic environment as director of the Naval Post Graduate School, then located at Annapolis. This school prepared navy officers to earn master's degrees at various universities.[4] He scuttled the strict teaching methods inherited from the academy and instead stressed critical reasoning. He also wrote another noted article for the *Proceedings,* arguing in favor of larger, if fewer, battleships. And he was a member of a three-man board that developed the hierarchical training program for the navy that is still in existence today.

Next, he qualified in submarines and took command of submarine division 11 and, later the submarine base at New London.[5] During the latter tour, King was asked to raise the *S-51,* a submarine that had been rammed and sunk in more than 130 feet of water. Since there was no precedent, it took six months to do the job; but it was done so well that King was awarded the Distinguished Service Medal. Yet, in his official report he gave most of the credit to his subordinates; and in a subsequent article in the *Proceedings,* he saw to it that this praise was more widely disseminated.

Later, after King had gone into aviation, he was called on to raise another submarine—the *S-4.* This time, there were survivors trapped in the hull. King gave it everything he had, often pushing himself past the point of exhaustion; but weather conditions doomed the rescue attempts to failure. His only consolation was obtaining the Medal of Honor for the senior diver, Thomas Eadie.[6] Eadie had risked his life for two hours under harrowing conditions in order to rescue another diver who otherwise would have met certain death. In turn, the navy awarded King a second Distinguished Service Medal and with it the respect of a great number of admirals as well as the Secretary of the Navy. It may have been these perfor-

mances, more than anything else in his career, that pulled him through
the enmity that he had sown unwittingly by his arrogance.

King increasingly realized that the future of the navy depended on aviation. Thus, he did not hesitate when he was given the opportunity to go to
flight school. After graduation he took command of a squadron of seaplanes
and the seaplane tender *Wright* as his flagship. From there he became assistant to Rear Admiral William "Billy" Moffett, chief of the Bureau of Aeronautics. King had conflicts with this admiral, too; but this time there was a
difference. Moffett believed in decentralization and individual initiative, was
a mentor of sorts to many officers, and was a recipient of the Medal of
Honor. The breaking point occurred when the admiral tried to take over
personnel functions for pilots from the Bureau of Navigation. King demurred, and they parted company—albeit on friendly terms.

Next he commanded the air base at Hampton Roads, Virginia, followed
by command of the carrier *Lexington*. In the latter assignment, he made
the pilots toe the line by reminding them rather forcefully that they were
part of the ship's complement and not just passengers. He also developed
checklists to be used before a plane took off, which markedly reduced
accidents and mishaps in flight. Then in 1932, during Fleet Problem XIII,
he took the *Lexington* to a position about two hundred miles northwest of
Oahu and from that point he staged a surprise "attack" on Pearl Harbor.
It caught the "defenders" totally by surprise. As a flag officer, he would
repeat this drill with the same success. Apparently, the Japanese navy took
more copious notes than his fellow officers.

In all, King's happiest tour was on the *Lexington*. When it came time to
depart for the Naval War College, his officers presented him with a scroll
of accomplishments during his tenure as captain. He admits to being
moved to tears in his otherwise dry autobiography, adding: "I can never
feel a ship is merely an inanimate assembly of pieces of wood and metal.
To me it is a living thing with a soul that one can love."

King relished his year at the war college, but left a few weeks early for
the best of reasons. He had been selected for early promotion to rear admiral and reported to Main Navy as chief of the Bureau of Aeronautics.
Accepting the realities of the navy budget in a depression, he concentrated
on squeezing out the last cent from every dollar by haggling with contrac-
tors, by eliminating impractical schemes, and by focusing on priorities—
so much so that he was identified as the man who should take over in the
Pacific in the event of a war with Japan.

In the interim, King returned to sea as Commander, Base Force; and
shortly afterwards he was elevated to three-star rank as Commander Aircraft Battle Force. During this time he experimented with combined carrier operations and synchronized launches to achieve maximum concentration of firepower. Yet when President Roosevelt visited King's flagship,

Official U.S. Navy photograph. Courtesy U.S. Naval Institute.
9. The Carrier as the Essence of Naval Warfare. The navy had its own aviation prophet, namely, Rear Admiral William "Billy" Moffett—but the officer who advanced its development and tactics and who twice demonstrated how the Japanese would mount a sneak attack on Pearl Harbor was Admiral Ernest J. King.

the admiral rendered the appropriate courtesies but declined, unlike his colleagues, to butter the president up. King's philosophy was to let one's record speak for itself and to limit the tentacles of ambition to seeking favorable assignments.

Unfortunately, not every senior admiral possessed the same forbearance, and many of them were sensitive to slights. Accordingly, Admiral King fell from grace and was banished to the General Board. Officially, this board was an in-house admiralty think tank. In reality it was a decompression chamber for senior officers who had surfaced from their last significant assignment and felt obliged to stay on until they reached the statutory age for retirement. King's hope of succeeding Admiral Leahy as Chief of Naval Operations never had a chance. Leahy himself opposed it, and Harold Stark got the job instead.

King charged into his work on the board with so much enthusiasm that his colleagues encouraged him to go back to sea. He did this, accepting continued reversion to two-star rank to take the only billet available—the Atlantic Squadron. This drive and humility, of sorts, impressed Admiral Stark, who then laid the groundwork for King's resurrection. Stark had King repromoted, this time to four-star admiral; and a few days after Pearl Harbor elevated him to Commander in Chief, United States Fleet. Later, when Roosevelt relieved Stark on the grounds that he was in part responsible for the disaster at Pearl Harbor, King also picked up the job of Chief of Naval Operations. Later King argued for years that Stark had been railroaded for political reasons.[7] In this he was partially successful for in 1948, the navy presented Stark with the Distinguished Service Medal.

At any rate, in his new role, King faced the following. First, the defeat of Germany had priority. This meant that the effort in the Pacific, which was predominantly a navy theater, would be allotted only fifteen to twenty percent of available resources. Second, much of the Pacific fleet had been sunk or damaged. Although the aircraft carriers escaped, the United States had only five, whereas Japan had ten and a larger fleet to protect them. Third, the navy was woefully unprepared to conduct anti-submarine operations in the Atlantic, an unpreparedness which led to the loss of twenty-three million tons of shipping before the so-called Battle of the Atlantic was won. Fourth, China had to be supported in order to tie down the bulk of the Japanese army on the Asian mainland at a time when the British regarded that theater of war as unimportant. King especially understood this need and championed it when others focused on immediate problems even though it meant a cutback in material for his own fleet.

Within this framework, King's orders were simple: (1) maintain the line of communications from the West Coast to Hawaii and Midway, and (2) maintain the line of communications to New Zealand and Australia by way of Samoa. Against that onus he brought three simple rules to bear: (1) do the best with what you have, (2) don't be concerned with water that has gone over the dam, (3) difficulties exist to be overcome.

These rules may sound simplistic, but simplicity is one of the nine principles of war. The problem was King's caustic personality, which rubbed Secretary of the Navy Franklin Knox the wrong way. As a result, Knox tried, without success, to maneuver King to the Pacific. Furthermore, King totally ignored Assistant Secretary of the Navy James Forrestal. This would cause problems when Knox died in 1944 and Forrestal succeeded him as Secretary of the Navy. Other difficulties arose from King's initial indifference to General Marshall and Hap Arnold on the Joint Chiefs of Staff.

On the other hand, King, like Marshall and MacArthur, understood the need to take the offensive against an enemy as soon as possible. In practice, that meant preventing the potential Japanese occupation of Guadalcanal and Tugali in the Solomons, an occupation that would have threatened the line of communications between America, Australia and New Zealand. This offensive put the United States at the extreme limit of its ability to support a major operation at that time; hence, the navy and the marine corps had to fight tenaciously and accept heavy casualties. Worse, under command of Rear Admiral Robert L. Ghormley, the operation was failing. Nimitz visited Ghormley on the latter's flagship, realized that Ghormley was not the man for the job, and discussed the matter with King, who agreed that it was time to relieve Ghormley.[8] They replaced Ghormley with Halsey, who immediately galvanized the American forces. The navy continued to lose an untoward number of ships in separate battles, which generated a great deal of negative public opinion; but King and Nimitz stuck to their choice.

King was not oblivious to these losses and never again advocated that kind of heroic warfare. He came to realize that a policy of attrition would win in the Pacific, notwithstanding any brilliant strategy during specific operations. A case in point occurred when Admiral Spruance declined to pursue the Japanese fleet after his victory in the battle of the Philippine Sea. Spruance believed that, as at Midway, the pursuit would have meant too high a risk without commensurate gain. His fellow admirals criticized him vociferously for this supposed lack of resolve, but King saw the matter differently and defended Spruance's actions.[9]

Then came the aggravating Formosa versus Philippines decision. The issue was to decide which objective would provide the greater advantages for subsequent operations against the Japanese mainland. King held to Formosa; MacArthur, for obvious reasons, to the Philippines. The compromise of taking both was out of the question.

The pot boiled over when Nimitz began to support MacArthur. King grew furious at both of them. As discussed in subsequent chapters, Roosevelt had to step in and resolve the impasse. This notwithstanding, King and Nimitz continued their fine working relationship, holding eighteen conferences during the war. King also faced a major problem in the Atlantic, courtesy of the enormously effective German submarine warfare. At least nine problems stood between this situation and what needed to be done. In time, King put all of them to rest, as discussed in more detail in chapter 14. Similarly, he finally resolved some massive logistical bottlenecks in the Pacific by creating the Western Sea Frontier Command to unify supply efforts.

King also repaired his deteriorating relationship with the press. This relationship had become so bad that journalists were circulating unfounded stories in order to force Roosevelt to relieve him. King's attorney, Cornelius H. Bull, recognized that this dismissal would not be in the country's best interests; so Bull got together with Glen Perry, the assistant chief for the *New York Sun,* in the *Sun's* Washington office. Together they proposed that King meet privately with a selected group of journalists at Bull's home in Alexandria, Virginia, and level with them off the record. King agreed reluctantly, predicting that there would be only one such meeting. In this he was dead wrong. Those meetings continued for the balance of the war, by the end of which the "members" came almost to revere King. He in turn developed a great deal of respect and regard for them. And he kept his job.

What he didn't get to keep were the new uniforms he imposed on the navy. These included: (1) combining the navy blue winter jacket with the summer white trousers, (2) the reverse of that, and (3) the summer grey worsted uniform with black insignia. The first two were laughed out of existence; the third survived as an optional uniform until the end of the war, but it was an endless source of jokes. Admiral Leahy wore them once in a while to keep the peace, but he called them dungarees.

As for keeping his sanity, King made it a habit to read the comic pages of the *Washington Post* every morning aboard his flagship; and he frequently circulated his favorite cartoons throughout the fleet. Then, too, when an eighth-grade girl wrote to him for information for a school essay, he took time to respond:

> Dear Harriet:
> I have your letter of January 6th—and am interested to learn that you have to do my biography as part of your English work. As to your questions: I drink a little wine, now and then. I smoke about one pack of cigarettes a day. I think I like Spencer Tracy as well as any of the movie stars. My hobby is crossword puzzles—when they are difficult. My favorite sport is golf—when I can get to play it—otherwise, I am fond of walking. Hoping that all will go well with your English work, I am
> Very truly yours,
> [signed] E. J. King
> Admiral, U.S. Navy

The reference to "a little wine now and then" is essentially correct. King had been a hard drinker during most of his career but curtailed the habit during the war. And it was the mark of his character that while he openly flouted the ban against alcohol on board naval vessels, he never turned against any officer who spoke too freely while in his cups.

Admiral King retired in December 1945, by then sixty-seven years of age, and concentrated on writing his autobiography in concert with Commander Walter Muir Whitehill. King suffered a stroke two years later, became progressively invalided, and died at Portsmouth, New Hampshire, on June 25, 1956. He is all but forgotten now, on the one hand, overshadowed by Nimitz and Halsey, and on the other, by the photographs of Leahy seated next to, or standing directly behind, President Roosevelt at the various Allied conferences. Even the *Encyclopaedia Britannica* chose to exclude him, alone among the ten principals, from the distinction of a biographical article.[10] His record deserves better, witness the tribute rendered by Harvard University on the occasion of awarding him an honorary degree:

> A strategist unshaken by adversity, determined organizer of final victory; we honor his brilliant leadership of our navy and pay tribute to the fighting men he commanded.

6

HENRY HARLEY ARNOLD

The man of true greatness never
loses his youthful heart.

—Mencius

In the army, there's nothing much lower than a newly commissioned second lieutenant; yet from that humble beginning, or from the equivalent in the navy, all of the principals began their careers. "Hap" Arnold decided to begin his career with a bang. He yearned for the cavalry, but his low class standing consigned him to the infantry. Unhappy with that turn of events, he took his veteran father, his senator, and his congressman in tow, and paid a call on the Adjutant General to demand that he be transferred to his preferred branch.[1] The ploy failed, of course; but over the next thirty-eight years he never tired of attempting variations on it. This included celebrating his promotion to brigadier general by picking a bone with President Roosevelt. He got the bone, more or less, but was sent to the doghouse for six months to gnaw on it.

Yet it was not windmills he was tilting with, but propellers. He dragged—at times almost single-handedly—a reluctant military establishment into the air age in barely sufficient time to use that class of weapons effectively in World War II. That he was often banished in the process is a matter of record. That he always got back up is a tribute to his rare combination of an infectious smile, lack of guile, perceptive foresight, innovative mind, willingness to experiment—and, above all, his vast energy. He was a modern Icarus who figured out how to keep the wax from melting. Most of the time.

To fully appreciate his accomplishments, one needs to grasp the inherent disadvantages of an airplane. Ships float easily because the *average* weight per unit of space—density—is lighter than water. Stronger power plants and plates of armor are comparatively easy to add. If they weigh too much, the naval architect designs a bigger ship. That's an oversimplification but the airplane has no such luxury. In effect, it tries to float on air, an impossibility for all but clumsy dirigibles. It requires motive power just to stay up. Anything added to the apparatus taxes the power source at an exponential rate, which therefore increases weight, which consumes more fuel, which requires larger and heavier fuel tanks, which require more motive power, and so forth. Additionally, aircraft maneuverability requires complex design features that are more intricate than those found in vehicles and ships. The Wright brothers spent more time engineering maneuverability into their invention than they did the invention itself.

Scaling this technological cliff in the presence of scoffing observers pouring the burning oil of sarcasm from the heights of power does not always make for easy climbing. Worse, as the size and capacity of aircraft increase, the technical demands compound. Thus prototypes of the B-29 bomber, which had roughly twice the capacity and double the features of the B-17, presented four times the headaches. Finally, early attempts to saddle aircraft manufacture on automobile makers proved to be a disaster. General Arnold contended successfully with all of these problems by placing himself in the eye of the information storm, keeping pace with it, and making the hundreds of necessary decisions with little hesitation.

Henry Arnold was born in Ardmore, Pennsylvania, on June 25, 1886, the third of five children, the second of four sons, and the first among the mischievous. His father, a doctor and something of a martinet, served briefly in the Spanish-American War and was determined that one of his sons would graduate from West Point. When Arnold's older brother refused to go, the good doctor turned all his energies on Hap, who didn't want to go either but didn't quite know how to stand up to his father. So Hap went.

The future general had ample native intelligence. However, as a cadet he was indifferent to his studies, graduating sixty-sixth (of 111) in the class of 1907, excelling only in mischievousness. As a ringleader of the underground activity known as the Black Hands, he masterminded their pièce de résistance—an extensive fireworks display set off from the roof of the cadet barracks after taps one night. He was caught and spent a great deal of time getting better acquainted with his room and trudging the pavement in the Central Area of barracks.

Upon graduation, his first tour of duty, not counting the Adjutant General's office, was on the island of Luzon in the Philippines. His job was mapping part of the interior, which put him largely on his own away from his unit and the harassment of his fellow infantry officers, all of

Official U.S. Air Force photograph. Courtesy U.S. Army Military History Institute.
10. General of the Air Force Henry "Hap" Arnold. Arnold's original rank was,
like the others, General of the Army. The title was changed to General of the Air
Force in 1947, concurrent with establishment of the air force as a separate service.

whom had heard the story of his grand entry into the army. By the same token, the mapping gave him more opportunity to develop self-reliance in his first eighteen months than most new officers get in ten years. Thus, when the chance for pilot training opened, he applied notwithstanding the high risk. At the time, forty percent of the pilots could look forward only to death or debilitating injury.

Two officers were selected for the initial class. Thomas DeWitt Milling earned army pilot license number 1 and Arnold got number 2. They trained directly under Orville Wright in planes that were little more than motorized gliders. That did not hinder Arnold. He pushed them to their limit, and in the process he earned the first award of the Mackay Trophy for advances in aviation. He proved that aircraft, flimsy as they might be, could be used for distant reconnaissance under difficult flying conditions. That was the year 1912.

In the same year, he made another flight with a different outcome. His plane went out of control and spun rapidly toward the earth. Try as he might, nothing would pull the plane out of that dive. With death seconds away, he did something—he never remembered what—that made the plane level out just enough to make a rough landing. This saved his life but it also shattered his nerve. He quit flying and went back to the infantry, presuming it would be home for the rest of his military career.

In the interim he renewed his on-again, off-again courtship with a young lady named Eleanor Pool. Although Eleanor had become engaged to another man, Hap decided that this time he was serious. It took more than a year; but his smile, it seems, was irresistible. While they were taking a walk in Washington, in front of the White House, no less, he blurted out a proposal of marriage. Bee, as she was often called, accepted. They would have five children, one of whom died in childhood from a ruptured appendix. Their daughter Lois married a career naval aviator and the three surviving sons all graduated from West Point (one of them after first trying Annapolis). At times Hap's inattention to Bee, generated by his single-minded quest to build an air force, severely strained the marriage; but they always managed to get it back on track.

Shortly after the wedding, Arnold was sent back to the Philippines, where (as mentioned earlier) he began a lifelong friendship with George C. Marshall. While there, Arnold's desire to fly reemerged. He got his wish and flew into World War I. Behind a desk. He was made the assistant director of the air section in the Signal Corps and promoted temporarily to colonel. Try as he might, he could not swing a transfer to France. Then, in the fall of 1918, General Pershing requested a demonstration of a radio-controlled drone bomber. Arnold decided to conduct it personally, arriving on the front lines on the morning of November 11, 1918. That was the day of the armistice. He did not see a battlefield until he had earned his fourth star twenty-five years later. It was a bitter disappointment, for he presumed that only aviators with combat experience would get anywhere in the army.

What Arnold failed to realize at that moment was that piloting aircraft was only five percent of the military aviation picture. Not a single plane of American design flew in World War I. The American-made planes that did fly were copied under license from French and British models, and only one—the British DH-4—seemed to have had any merit. Even that model had its gas tank placed between the pilot and the observer, earning it the nickname of "the flying coffin."

Put another way, lofting airpower in significant numbers required a sustained ground assault of sorts on lawmakers, manufacturers, and the army in general. This included other aviators, who on occasion made more trouble than their opponents. For example, Billy Mitchell quarreled so frequently with the AEF air staff officer Ben Foulois that General Pershing had to separate them. Pershing let Mitchell stay in a combat role but replaced Foulois with Brigadier General Mason M. Patrick, an officer from the Corps of Engineers with no flying experience. When Pershing later became Chief of Staff, he appointed Patrick as the chief of the Air Service, relegating Mitchell to deputy.[2]

After the war, Arnold did not fare especially well either. He was given command of Rockwell Field in San Diego, but only for the purpose of demobilizing it. Afterward he became air officer for the IX Corps headquartered in San Francisco. There he developed the forerunner of the air observer section of the forestry service (while Billy Mitchell did the same for the border patrol). The bright spot was that Pershing had come to understand the immense role that logistics played in war and, as a result, established the Army Industrial College adjacent to the War College in what is now Fort Leslie J. McNair in Washington. Arnold was selected to attend the first class and began to realize what it would take to create an air force.

No amount of schooling, however, could teach an officer how to deal with a prophet, and Arnold learned that just being associated with one can damage a promising career. The prophet, of course, was Billy Mitchell. Arnold had become information officer for the air service after completing the industrial college. In this capacity, he worked hard to get Mitchell to tone down his remarks and to stop boring Congress and the press with his harangues and long readings from his own books. All in vain. General Mitchell had worn out his welcome in the War Department, and early in 1925 he was exiled to Fort Sam Houston, Texas. He was also reduced to his permanent grade of colonel. In short, Mitchell was washed up and he knew it.

That summer witnessed the so-called Scopes monkey trial, which began on July 10, 1925. Scopes was a high school teacher who had taught evolution in his classroom in direct violation of a Tennessee law. Although the conviction was later overturned on a technicality, there was little doubt about his guilt. The real issue was the validity of the law involved. Accordingly, William Jennings Bryan and Clarence Darrow turned the courthouse into a public forum, popularized by the play and film *Inherit the Wind*. About eight weeks later, on September 3, the dirigible *Shenandoah* crashed in Ohio. Mitchell wrote a caustic article for *Aviation Week* magazine, published on September 14, accusing the War Department of malfeasance and a host of other sins. Unless he had lost total control of his faculties, he had to realize that this would bring about a court-martial.[3]

That, of course, is what happened. And just as surely the testimony devolved into a debate on the larger issue. Arnold supported Mitchell by providing various documents, some of which he should have left in the filing cabinet. For his troubles, Arnold was banished to Fort Riley, Kansas. Strangely, he had been giving serious consideration to leaving the service to head up Pan American Airways, but the sacking motivated him to remain. He arrived at Fort Riley on a typically cold winter day and paid the obligatory call on the post commander, Major General Ewing E. Booth, who had served on Billy Mitchell's court-martial. This is called looking up at bottom.

To Arnold's complete surprise, General Booth warmly welcomed him to the post and offered to help him get back on his feet professionally. Booth understood what Mitchell was trying to do; it was just that his methods could not be tolerated. Although Arnold's methods were not always the best either, they never went that far and his smile was genuine. Thus, he regained the confidence that he might make it to the top yet. The first step was to get to the Command & General Staff College at Fort Leavenworth. When the commandant (another veteran of the Mitchell trial) stood against it, Booth called his friends in the War Department. The orders were cut.

After graduation, Arnold served first as commanding officer of the first wing of the general headquarters of the air force. This headquarters was separate from the air staff section of the War Department, a divide-and-conquer maneuver that may have been intentional in order to dilute the influence of aviation on other army priorities. At any rate, it was from this position that Arnold began to make his mark.

The first installment began when the government canceled contract airmail service and saddled it on the army as an additional mission. Unfortunately, the air corps had neither the equipment nor the experience to take on this kind of traffic, especially over high mountain ranges in bad weather. Planes crashed and pilots died in unacceptable numbers, except in Arnold's sector of responsibility. His energetic personal leadership and management made the difference, a fact that was not lost on more senior officers.

Arnold's other accomplishments during this period included: (1) a round-trip air race to Alaska with B-10 bombers, which netted him a second award of the Mackay Trophy; (2) organization of systematic weather reporting for the air force (a sore point raised by Billy Mitchell in his fatal article); and (3) participation in a 200-plane training exercise, spread over several states, that taxed the support system to its limits. His energy level seemed to increase, not decrease, with age.

Afterward, Arnold was assigned to command March Field near Long Beach, California, where, on one occasion, he volunteered the assistance of his squadrons in order to provide emergency relief to nearby earthquake victims. Because he did not have authority to do that, however, Arnold was summoned to IX Corps headquarters at the Presidio in San Francisco. Flying in, he intentionally buzzed the headquarters building. For that impudence he was met by a military police escort at the airfield and taken directly to the commander, Major General Malin Craig (who had been First Captain of the West Point class of 1898). Although Craig was at first furious, Arnold charmed him into becoming a mentor of sorts. When Craig was appointed Chief of Staff in 1935, he in turn agreed to make Arnold the assistant chief of the Air Corps, with temporary promotion to brigadier general. It was shortly after this assignment that Hap tangled with Roosevelt in an argument over priorities.

While Arnold was cooling his heels, his boss, Major General Oscar Westover, was killed in a plane crash. Westover was a solid officer but a terrible pilot who insisted on flying anyway. The debate on his successor went on for several months. Fortunately, Arnold had the support of a few key friends, the most important of whom was Harry Hopkins. Even better than Roosevelt, Hopkins understood the crumbling world situation and made a point of learning about the various services. In a way, he acted as a behind-the-scenes chairman of the joint chiefs before they ever met as such. The second friend, of course, was General Craig. The third was Major General George C. Marshall, who had moved up to Deputy Chief of Staff for the army. Arnold got the job as successor to Westover.

From that point forward, Arnold hardly ever knew a day's rest, except when heart attacks forced him into the hospital, and also when he took one brief fishing trip with Marshall late in the war. Among other things, Arnold learned about the byzantine world of politics, at least as it related to the conflict inherent in providing aircraft to Great Britain at the price of not building up American airpower. Roosevelt tasked Secretary of the Treasury Hans Morganthau sub rosa with the former, and it cost Arnold several months of hard knocks to understand how the president operated in an era of isolationism. On the other hand, the mother country was fighting for her life, whereas the United States was still at peace. It finally dawned on Arnold that building his air force was going to be an uphill struggle. He would need to exert the force of his character and personality at every turn.

Part of this struggle meant persuading manufacturing firms to start production without funding or even congressional authorization, asking them to have faith in his ability to get it later. It also meant contracting with civilian flight schools to provide preliminary instruction to air cadets. And it meant risking Roosevelt's wrath again by consulting with Charles A. Lindbergh.

Because of his avowed isolationism, Lindbergh was anathema, to the point that when the United States finally entered the war the President refused to let him come back on active duty. Arnold could not afford such grudges. Lindbergh had been to Germany several times and had developed an acute perspective on the *luftwaffe,* and Arnold needed that information. The two of them met secretly several times, once in the stands at a baseball game at West Point, where they sat behind reporters who were trying to track them down.

Next, Arnold created an advisory group within his own staff, different from all others. Arnold insisted that this group become an extension of his eyes and ears worldwide—a high-level intelligence-gathering mission—and hounded them whenever he felt they had become too comfortable in their jobs. He also made a point of flying to every theater repeatedly to get information first hand. He then organized the hundreds of air-shuttle runs into a formal Air Transport Service and a somewhat parallel air evacuation service staffed with flight nurses and other medical personnel.

He set up Eglin Air Force Base in Florida as a research and development center and spent considerable time with scientists trying to head off the technical problems that inevitably arose as new aircraft were developed, especially the jet-powered aircraft in which he took a keen interest. At first, even Marshall was puzzled at why Arnold associated with university "eggheads" when there was a war to be won. Lastly, Arnold all but eliminated staff meetings. Key officers had direct access to his office, and he made a point of seeing them perhaps more frequently than they cared for.

Then, too, he had a hard time gaining the acceptance of the navy on the Joint Chiefs of Staff. At first, King rudely ignored him or treated him as a junior upstart who should not be there except to make presentations when asked. Dealing with MacArthur was another problem. The first time he met him, the general was almost paranoid, prophesying doom at every turn. Arnold's good nature was sorely tried, and at times he became quite abrasive, especially when it came to the bomber campaign issues.

This campaign comprised several distinct "battles" beyond the obvious one of actual bombing. First, the proportionality of funds and support for strategic bombing versus other elements of war—to include tactical air support—was never clearly resolved. Second, the debate about night versus daylight bombing—to include the subissues of fighter escorts and appropriate targets—remained a sore point almost to the end. Third, development of the B-29 bomber drained funds away from the B-17 production, notwithstanding that technical problems with the former—primarily overheating engines—lingered until 1945.

Worse, the earlier predictions on how strategic bombing would bring victory without the necessity of a campaign on the ground proved utterly wrong. The most embarrassing moment came when the army air force initially took the credit for victory in the battle of Midway. Later analysis determined that one bomb had caused minor damage on one small Japanese ship. On the other hand, the bombing campaign over Europe, and later over Japan, inflicted tremendous damage that contributed significantly to final victory.

In all, Arnold was so used to going it alone that he never really stopped to organize his staff and key commanders to share that load. Moreover, he took time to care for his men at every opportunity. For example, when the mess hall at Goose Bay in Labrador lost its five-star rating, so to speak, Arnold instantly recognized that the morale of the personnel stationed in that forsaken outpost would plummet. He raised hell and did not let up until the food improved markedly. In another case, while flying back from China by way of the Indian Ocean, he went out of his way to inspect a small air base on what is now Diego Garcia. He asked the officer in command, who was only a lieutenant, if anything was needed. The reply was negative, but Arnold realized that few lieutenants complain to four-star generals. He made the lieutenant feel at ease and then asked again. This time he got some answers and promptly saw to those needs.

Still another aspect of his character was demonstrated in the way he handled the displacement of Major General Ira Eaker as the senior air force officer in the European theater. As long as Eisenhower was engaged in Africa in Operation TORCH, there was little need for Eisenhower's air officer Tooey Spaatz to be involved with the bombing campaign run out of Great Britain. When Eisenhower was appointed Supreme Commander for OVERLORD, he specified that he wanted Spaatz, not Eaker, as his senior American aviator. Arnold went to London personally to inform Eaker of the change, indicating that it was his decision. In light of the long-standing friendship between Arnold and Eaker, taking the onus off Eisenhower's back for the good of the cause showed remarkable courage.

This burning of the candle at both ends had its price, and that was the series of heart attacks mentioned previously. Arnold's good friends, especially Marshall, pulled the necessary strings at Arnold's request to keep him on active duty until the end of the war. But when the war was over, so was his career. He and Bee settled on a small ranch they had purchased earlier in Sonoma, California; and at times he reverted to his earlier playfulness.

One incident in particular stands out. When he visited his son David at West Point, he brought a model railroad and set it up in David's room. A

Official U.S. Air Force photograph. Courtesy U.S. Army Military History Institute.

11. Bombing Raid over Germany. Although strategic bombing was not *the* decisive arm of war, it was an indispensable element. General Arnold's vast personal energy ensured that sufficient airpower was produced in time to make that contribution.

cadet guard came by and wanted to know just who was responsible for this childishness. General Arnold stepped out from behind the alcove wall and said "I am." That, of course, brought the inquiry to an end.

He was also the most strapped for cash among the ten principals; and as a consequence he decided to write his autobiography *Global Mission*. Unfortunately, it did not do well in the marketplace. Apparently, the battles he fought were not the kind that interest the majority of potential readers.

In the interim, the Department of Defense was formed in 1947, with designation of the air force as a separate service. Concurrently, Hap Arnold's rank was changed to General of the Air Force, the only person ever to hold that title. By then, however, it no longer meant much to him. His health was deteriorating, and he sought happiness only with his family and friends, one of whom had been his driver throughout World War II and now lived in a house adjacent to the ranch. Arnold died on January 15, 1950, the first of the World War II five-star officers to pass from the scene. All things considered, it is fair to say that Hap Arnold gave his life for his country and for his fellow man.

7

Douglas MacArthur

In men of the highest character and noblest genius there is to be found a desire for honor and command, for power and glory.

—Cicero

An apocryphal story tells about General MacArthur transferring from one cruiser to another during a conference afloat in the southwest Pacific. Just as the launch hove to, a sudden wave smashed it against the hull of the ship. The officer in charge apologized and said he would get another one in a few minutes. The general replied, "Don't bother; I'll walk." By contrast—and this is not apocryphal—when a radio broadcast led to his being informed that President Truman had relieved him of command, his expression registered shock only for a moment. Then he turned to his wife and calmly said, "Well, Jeannie, we're going home at last."[1] Thus in his last moment of active service after fifty-two years in uniform, he demonstrated a remarkable simplicity and control over his temper.

The irony of it all, then, is that if MacArthur hadn't sometimes acted like a god, he really could have passed for one. No other man in modern history was endowed with so many high attributes: absolute fearlessness and personal courage, intellectual genius, an acute strategic sense, nearly unequaled battlefield acumen, and the ability to lead a conquered militant nation into a more democratic model. Even with his flaws—and he had a number of them—he makes the gods of Homer's *Iliad* pale by comparison. Without those flaws, there would be no comparison at all. To put the case another way, when the Creator puts that many marbles in one ring, some of them are bound to knock about in an untoward way.

MacArthur was one of the two principals who were sons of career officers—Halsey was the other—and his father was probably the most renown

Official Department of Defense photograph. Courtesy National Archives.
12. General of the Army Douglas MacArthur. MacArthur's role as proconsul of Japan during the occupation remains unique in history. Notwithstanding his well-known flaws, he exerted an influence on Japan equal to that of Washington and Jefferson on the United States during the American Revolution and its aftermath.

officer of his day. Arthur MacArthur rose to the rank of temporary colonel at the age of twenty during the Civil War and won the Medal of Honor in the process.[2] Afterward, he married Mary Pickney Hardy of Virginia, climbed from Regular Army lieutenant to major general, fought in the Philippines during the Spanish-American War, and quarreled incessantly with the commissioner William Howard Taft. He was relieved of command, brought home, promoted to lieutenant general as a reward for his services; and then retired.

Arthur and his wife "Pinky," as she was called, had two sons. The elder son, Arthur, graduated from the Naval Academy, class of 1896, one year before Leahy. Arthur was compiling his own distinguished career when a ruptured appendix took his life in 1923.[3] As for the younger son, Douglas, "Pinky" took on the job of mentor and followed him everywhere possible, until she died in her eighties. She saw to it that Douglas entered the Military Academy; and once he had been admitted, she took up residence in the local hotel and stayed there until his graduation four years later. While a cadet, MacArthur rarely made a personal decision of any consequence without first consulting her, perhaps extending even to his choice of a roommate.[4] How a momma's boy could grow into such independence of spirit and indomitable courage is surely a mystery for the ages.

Many stories are told about Douglas's cadet days. The best-known story is his refusal as a plebe to rat on upperclassmen after they nearly killed him in a hazing incident. He compiled an academic record that had been exceeded only once before and has never been exceeded since.[5] Like Pershing and Marshall (at VMI), he was the ranking cadet in each of the last three years.[6] Thus, by graduation Douglas had captured triple honors as First Captain, first man in his class, and captain of a varsity sport, namely, baseball.

However, there was one incident that clearly foreshadowed his egotistical bent. Normally cadets who earned high marks in a subject were exempt from certain examinations. This was Douglas's situation until a brief hospitalization for influenza caused him to miss several classes; therefore, his professor scheduled him for those exams. MacArthur staged something of a ruse and went over to the professor's quarters without authority, threatening to resign if the order was not rescinded. The professor humored him, but this conduct was noted in his disciplinary record.[7]

MacArthur's first four years of service were not auspicious. He did poorly at the engineer officer school, barely making passing marks. Next he absented himself repeatedly from his duties at the district engineer office in Milwaukee, primarily to cater to the demands of his parents who lived in that city. Then he balked at temporary harbor construction duty located sixty miles north. This exhausted the patience of the district engineer, who wrote a scathing efficiency report on him. In short, MacArthur was acting like a spoiled brat, which at the moment he was.

The turning point of MacArthur's early career came at Fort Leaven-worth, but it was not at the Command & General Staff College. It was with troops, specifically the worst of twenty-one companies on post. From the first day, he set down standards and then drilled, marched, and instructed his men until they jumped from last place to first by the time of the next annual inspection. Off duty, however, he had a tendency to swagger about the grounds with a Napoleonic gaze in his eyes. This rubbed Lieutenant George C. Marshall the wrong way, but there was just no denying MacArthur's leadership abilities.

Certainly his superiors recognized his leadership qualities. It wasn't too long before MacArthur gained assignment to the general staff at the War Department. While there he exerted an unusual influence on major deci-sions, including the selection of Pershing to command the AEF during World War I. In the interim, the potential for war with Mexico took pre-cedence. MacArthur volunteered to lead a reconnaissance expedition deep into Mexican territory at Vera Cruz. The account of this harrowing expe-rience reads like the script for the film *Raiders of the Lost Ark*. Bullets ripping through his shirt, MacArthur narrowly escaped death at least four times, once while pumping a hand-powered railroad shuttle car in a mad dash to safety. Afterward, he buttered up Chief of Staff Leonard Wood, who in turn nominated him for the Medal of Honor. The awards board turned it down, but the bravery was real.

When the United States entered World War I two years later, MacAr-thur was picked as chief of staff for the 42nd "Rainbow" Division that he had created, and from which he had himself transferred to command of one of the brigades. In that capacity, he distinguished himself on the field of battle as no other person has ever done before or since. In the space of eight months he earned seven rows of ribbons, including two Distin-guished Service Crosses, one of which was a downgrade from his second recommendation for a Medal of Honor (probably because of his higher rank). In part, the citation read: "On a field where courage was the rule, his courage was the dominant factor." In the process, he went from com-mand of a brigade to command of an entire division.

That was the bright side. The negative was that his mother badgered General Pershing and the War Department, including Secretary of War Newton Baker, with a letter campaign to advance the case of her son.[8] Whether this interloping ever had any effect is speculation. The chances are slim. Pershing was his own man, and in his old age had a unique way of designating those for whom he had the most respect. He would simply say, "A fighter." For exceptional fighters, he intoned, "A fighter . . . a fighter." And for a rare handful, MacArthur among them, it was, "A fighter . . . a fighter . . . a fighter."[9]

At any rate, when MacArthur returned to the states, he was given the superintendency of the Military Academy. This made his temporary rank of brigadier general permanent, but it was not a reward for his services. The academy had been drained of all but one class in order to supply officers for the war. Another class was recalled as student officers for a year, but it wasn't enough. The institution needed a renaissance and MacArthur obliged. He forced the academic board to bring at least part of the curriculum up to date, made participation in athletics mandatory (either in varsity or intramural sports), and eliminated some of the more petty restrictions that had been imposed on cadets. His adjutant said later that he radiated "a gifted leadership, a leadership that kept you at a respectful distance yet at the same time took you in as an esteemed member of the team, and very quickly had you working harder than you had ever worked before in your life."[10]

While superintendent, he married a young divorcee named Louise Cromwell Brooks, who had recently declined Pershing's proposal. Within a year, Pershing reassigned MacArthur to the Philippines, before the latter's normal tenure at West Point would have ended. However, the connection between the two events is not as insidious as it appears. First, MacArthur's reforms had gone too far, and he sometimes countermanded failing grades of promising athletes. This lead to a ground swell among graduates and faculty (including Major Omar Bradley) to oust him. Second, the Philippines were then considered the most important overseas post. Third, command assignments, then as now, were stepping stones to higher rank. In short, Pershing had to act and did so in a way that would not jeopardize MacArthur's career. If he satisfied his pique at the same time, that was merely a bonus.

MacArthur spent three years in the Philippines; and upon his return to the states, he was given command of several corps in succession, although the event that marks this period was the court-martial of William "Billy" Mitchell. As mentioned in Chapter 6, Mitchell was guilty beyond all doubt; the trial was a formality required by law that Billy turned into a forum on airpower. As such, MacArthur's vote took on its own importance. Because conviction required only a two-thirds vote of the court, a "not guilty" vote on McArthur's part could have no effect; but such a vote would indicate that McArthur believed virulent insubordination to be justified. This meant that MacArthur believed a prophet in uniform was above regulations intended to maintain order and discipline. Although not conclusive, the evidence suggests that is how he voted.[11]

At any rate, MacArthur returned to the Philippines, but it was short and alone. The first Mrs. MacArthur filed for divorce and would later try two more husbands, the first of whom was the actor Lionel Atwill. Then within a year, MacArthur was offered the job of Chief of Engineers. He declined on the grounds that he had not accrued any significant engineer experience since his early days as a lieutenant. That was true, but the real reason was that he was holding out for Chief of Staff of the Army. Although his fellow officers concluded he had just ruined his career by that maneuver, MacArthur had an uncanny sense of how events transpired in the upper echelons of power. A few months later, he put on the four stars that went with the army's most senior assignment.

His tenure coincided with the low point of the army's fortunes. The potential for future war was faint, while the depression further reduced the penurious budget; and the already low pay was cut by fifteen percent. Additionally, officers were placed on unpaid furlough one month each year. Still, military personnel had an income when millions did not; and this set the stage for a serious lapse of judgment on MacArthur's part, namely, the way he handled the so-called bonus marchers.

At the end of World War I, Congress declared a bonus for veterans payable in 1945. The depression motivated thousands of them to descend on Washington and demand immediate payment thirteen years in advance. MacArthur was ordered to use the army to prevent an insurrection but not necessarily to rout the marchers. Against the advice of his aide Major Eisenhower, MacArthur took to the field. On the false premise that the marchers were communist sympathizers and other radicals rather than veterans, he had some of their tents on the Anacostia flats fired and then drove them from the city.[12] It was not his finest hour, though it did not detract from his standing with Roosevelt.

On the contrary, MacArthur would serve five years as Chief of Staff. Then, reverting to his permanent grade of major general, he returned to the Philippines again. On the way over, he met Jean Marie Faircloth, a young lady from Tennessee with a delightful accent to match. They became engaged and were married two years later while on a short trip to New York. They had one son, Arthur MacArthur IV, on whom his father would dote and who later gravitated to the field of music under an assumed name.

Coinciding with this marriage, MacArthur was given the choice of returning to the states to serve in another two-star billet somewhere or of retiring and staying on the payroll of the Philippines as a local field marshal. He chose the latter and continued to do what he could under limited budgets to prepare the islands for defense. He believed it would take at least ten years. The Japanese gave him five. At the end of those five years, Japan attacked Pearl Harbor and nine hours later commenced their offensive against the Philippines.

Much has been written about MacArthur's roughly one hundred days between this outbreak of war and his evacuation to Australia under orders from the President.[13] Most of it is a record of failure, punctuated by frequent and willing exposure to enemy fire directed at Corregidor. First, MacArthur did not ensure that all of the recently arrived B-17 bombers at

Clark Field were evacuated to Mindanao, out of range of Japanese fighter planes. Second, he failed to place sufficient food and medical supplies on Bataan, causing untold suffering among the defending troops that retreated there. He even moved some of the supplies that were on Bataan to Corregidor out of proportion to needs.[14] Third, he visited Bataan only once—in January before matters grew desperate. Fourth, he accepted a gift of several hundred thousand dollars in Filipino state funds from President Quezon and banked it in his personal account. The list goes on and on.

What explains this extended lapse of character and judgment? William Manchester posited that it was "information overload."[15] Other writers have concluded that MacArthur's performance was very much *in* character for him. Perhaps the answer lies in the fact that he had retired four years earlier after thirty-four years of active service and became inured to a life of passive luxury. Paralleling his first years of active service, it seems to have taken a while for events to jar him out of this lethargy, and that happened only after he reached Australia. The situation he faced there, combined with the award of the Medal of Honor, broke the spell.

For starters, he challenged the Australian defensive mentality that was inherent in the so-called Brisbane line. This was an imaginary line drawn from Brisbane to Adelaide behind which the Aussies intended to fight to the death against any Japanese invasion. MacArthur demurred. He was going to take whatever troops were available and go after the Japanese forces on Papua-New Guinea. If MacArthur could occupy that island, there was no chance the Japanese could ever invade Australia. And that's where he went. Moreover, his campaign sustained the lowest casualty rates of any in World War II.[16]

The ultimate objective of this campaign was the Japanese stronghold at Rabaul. Fortunately, MacArthur (and Nimitz) came to realize that Rabaul could be isolated and, hence, neutralized without mounting a direct offensive. The key to this isolation strategy was the Admiralty Islands, one of which offered a fine harbor at Manus. MacArthur wanted the base solely for his own southwestern theater, notwithstanding its ability to also support naval operations under Nimitz's command. In effect, he told Nimitz, "If I cannot control your navy, you cannot use my island."

Admiral Halsey was the man caught in the middle of this childishness. He remained under Nimitz's command but came under MacArthur's thumb for operational control. Command arrangements in the Pacific left much to be desired. Halsey and MacArthur discussed the issue at some length, until Halsey in exasperation stood up to MacArthur and said, "General, I disagree with you entirely. Not only that, but I'm going one step further and tell you that if you stick to that order of yours, you'll be hampering the war effort." MacArthur backed off, albeit not before pleading with long-winded rebuttals that evening and again the following morning.

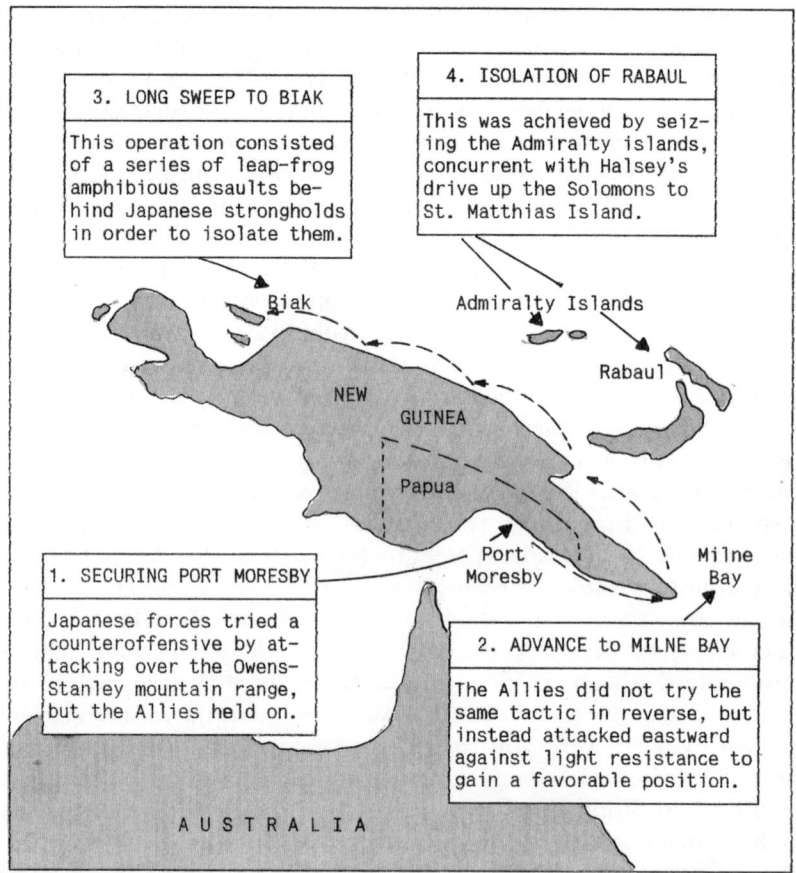

3. LONG SWEEP TO BIAK

This operation consisted
of a series of leap-frog
amphibious assaults be-
hind Japanese strongholds
in order to isolate them.

4. ISOLATION OF RABAUL

This was achieved by seiz-
ing the Admiralty islands,
concurrent with Halsey's
drive up the Solomons to
St. Matthias Island.

Biak

Admiralty Islands

Rabaul

NEW
GUINEA

Papua

Port
Moresby

Milne
Bay

1. SECURING PORT MORESBY

Japanese forces tried a
counteroffensive by at-
tacking over the Owens-
Stanley mountain range,
but the Allies held on.

2. ADVANCE to MILNE BAY

The Allies did not try the
same tactic in reverse, but
instead attacked eastward
against light resistance to
gain a favorable position.

AUSTRALIA

Figure 2. The Campaign for Papua-New Guinea. Although MacArthur's envelopment of North Korean forces at Inchon remains his most famous success, the campaign to rid this 1500-mile-long island of the Japanese army early in World War II was an even more remarkable accomplishment.

By mid-1944, the separate theaters under MacArthur and Nimitz had merged in practical, if not legal, terms. This meant that agreement on the next object had to be negotiated. MacArthur wanted the Philippines; King wanted Formosa. Nimitz leaned towards MacArthur, but King was his boss. The impasse was not resolved until Roosevelt intervened personally. First, King was told to stay home, while Leahy stayed in the background.[17] Then combining a campaign publicity trip to Hawaii with the hard business of war, Roosevelt listened to the two protagonists for two days. With the deck stacked in his favor, MacArthur's power of persuasion prevailed, helped immeasurably by Nimitz's lack of enthusiasm for the Formosa option.

The ensuing campaign in the Philippines was hard fought, especially on Luzon where the Japanese forces were still holding out in the northeastern sector at the time of the surrender. Walter Kruger's Sixth Army made the attack south from Lingayen Gulf through the central plains towards Manila, the same approach that the Japanese used in 1942. When Kruger bogged down, MacArthur sent Eichelberger with a major task force on an amphibious end run south of Manila, which then forced the Japanese commander, General Yamashita, to order the evacuation of that city. Unfortunately, Vice-Admiral Denshichi Okochi decided to defend Manila and, while doing so, massacre the residents in a holocaust. MacArthur witnessed this up close as he accompanied the lead elements into the city, braving death at every instant. This was probably the bitterest week in his life, and he would later exact vengeance for it.

A less distressing subject was MacArthur's relationships with other senior officers. He had unreserved pride in his air force chief, George C. Kenney. Whenever Kenney by a stroke of luck picked quarters that proved to be in a more favorable spot, MacArthur exercised eminent domain proceedings. Then he would apologize sheepishly like a little boy who had just been caught with his hand in the cookie jar. By contrast, when he turned against his chief of staff, Lieutenant General Richard K. Sutherland, for a minor shortcoming as wars go, he poured forth a torrent of profanity that stunned those who overheard it.[18] And then there was the admiral who just simply hated MacArthur, or so the former believed. The two of them were inspecting front lines when a Japanese shell hit nearby. The admiral hit the deck while the general just stood there watching. When he got up, MacArthur remarked, "I'm glad somebody around here has enough sense to get out of harm's way," or words to that effect. From that point forward, the admiral became a devoted follower, one of forty or fifty senior officers to accept membership in "the association of former heretics." General Maxwell D. Taylor joined this club as late as 1955![19]

MacArthur's skill at winning people to his viewpoint became the mainstay in a campaign of a far different sort after the war—one which placed him among the true worthies of all time. This performance was heralded by the remarks of Toshikazu Kase, who was with the Japanese surrender party aboard the *Missouri*.

When the Supreme Commander finished, I wrote in my report the impression his words had made on me. He is a man of peace. Never has the truth of the line "peace has her victories no less renowned than war" been more eloquently demonstrated. He is a man of light. . . . I raised a question whether it would have been possible for us, had we been victorious, to embrace the vanquished with a similar magnanimity. Clearly it would have been different.[20]

As commander of occupation forces in Japan, MacArthur's approach was the antithesis of militarism. He combined persuasion with an absolute trust and faith in the Japanese people. At the same time, he maintained an aloofness that is more highly regarded in the Japanese culture than in America and, therefore, is harder for critics to understand. He also knew instinctively how to work with the Japanese emperor, striking just the right balance between eliminating the deistic pretenses but still allowing him to be the revered head of the nation.

Perhaps MacArthur's greatest single contribution was the rewriting of Japan's constitution. He appointed a Japanese committee to prepare a revision. The first draft was a whitewash and got nowhere. The second was radical and included a bill of rights for all Japanese citizens. Among other things, women gained the right to vote, and everyone had the right to strike. At first, the citizenry were reluctant to exercise that latter right. For example, a chorus line—primarily to entertain occupation forces—expressed displeasure at their employers by kicking only half as high. In time, though, these reforms took root.

The one unpleasant task MacArthur faced was the prosecution of war criminals. The trials conducted in Japan were models of restraint; but the two in the Philippines, against General Homma and General Yamashita, were not. This was MacArthur's vengeance pure and simple, and nothing was going to stand in the way of it.[21] Even if those two commanders had not directly ordered the heinous crimes committed against tens of thousands of Filipinos and Allied prisoners of war, they were responsible for the conduct of their troops. All things considered, then, it was indeed a mild retaliation.

Then came the invasion of South Korea by North Korean forces. This piece of world history is well-known; and because the events and decisions became entangled in different levels of perspective, it is included among the case studies in chapter 14. Briefly, once the United States made the decision to counterinvade North Korea and China reacted with a massive intervention, MacArthur's theater-level perspective clashed with the national purpose, or, more accurately, with the changing national purpose. Eventually, this clash reached an impasse, which left Truman no other choice but to relieve MacArthur of command. Interestingly, MacArthur later admitted that Truman had a perfect right to dismiss him but was embittered by the way he went about it.[22] Apparently, Truman had a poor understanding of the value of social grace.

Upon his return to the states, MacArthur made the rounds of the country, giving many speeches. Among these speeches was the keynote address at the Republican National Convention in 1952, when he was resurrecting his old hopes of running for president. The idea of becoming president was not all that far-fetched. For if Robert Taft had received the Republican nod, MacArthur would have been his running mate; and if Taft had won,

then upon his death shortly afterward it would have been President Mac-
Arthur rather than President Eisenhower in the White House. Whatever
the case, MacArthur's speeches did little to improve his stature. States-
manship does not evolve from bilging one's grudges.

"The General," as his wife Jean always called him, lived on for thirteen
years, passing into history on April 4, 1964. MacArthur was interred in
his own memorial, the former city hall in Norfolk, Virginia, somewhat
reminiscent of the mausoleum in Paris that holds Napoleon's remains. But
his spirit isn't there; it is on the Plain at West Point, the First Captain of
the Long Grey Line. Consider his remarks on the occasion of the award
of the Sylvanus Thayer medal:

> You are the leaven which binds together the entire fabric of our na-
> tional system of defense. From your ranks come the great captains
> who hold the nation's destiny in their hands the moment the war
> tocsin sounds. The Long Grey Line has never failed us. Were you to
> do so, a million ghosts in olive drab, in brown khaki, in blue and
> gray, would rise from their white crosses thundering those magic
> words—Duty, Honor, Country.

It is true that some contemporaries—and a few historians, for that matter—came to despise his memory. He did have his flaws and his conduct
on Corregidor in the early days of the war was tantamount to a disgrace.
Yet from the perspective of time, it all means nothing. Like Alexander,
like Caesar, like Napoleon, these flaws are transcended by his virtues and
accomplishments—and in MacArthur's case the ratio is much higher. *National Geographic Magazine,* in a rare biographical article, put the case this
way:

> Proud mixture of vanity and valor, a figure of legend and contro-
> versy, Douglas MacArthur was a military prodigy unlike any other
> in U.S. history. A veteran of three major American wars, his honors
> and influence grew with each new command. In the end his pride
> exceeded his authority, and like a figure of Greek tragedy he fell
> precipitously from power. Yet a strong MacArthur heritage remains.
> No American had more influence over the destiny of modern Japan,
> and consequently the resurgence of democracy in the Pacific, than
> this all-too-human five-star hero.[23]

One might add that he touched the spirit of man as few soldiers ever have.

CHESTER WILLIAM NIMITZ

Adversity reveals the genius of a general; good fortune conceals it.
                                                              —Horace

Every service has its own cardinal sins. For the navy, one of the most serious offenses is running a ship aground. This normally results in the termination of a promising career, and it certainly isn't the normal route to fleet admiral. However, one culprit did manage to overcome the stigma of a court-martial conviction on this account, although it is doubtful if Ensign Nimitz believed he would be that lucky.[1] What got him off the hook, it seems, was that (1) ensigns are rarely given command of ships, (2) the site was poorly charted, (3) his service record to that point was spotless, (4) he extricated his ship without serious damage and then re-ported himself, and (5) he had a twinkle in his eye.

That twinkle was deceptive. Its possessor could be forceful, more so than Nimitz's colleagues wanted his first biographer to relate. In his original manuscript, E. P. Potter told how the late Admiral Nimitz had once queried each member of his staff on the advisability of attacking Kwajalein directly or first taking some outer islands. To a man, they all voted for the latter. Nimitz pondered these replies for a moment, then said, "Well, gentlemen, it appears that Kwajalein will be our next objective." Then he added that there were many officers stuck behind desks stateside itching for sea duty, and if any member of his staff could not see his way clear to supporting that decision he would arrange for an immediate exchange. Given that Potter and Nimitz had once collaborated on a major history of seapower, the reviewers prevailed on him to cut that item.[2]

Chester Nimitz was born on February 24, 1884, in the small town of Fredericksburg, Texas. He seems to have been an outgoing lad from the beginning, and like Leahy he sought an appointment to West Point. When that proved unavailable, Nimitz trained his sights on Annapolis. He graduated with the class of 1905—a year after Halsey and two years before Spruance—and was seventh in order of merit. In his last year he was a "three stripper," commanding a company, which placed him in the upper ten percent of his class in military bearing. In the *Lucky Bag,* his classmates wrote: "He seems of cheerful yesterdays and confident tomorrows."

Following graduation, Nimitz's first cruise brought him to Japan, where, as mentioned earlier, he met and developed a great respect for Admiral Togo. He maintained this respect during World War II, arguing for a more dispassionate attitude toward the Japanese while destroying their war machine as fast as possible. His reasoning was that the two nations would be allies afterward; and, therefore, too much enmity would make the peace process more difficult than necessary. After the war, Nimitz was distressed at the desecration of Togo's flagship *Mikasa,* by then anchored in concrete and used as a recreation center. He organized a fund drive to restore the old battleship and made a handsome contribution of his own.

Nimitz's early assignments included command of the gunboat *Panay* and the destroyer *Decauter.* He then gravitated to submarines; and while serving on the *Skipjack,* he risked his life to save a sailor who fell overboard in a storm. For this deed he was awarded the Silver Lifesaving Medal.

And speaking of submarines, they were almost as dangerous as aircraft at the time and, worse, they were powered by gasoline engines that caused no end of mechanical problems and hazards. Nimitz set his sights on changing over to oil as a source of fuel and became something of an expert on diesel engines. He also considered the use of submarines in time of war and was invited as a lieutenant to lecture at the Naval War College on the subject. The talk was latter expanded and published in the *Proceedings* under the title "Defensive and Offensive Tactics of Submarines."

In April of 1913, Nimitz married Catherine Freeman which developed into a relationship that by all accounts, was as idyllic as Pershing's. They raised four children, a son and three daughters, one of whom became a nun. Their son followed in his father's footsteps at Annapolis and rose to the rank of rear admiral. According to all of the children, the parents rarely argued or bickered, not even when as youngsters they raised cane in the family car on cross-country trips. When daughter Mary announced her decision to become a nun, her father replied that he was not losing a daughter but was gaining 345 of them. And when another daughter, Nancy, became a communist sympathizer for a while, her father tolerated it with remarkable patience, except that he would not allow any disrespect to be shown towards the symbols of the nation, not even from a distance.

Admiral Nimitz had many positive attributes, and almost all of them

Official U.S. Navy photograph. Courtesy U.S. Naval Institute.

13. Fleet Admiral Chester W. Nimitz. The most likable of the ten principals, Nimitz was forever telling stories; but he told them to make his point and to keep the intensity of his responsibilities from turning him sour. This aspect of his personality often obscures his true greatness.

contributed to making his career an unqualified success. In addition to being one of the most likable officers in naval history, he made the most of every assignment, including command of a flotilla of decommissioned destroyers. He had more fun when tasked to build the submarine base at Pearl Harbor. Shortchanged on the requisite funding, he elevated the practice of "midnight requisitioning" to an art form. The stuff he and his band of "thieving" petty officers lifted from various commands would have warmed the heart of the most conniving army supply sergeant. There was no crime, of course. Every scrape was used to fulfill a mission imposed on Nimitz by the navy; and even some of the flag officer "victims" admired him for his ingenuity, even the one who "contributed" his staff car.

His career also included teaching at Annapolis, and later he was made director of the new naval reserve officers training corps program at the Berkeley campus of the University of California. Of special interest to him was the reform of teaching methods. As a midshipman at Annapolis, he had been forced to learn bite-sized nodules of information gathered on his own steam. This enhanced the self-reliance essential to command, but it did little to exercise the mind. Like King and Marshall, he wanted his students to think for themselves. He understood the need to employ initiative in an environment as regimented as the armed services. At Berkeley, he railed against the publish-or-perish syndrome. On that point, however, he had no luck whatsoever; neither then nor years later when, as a retired and idolized fleet admiral, he was invited to serve on the Board of Regents.

Nimitz extended his educational approach beyond the classroom by on-the-job instruction for dozens of young officers. He gave them a chance to exercise command or take on difficult tasks while he stood by and guided them passively, even to the point of emphasizing his own errors. Once when his cruiser *Augusta* was refueling oil at sea in heavy weather, he took the conn personally and by misjudgment glanced the oiler. Nimitz gave the watch officer, Lieutenant E. M. Thompson, an order to disengage; but it was infeasible. Thompson told him why "Your anchor is in the other ship," and recommended another procedure. Nimitz agreed and afterward asked how he had gone wrong. Thompson obliged, "You were overconfident and misjudged the wind." Nimitz thanked him in a colorful sort of way, "That's right, and don't you ever forget it!"

About the time of World War I, Nimitz gained a mentor in the person of Captain Samuel S. Robison (later Rear Admiral), who was Commander, Submarine Force Atlantic Fleet. Nimitz was initially assigned as engineering aide, a tough job in submarines; and Robison took him under wing on a tour of European naval stations. Later, when Robison became the Superintendent of the Naval Academy, he began to implement some of Nimitz's ideas on teaching, so that the relationship became something of a two-way street. Most of all, it was Robison who encouraged the future admiral to veer away from engineering into general staff and command, which is where Nimitz's superlative talents lay.

Thus, Nimitz progressed through a variety of assignments, such as senior member of the Board of Submarine Design and executive officer on the battleship *South Carolina*. He took a keen interest in amphibious operations. He also tried to get to the flight school at Pensacola, but other duties intervened. In 1927, he was selected for flag rank with command of Cruiser Division Two. Unfortunately, at that moment he was hospitalized with a hernia, which cost him the command of the cruisers. But upon recovery he received an even better assignment—command of Battleship Division One.

In many ways Nimitz followed in Leahy's footsteps, because when he completed that tour he was appointed as the chief of the Bureau of Navigation. While in that assignment, he was offered command of the Pacific theater at Pearl Harbor, declining on the grounds that he was too junior a flag officer for that critical post. Two years later—nine days after Pearl Harbor—the Navy Department turned the offer into a command, whereupon Nimitz jumped from two to four-star rank as Commander in Chief, Pacific (CINCPAC), the job he would hold for almost four years.

When Nimitz arrived at Pearl Harbor, most of the personnel were demoralized. They had blamed themselves for the failure to adequately defend against the Japanese attack and were almost certain that they would lose their jobs. But Nimitz kept them just where they were and proceeded with the war. In time, he did replace or rotate most of them (as he should have done), but there is no doubt that morale shot up.

For his chief fighter, Halsey was the obvious choice. The carriers were the only significant ships left to fight, and Halsey would take on any assignment when the risk was less than suicidal. For his chief of staff, he selected Rear Admiral Raymond Spruance. As with most of Spruance's former bosses, Nimitz's respect for him grew steadily. Spruance was a quiet officer with an intelligence that exceeded Nimitz's, and King's, for that matter. He devoted his energies entirely to matters at hand, was without a trace of arrogance, and would later prove to be a fighter.

Nimitz's management style was similar to current Japanese business practices, in that he would often formulate an idea orally with his chief subordinates and then let it filter down the ranks for comment. He often tried the same method in the upward direction with Admiral King, and sometimes it worked there, too. He was also a strong advocate of joint staff operations, although he had his share of troubles with the army and the air force. The latter, including Major General Curtis LeMay, were often distraught over the navy's inability to understand the supremacy of

Official U.S. Navy photograph. Courtesy U.S. Naval Institute.
14. Nimitz with Admiral Raymond Spruance. Spruance was the only serious contender for the remaining five-star billet that instead went to Admiral Halsey. Halsey's contributions were enormous, but privately Nimitz came to place his greatest trust in Spruance.

strategic airpower. In time, though, Nimitz persuaded the air force commanders that they needed islands on which to land their planes and that the planes by themselves could not secure those islands.

This management style also meant noninterference in the prerogatives of subordinates once they commenced operations. Nimitz might sweat out messages; but unless the situation was critical, he believed that the commander on the scene knew more than he did. This led to the famous message to Halsey when the latter abandoned Leyte Gulf to go after the Japanese carrier task force steaming in from the north. Admiral Kinkaid, commanding the smaller Seventh Fleet, thought that Halsey was leaving battleship task force 34 behind. Halsey didn't. But when the going got rough, Kinkaid repeatedly sent messages asking where the task force was, one of which was in the clear. At that point, Nimitz at CINCPAC headquarters realized that Kinkaid was desperate and signaled Halsey with the same question. Yet he didn't *order* Halsey to change his decision. Instead, he assumed that if *he* asked the question, Halsey would reconsider.

Unfortunately, it was the practice of cryptographers to pad messages with meaningless headers and trailers to confuse the enemy code breakers. The addressee's cryptographer normally stripped these fillers out; but in this case Nimitz's encoder was a student of literature and added the phrase "THE WORLD WONDERS" [from Tennyson's *Charge of the Light Brigade*] after "WHERE IS TASK FORCE THIRTY FOUR." At the receiving end, the decoder wasn't sure about the status of that trailer and left it in. When Halsey saw it, he became enraged.[3] It was totally out of character for Nimitz to send a sarcastic message like that. Still, he reversed course immediately, foregoing a strike on the Japanese carriers and arriving at Leyte Gulf too late to influence the battle there.

Yet another mark of Nimitz's skill was his reaction to the carnage sustained on Tarawa. That operation incurred thousands of casualties in a period of two days because the extensive prebombardment failed to knock out the Japanese entrenchments. Nimitz ordered replicas built on the uninhabited Hawaiian island of Kahoolawe and bombarded them until the reasons became clear. Sustained precision gunnery with armor-piercing shells was what was needed. As a result, the Japanese defenders on Kwajalein and several other islands found their defenses to be less effective than they had expected. He ordered a similar exercise to be conducted when too many submarine-fired torpedoes failed to explode on impact. In that case the problem lay in the type and design of the fuzes. Nimitz also answered many aggrieved letters from parents who had lost their sons in these early operations, some of whom called him a barbarian or worse. He made no excuses.

Nimitz was a voracious reader. At CINCPAC he set his alarm clock for three A.M., read for two hours, and then went back to sleep for another hour and a half. He was also a serious student of the principles of war and kept a copy on his desk. Of these principles, he most admired that of simplicity. In this vein, he kept three questions in mind for each operation:

• Is the proposed operation likely to succeed?
• What would be the consequences of failure?

- Is the operation in the realm of practicability of materials and supplies?

He also placed himself at the center of the maelstrom of information flow. Some of the ways in which he did this were scheduling dinner parties at his quarters almost every night and inviting the captain of every ship that came into Pearl Harbor to call on him personally. On these occasions, he spent most of the time listening. In short, he integrated genuine sociability with information gathering and exchange of ideas. This approach also gave him a sharper perspective on the needs of his personnel.

Related to this high-level information processing was his initial negative attitude toward cryptoanalysis. Although it "failed" to predict the attack on Pearl Harbor, he came to realize that total radio silence on the part of an opponent not yet at war is open to speculation. Consequently, he began to reverse his attitude. His intelligence officer, Commander Edwin T. Layton, and his chief cryptoanalyst, Commander Joseph J. Rochefort, finally convinced him by way of a ruse. As the battle of Midway approached, Nimitz was still skeptical about the value of cryptoanalysis, so the two officers "planted" a message about bad water supplies at Midway island. Sure enough, this was retransmitted by the Japanese in their own code, which the United States had broken some time before. Interestingly, although Layton hesitated to hazard specific estimates, Nimitz insisted that he state his best guess as to when and where the Japanese fleet would approach Midway. Layton complied, misgauging the actual event by only five minutes on the clock and five degrees on the compass.

As for his own angst, Nimitz kept that to himself except to let off steam in his daily letters to Catherine. Many of those letters were so derogatory that she wisely destroyed them after the war. She knew instinctively that he never intended them for perusal by anyone else, much less for publication. He also told stories, especially at the end of briefings for major operations. Most of them are unprintable, but one exception tells about a young soldier who was apprehensive before his first parachute jump. The sergeant took him aside and said that he had nothing to worry about. A static line attached to the plane would open his chute for him. If for any reason it failed, he need only pull the ripcord on his reserve chute. Then a truck would be waiting at the edge of the drop zone to bring him back to the barracks. Sure enough, on the jump itself his main chute streamered. Then he pulled the ripcord on the reserve only to watch a lot of sawdust fall out, whereupon he said, "That's just like the military. I bet that damn truck isn't down there either."

Nimitz was also a humble man when the circumstances called for it. When landing in his seaplane in San Francisco Bay for a conference with Admiral King, the plane hit debris and flipped over. Nimitz was injured and others were mauled. During rescue operations he stood on the wing, reluctant to leave while the more severely injured were still in the aircraft. A sailor, who had only vague notions of rank, said, "Commander, if you would only get the hell out of the way, maybe we could get something done around here." Nimitz complied. A few minutes later, he continued to watch the rescue operations standing up in the stern of a launch taking him to shore, wrapped in a blanket. The coxswain—who is no less responsible for the safety of his passengers than a captain is responsible for the safety of his ship and crew—yelled, "Sit down, you." When Nimitz turned around, revealing the gold braid of a four-star admiral, the coxswain tried to apologize. Nimitz stopped him and said, "Stick to your guns, sailor, you were quite right."

If Nimitz had a fault, it was that he was punctilious, especially on matters of protocol. During the first few weeks of the occupation of Japan, he chewed out Admiral Halsey for raising his four-star flag on base when a five-star admiral (himself) was present. Perhaps that was in retaliation for Halsey's occasional sneering at Nimitz's respect for the Japanese during the war. When Japan signaled her willingness to surrender, the word did not immediately trickle down to all Japanese commands. Consequently, sporadic attacks continued for a few days, to which Halsey responded by issuing an order: "Shoot down all snoopers, not vindictively but in a friendly sort of way."

At any rate, the war was over and Nimitz's lifelong ambition was to become Chief of Naval Operations. Unfortunately, Secretary of the Navy James Forrestal was not so inclined. One stubborn Dutchman (King) was enough for him. However, Admiral King was in favor of it; so when it came to an impasse he went over Forrestal's head to Truman and laid it on the line. Nimitz got the job, although Truman compromised by agreeing to Forrestal's stipulation that he serve only two years rather than the normal four. It was just as well. This way, Nimitz avoided the disgraceful "revolt of the admirals" incident that ruined the career of his successor. More on this in the Bradley chapter.

Perhaps his most painful decision was whether Halsey or Spruance would get the remaining five-star promotion. King and Nimitz finally decided on Halsey, and King took the onus by announcing it two days before he officially turned the office over to his successor. To compensate Spruance, Nimitz as Chief of Naval Operations repeatedly asked Congress to create a fifth fleet admiral position. Congress demurred just as frequently, but Nimitz's persistence must have had some effect. In June 1948, Congress granted Spruance permanent four-star rank with full pay and allowances for life.[4]

When the two years were up, Nimitz and Catherine bought a home in Berkeley, California, which they named Longview. It was their first and only home, and home it would be. Although he was given countless lucrative offers to work in business, he turned them all down. To quote from his son, the admiral felt "that he represented the navy to a lot of people who had lost relatives in the Pacific war, and that it would somehow undermine their feeling for the navy if the man who had been the naval commander under whom their relatives had served acquired an image as other than that naval commander."

As mentioned earlier, Nimitz did agree to serve on the Board of Regents for the University of California. He also accepted an interim position as plebescite administrator of the U.N. sponsored vote in Kashmir to determine whether it would become part of India or Pakistan. Yet when it became apparent that his services would not be needed—not owing to any fault on his part—he resigned and returned to Berkeley in permanent retirement. Public service was one thing; sinecures another. Nimitz also refused to write his own memoirs, notwithstanding repeated pleas from distinguished scholars. He recalled the Sampson-Schley controversy that raged while he was a midshipman at Annapolis and also noted that many of the memoirs then pouring forth from other military and naval figures were generating an untoward intensity of bad feelings.[5]

He *did* want to see his friends and dote on his grandchildren. Accordingly, Longview witnessed an endless stream of visitors, although one of his daughters said of him that he had a "restless need to have an enterprise worthy of him to do, an inability to generate it within himself, and a cold rage at not having something which demanded his effort."

In time, Nimitz grew weak and the family moved to quarters #1 on Yerba Buena, the small navy-base island in San Francisco Bay that connects the two major sections of the Bay Bridge (and from which the man-made Treasure Island is an appendage). Here he could be near medical attention and still be accessible to friends and family. He died on February 20, 1966, and was buried in Golden Gate National Cemetery just south of San Francisco. By his own wishes he was interred in a simple graveside ceremony. His headstone was the same size as all others buried there, except that he requested it display his five-star insignia of rank instead of the traditional religious symbol. Shortly afterward, his wife Catherine responded to a letter of condolence: "I'm not feeling sad. To me, he has just gone to sea, and as I have done so many times in the past, some day I will follow him. In the meantime, he's always in my heart, and I can hear him laugh when I do something silly."

Nimitz did not care for effusive tributes. His biographer Potter knew this and, therefore, did not quote the citations from Nimitz's many awards and decorations; but Potter did say that the admiral was "an officer who had wielded enormous power without arrogance or ostentation, a forceful leader who had remained simple, friendly, and approachable while commanding millions of men." Potter also mentioned that Truman's respect for Nimitz grew until it was on a par with the regard he held for Marshall. That's not a garden-variety compliment.

WILLIAM FREDERICK HALSEY, JR.

The Spartans do not ask the number of the enemy, but where they are.
—Agis II, King of Sparta

Every war produces a number of apocryphal tales. Some are meant in pure jest while others are based on real events exaggerated to make a point. MacArthur and his good friend Bill Halsey seem to be the subject of these tales more so than the other principals. One of the better tales revolves around a Japanese message intercepted by Halsey's intelligence officer. The message was "Where is the American fleet?" Halsey, so the tale goes, responded, "Send them our latitude and longitude." What he actually said was, "If Admiral Nimitz would let me, I'd send them my latitude and longitude." This illustrates Halsey's aggressive spirit at sea— the navy's counterpart to General Patton, with few of the offsetting flaws of the famed general.

William Halsey was born in Elizabeth, New Jersey, on October 30, 1882, descended from a seafaring family. His father was a graduate of the Naval Academy, class of 1873, and rose to the rank of captain. As a navy junior, the younger Halsey moved six times before entering Annapolis in 1900. He had set his sights on that path early in life, but for a few years after high school the prospects seemed dim. He even started college at the University of Virginia in the premed program, as a different way to get into the navy. Fortunately, Congress had recently granted a number of direct appointments at the President's discretion; so Halsey's mother camped out in the White House, so to speak, and badgered McKinley until she wrested one for her son.

At the Naval Academy, Halsey's academic record was less than out-standing, graduating forty-second in a class of 62 in 1904. But he was within the upper fourth of his class as far as military aptitude was concerned, and he won the Thompson Trophy for contributing the most to athletics. Of the latter, he liked to joke about being the worst fullback in Naval Academy history. When Eisenhower met him for the first time, the general asked if that record were true. Halsey, somewhat at a loss for words, admitted to it; whereupon Ike said, "Well, I want you to meet the worst halfback in Military Academy history."

Halsey's first cruise after graduation was aboard the old battleship *Missouri*. Many years later, his flagship in World War II would carry the same name—displacing nearly four times the weight—and would host the final moment of World War II. One of his first moments aboard the original *Missouri* was less auspicious. A gunpowder explosion in a turret incinerated thirty-one lives. He bore no responsibility for it, yet it seems to have engendered in him a concern for his men that would become the hallmark of his career.[1]

After temporary duty at Annapolis to coach football, Halsey's next cruise was aboard the battleship *Kansas* as part of the around-the-world cruise with Theodore Roosevelt's "Great White Fleet." In 1909, Halsey was assigned to destroyers. With one brief exception, all of his sea duty for the next twenty-three years would be on that type of ship. This meant early command and more of it than most naval officers experience.

During the first of those years, a young lady happened to observe Halsey from a dock and asked the executive officer's wife who the young man was ("The one over there who takes himself so seriously," she said). Upon learning his name, she—Frances Cooke "Fan" Grady—threw her muff at her future husband. Within a year they were married, with his classmate Husband E. Kimmel serving as an usher. They had a son and a daughter. But unfortunately—as Halsey himself has indicated by several asides in his autobiography—Fan had a sharp tongue. After World War II, they lived separate lives.[2]

At any rate, following a tour as executive officer on the destroyer *Lamsom,* Halsey was ordered to the training ship *Franklin,* berthed at Norfolk, where he became the officer in charge of the basic training of recruits (commonly called "boot camp"). While there, he was tempted to resign, and was further encouraged by Fan to do so. He applied for an engineering job in civil life, but a friend advised him to stay with the navy. He did, and took command of the *Flusser* and, later, the *Jarvis* under the flag of Admiral Sims.

On the first of these two assignments, Halsey sailed to Campobello Island to pick up Assistant Secretary of the Navy Franklin Roosevelt for the purpose of inspecting naval installations in Frenchman Bay. Roosevelt asked to take the helm, whereupon Halsey discovered that the future President really knew how to handle a ship.[3] The two became casual friends; during World War II the president took the admiral into his White House office and told him a number of official secrets that Halsey afterward

Official U.S. Navy photograph. Courtesy U.S. Naval Institute.
15. Fleet Admiral William F. Halsey, Jr. After the surrender ceremony on board his flagship *Missouri,* MacArthur turned to his favorite admiral and said, "Bill, when you leave, the Pacific will become just another ocean."

regretted hearing. Telling such secrets was one way Roosevelt conveyed his trust in a senior officer below the level of the joint chiefs. The President extended the same confidence to Bradley, with equal consternation on the recipient's part.

Like Admiral King and many other naval officers of his era, Halsey was a hard drinker. Notwithstanding General Order 99 that prohibited alcoholic beverages aboard ship, many officers simply disregarded this order or found a neat way to circumvent it. Admiral King was among those who ignored it, and it nearly ruined his career. Halsey had more self-control but went beyond merely ignoring the order. For example, during the campaign for the Solomons, he gave strict orders that no ships were to sail to Australia or New Zealand for repairs or supplies. Captain Arleigh Burke (later Admiral and Chief of Naval Operations) had different ideas and sent one of his ships to New Zealand ostensibly for repairs but in reality to obtain a fresh supply of liquor. Halsey immediately called him to mast for it. When Burke revealed his true purpose, the admiral pondered it for a moment and then let him off the hook, adding, "But if it had been for repairs, you would not have got off so easy." In yet another instance, Halsey directed his medical officers to keep a supply of ethyl alcohol for carrier pilots. The back-to-back missions and heavy casualty rates early in the war often generated severe stress, for which intoxicants were the admiral's tension reliever of choice.

One last point here. The admiral liked to tell the story of the bos'n's mate who could not hold his liquor very well and was, therefore, continually in trouble. His captain lectured him: "You're the best man on this ship and there is just no limit to the rating you could hold. Why don't you behave yourself and drink like an officer." The mate replied, "God Almighty, Captain, my constitution couldn't stand it."

In 1915 Halsey was assigned to Annapolis as a tactical officer, where he had quarters aboard the permanently berthed ship *Reina Mercedes*. Actually, it was more of a refurbished hulk than a ship, and midshipmen who were guilty of more serious infractions were temporarily confined on it. For serious offenses, this was no problem; Halsey threw the book at them. By contrast, he grew increasingly tolerant of minor infractions. Much later, during World War II, Admiral King had to pry away one of his incompetent chiefs of staff by "bribing" that captain with a carrier command.

From Annapolis, Halsey took command of the destroyer *Shaw*, serving in antisubmarine warfare and convoy duty during World War I. At the time, that was about the closest to combat American naval officers came. It was the unescorted ships that the German U-boats attacked, not those in escorted convoys; as a result, Halsey had the opportunity to sink only one submarine. For this, he was awarded the Navy Cross; but he later admitted that the medal had been distributed rather freely to captains in that period.

After the war, Halsey drew picket duty for the first flight of four navy seaplanes across the Atlantic. One of them—the *NC-4*—made it the entire distance and awoke Halsey's latent interest in flying. Before he had a chance to pursue this interest, however, he spent a tour as military attaché in Germany.

Upon return to sea duty, Halsey met up with Raymond Spruance the hard way. Halsey's destroyer *Chauncey* suddenly lost all power; and, accordingly he hoisted the breakdown flag. Unfortunately, the flag fouled in the rigging while the *Aaron Ward,* commanded by Spruance, was coming up hard astern. An inexperienced ensign on watch on the *Ward* did not respond in time and thus the *Ward* rammed the *Chauncey* abaft. Fortunately for the country, the navy let both of them off the hook. The two of them led most of the operations in the Pacific theater.

Gunnery drill provided another interesting episode. These drills used practice torpedoes with soft-metal dummy warheads; but they were propelled at the time by compressed air engines. When Halsey moved in for an attack, the distance sometimes closed to seven hundred yards, at which range the unexpended compressed air worked like an explosive. The navy admired Halsey's aggressiveness, but not the repair bill for several damaged battleships that came with it. From that point forward, the "players" were advised to fire torpedoes no closer than five thousand yards, unless they had a preference for life-long indentured servitude.

Promotion to captain came in 1927 and with it command of the familiar *Reina Mercedes* at Annapolis. He occupied the spacious captain's quarters with his family; and as that ship was the headquarters for naval aviation at the time, Halsey took up flying seriously and requested pilot training at Pensacola. Unfortunately, although he passed the physical, the 20–20 eyesight requirement had just been imposed—against which no amount of fighting spirit could help. As a consolation he was given command of a squadron of nineteen destroyers. In 1931, Halsey was selected to attend the Naval War College and immediately following that, the Army War College. These assignments were fairly significant because Halsey was not noted as one of the navy's scholars. At the Army War College, he played baseball with Lieutenant Colonel Jonathan Wainwright and Major Omar Bradley.

His big chance came a year later. Rear Admiral King, then chief of the Bureau of Aeronautics, offered him command of the new carrier *Saratoga* if Halsey would take the aviation observer's course at Pensacola. The 20–20 eyesight requirement would be waived, which left only Fan to convince. Aviation duty was still very hazardous in those days, and a man with a family had to give serious consideration to such duty before accepting it. Fan gave conditional approval—the condition being that Rear Admiral Leahy, then chief of the Bureau of Navigation, approve. Leahy was more than enthusiastic; and Halsey badgered his way into taking the full pilot's course, not just the observer's.

While in Pensacola, Halsey earned what was known as "the flying jackass" award. Whenever a pilot taxied over a runway light, he was obliged to wear a piece of medal shaped like a jackass across his chest except when actually flying, at least until the next student earned it. Although he was a captain among mostly ensigns, he wore the jackass without complaint. When the time came to pass it on, he took it off but declined to part with it. He said: "I want to keep it. When I take command of the *Saratoga,* I'm going to put it on the bulkhead of my cabin. If anybody aboard does anything stupid, I'll take a look at the jackass before I ball him out and say to myself 'Wait a minute, Bill Halsey, you're not so damn good yourself.' "

As captain of the *Saratoga,* Halsey grew in professional stature. He must have. After just two years he was selected for rear admiral and, consequently, command of the flight school at Pensacola. His only regret was that it cost him three thousand dollars. At the time only one flag officer could earn flight pay and that perquisite belonged to the chief of the Bureau of Aeronautics. At the end of the year, flight pay was restored to flag officers; and Halsey took command of Carrier Division 2. Admiral King had command of Carrier Division 1, as well as overall command of Aircraft Battle Force—another *pooh-bah* situation.

During this time, two incidents further proved the character and ability of the man. In the first incident, a subordinate was slow to launch planes. King on his flag carrier immediately signaled for the name of the individual at fault. Halsey named himself. In the second incident, he grew frustrated with the tangle of radio communications among ships and planes. As different wavelength allocations were to blame, he solved the problem by insisting on a common frequency. Similarly, he argued successfully for voice rather than key (Morse code) communication. This reduced the need for a second crew member in some aircraft and made flying more manageable for single-seat aircraft pilots. These may not seem like major accomplishments today, but it is surprising how few officers will take the initiative to do something about chronic problems.

In time, Halsey was moved up to commander of the entire Pacific-fleet carrier force—coupled with a promotion to vice admiral. It was in this capacity that he sailed into Pearl Harbor shortly after the Japanese attack and began to emerge from an obscure officer into the most popular admiral in American history. Simply put, he was a natural fighter—at the only time in the history of the United States Navy that there was a prolonged struggle in an ocean-based theater of war.

Halsey immediately conducted raids on a few of the outermost Japanese-held islands. The actual damage was not great, but it put Japan on notice that the United States was assuming the offensive. He also accepted the carrier support mission for the famed Doolittle raid over Tokyo in April 1942. The raid was a grave risk, not only to Halsey but to the U.S. fleet. If the fleet were spotted by the Japanese—which is what happened—and then sunk, it would have left the United States with only two carriers. Halsey's adroit maneuver tactics during the withdrawal avoided those consequences.[4] However, the successful raid and subsequent getaway motivated the Japanese to attempt to put the American fleet out of action once and for all. To do this, they planned a decisive battle near Midway, and Halsey itched for it. Unfortunately he had to give priority to another type of itch, this one a dermatitis so painful that he was hospitalized for several months. The disappointment planted a seed that would later engender serious problems at Leyte Gulf.

In the interim, Halsey was sent on an inspection trip to the Southwest Pacific, or so he thought. At the time, the navy and marine corps were fighting desperately to retain their toehold on Guadalcanal and thus prevent the Japanese from cutting the line of communications from the United States to New Zealand and Australia. As mentioned in previous chapters, the commander of this mission, Admiral Ghormley, was not up to the job. So just as Halsey's seaplane landed at Ghormley's headquarters, Halsey was handed a classified message telling him to assume command immediately.

Morale shot up, and sailors were sometimes overheard arguing whether Halsey was worth two or three carriers. That hyperbole is not as fanciful as it seems and comes under the expression "leadership as a combat force multiplier." A competent admiral will make much better use of his fleet, inflict more damage on his opponent, and suffer less damage to his own. Hence, in a very real way, Halsey was worth a carrier or two, if not three. It all depends on the consideration given to the factor of time. This is not to say that his leadership in the Solomons was perfect. He lost too many ships in various tactical battles without exacting a commensurate price on the Japanese. Yet like Grant at the Battle of the Wilderness, he persevered and that meant success.

Admiral Halsey could talk easily with any man regardless of rank. When he overheard one sailor say to another, "I'd go to hell for that old son of a bitch," he came up behind him and advised, "Young man, I'm not so old." On shore, he refused to grandstand by riding around like Field Marshal Montgomery and putting on a show of concern for the troops. Halsey's concern was too genuine for that.

For example, when men under his command suffered high casualties, he received a lot of hate mail from parents. Like Nimitz, Halsey answered as many letters as possible, without making any excuses or attempting to justify his actions. He considered those who died as much his sons as they were the sons of the bereaved parents. The proof of this is that when his own son, a navy pilot, was lost returning from battle, he refused to permit any search more extensive than that for any other pilot (though, to Halsey's great relief, his son was found and returned to duty).

Halsey also learned from all but the most serious of his mistakes and readily admitted to them in his autobiography. For example, he suggested building a supplementary airfield at the western end of Guadalcanal to support operations, and put his forces in motion before discovering that the terrain there was utterly unsuitable for the task. He immediately apologized and accepted full responsibility for the error. Another example occurred when Mrs. Eleanor Roosevelt, in her capacity as a representative of the Red Cross, wanted to visit the Pacific area. Halsey was dead set against it on the grounds that the Japanese were still too active and he didn't have the manpower to spare for her security. When informed that President Roosevelt felt differently, Halsey grudgingly made the necessary arrangements. Afterward, he was so impressed with her tireless and extended visits to nearly every patient in every hospital, he again admitted to an error of judgment.

Also notable was the early and infamous press interview during which Halsey confidently predicted the war in the Pacific would be over by the end of 1943. In 1945, Captain Harold Stassen, who had been Halsey's flag secretary, said:

> He made it during the darkest period of the Pacific War. We had very little navy afloat. Australia was very much concerned. The Japanese navy was still strong. It was a pretty gloomy situation. Halsey knew that if the Japanese navy had attacked our force, it was doubtful if our fleet, even with its magnificent fighting spirit, could hold the line. So he made this bold assertive statement both to mislead the Japanese and to cheer up our force. It worked. The Japanese didn't attack for six months. Instead they tried to find out what in the world Admiral Halsey had that led him to make that statement."[5]

Then of all the things that came out of World War II, the wonder of wonders was the friendship that developed between this most outspoken of admirals and the most histrionic of the generals. Almost to the end, Halsey remained under Nimitz but was placed in support of MacArthur and, therefore, Halsey was somewhat under MacArthur's operational control. Yet Halsey said of the general that he "did not force decisions on me. We discussed the issue until one of us changed his mind." More often than not, it was MacArthur who changed his mind.

In time, of course, the campaign for the Solomons wrapped up; and Halsey turned his command over to Vice Admiral Arthur S. Carpender, and his Seventh Fleet over to Vice Admiral Thomas C. Kinkaid. Then

16. Admiral Halsey Sharing Thanksgiving Dinner with His Crew. Halsey was dubbed "Bull" by the press, but he hated that nickname as much as he hated all pretense and showmanship. What he did not hate, he loved, and chief among the latter were his men.

with a promotion to four-star admiral, Halsey took command of the much larger Third Fleet. Actually, he rotated that command with Admiral Spruance (under whom it was known as the Fifth Fleet). The two admirals kept their own flagships and a few escort vessels; but otherwise the two fleets were one and the same, a situation that caused no end of confusion to the Japanese.

It was at this time that Halsey discovered that the central Philippines were less well defended than presumed. As mentioned earlier, this led to the planned invasion of Leyte being moved up from December 1944 to October of that year. In the ensuing campaign, Halsey had two conflicting missions stemming from the separate theater commands in the Pacific. Under the operational control of MacArthur, Halsey's mission was to cover the amphibious landings on Leyte. Under the general control of Nimitz, Halsey's standing orders were to decimate the Japanese fleet at every reasonable opportunity.

This conflict in orders led to the potential debacle. As mentioned in chapter 8, the Japanese had sent in a decoy task force of planeless carriers from the north to draw Halsey away from Leyte Gulf and thus leave it open to attack by Japanese battleships and cruisers steaming in from the west and southwest. Halsey took the bait, and the plan almost worked. The admiral was roundly criticized for his decision—but, in reality, it was in keeping with his experience and his mission. True, a more insightful commander with a higher level of perspective might have acted differently, but where Halsey can be faulted is in his postwar attempt at self-justification. He refused to acknowledge that the Japanese carrier task force was a decoy, even when its commander (Ozawa) himself confirmed it. More on this in chapter 14.

Halsey also "fought" two "battles" with typhoons, in which his fleets came out the worse for it. In both cases, boards on inquiry recommended that he be relieved of command. On the second occasion, Secretary of the Navy Forrestal was ready to order Halsey's retirement when King and Nimitz intervened on Halsey's behalf. It was Nimitz's practice to give a man two strikes before declaring him out. In this one case, the third strike was declared a foul and therefore, Halsey got to stay at bat for the remaining five months of the war. Then, on his way home after the surrender ceremony, Halsey received this message from MacArthur, reinforcing the latter's previously mentioned oral compliment: "Your departure leaves all your old comrades of the Pacific war lonesome indeed. You carry with you the admiration and affection of every officer and man. May your shadow never decrease." Three months later, the Navy Department promoted Halsey to fleet admiral.

Halsey retired in 1947 and pursued several business interests, primarily in a public-relations role. Three years later, Hollywood produced the film *The Gallant Hours,* starring James Cagney as Admiral Halsey. The only other principal to be similarly honored was Halsey's friend Douglas Mac-Arthur. He died at Fishers Island, New York, on August 16, 1959, and was buried at Arlington National Cemetery on a terribly hot afternoon. Admiral Nimitz made a point of being there as an honorary pall bearer. He owed much of his reputation to his fallen comrade-in-arms.

10

DWIGHT DAVID EISENHOWER

Nothing more becomes a ruler than to despise no one, nor be insolent, but to preside with impartiality.

—Epictetus

Early in World War II, General Marshall sent newly minted Major General Eisenhower to coordinate a matter with Admiral King. The admiral looked briefly at the paper from Marshall and said no. Eisenhower riposted that the admiral had not given Marshall's idea serious consideration, adding that the admiral's attitude could not do much to encourage cooperation between the services. Now King was not an individual who took well to insubordination. He stared icily at Eisenhower for a moment, motioned for him to sit down, apologized (in a manner of speaking), reconsidered Marshall's proposal, and then reversed his decision. It was the same scene that played dozen of times among the principals. Each admired the courage of a subordinate in risking his career to make a valid point, and each had done it himself.

Ike—and everybody except General Marshall called him that at times—was the Horatio Alger story of the era. Raised by exceptional parents in a small midwestern town, he rose to command the largest land invasion in history and later served eight years as President of the United States. Still, a path as distinguished as the one taken by Eisenhower doesn't open by magic or luck; the trekker must possess an unusual combination of substance and attributes. In Eisenhower, those qualities included intense perseverance, a sense of humility that went deeper than any of the other principals, an honest willingness to learn, a strong temper that rarely if ever went out of control, and a likable personality with a sadness rather than a twinkle in his eye. The humility is readily apparent in his reminiscences

At Ease: Stories I Tell Friends. One incident in particular reveals his fundamental character.

This incident occurred after Eisenhower finished his first year at West Point and was pressing a new plebe for various bits of information including his "previous condition of servitude." Before the plebe could answer, Eisenhower ad-libbed sarcastically, "You look like a barber." The plebe responded that he had, in fact, been one. Ike did not apologize and tried to make a joke of the incident, but when he got back to his own quarters he grew distraught at having made a man ashamed of the honest work he had done to make a living. He vowed never again to harass a plebe.

Dwight David Eisenhower was born on October 14, 1890, in Denison, Texas, to David Jacob and Ida Stover Eisenhower, the fifth of seven boys (one of whom died in infancy). Shortly afterward, the family moved to Abilene, Kansas. His mother was a devout Quaker and firmly opposed to war; yet she did not stand in her son's way when he chose the profession of arms as a career. Nor did she single him out for praise when he became famous. At the end of World War II, Eisenhower's mother was asked how she felt about her son. She replied, "Which one?"

Perhaps the most telling incident in Ike's childhood happened when he was forbidden to accompany his older brothers for Halloween trick-or-treating. He flew into a rage and started beating his head against a tree trunk. His father grabbed him by his shoulders, gave him a thrashing, and sent him off to bed. A little later, his mother came to his room and—adapting scripture to the exigencies of the situation—said that he who conquers his own soul was greater than he who took a city. Then she added that of all her boys, he had the most to learn. It took a while, but Ike admitted that he was wrong. Apparently that was the last time he ever lost control of his ferocious temper. On a more positive note, he often buried himself in history books to the point where his parents had to hide them in order to get him to tend to his chores.

Several years after high school, Eisenhower obtained an appointment to West Point by competition and entered with the class of 1915. This is sometimes called "the class the stars fell on." Among his classmates were Omar N. Bradley, Joseph T. McNarney, James A. Van Fleet, George E. Stratemeyer, and Charles W. Ryder. The more interesting point is that he graduated eight years later than the last of the classes (1897–1907) that produced all of the other five-star officers in World War II. Moreover, the army nearly denied Eisenhower a commission owing to a serious knee injury that he suffered while playing football; but his persistence impressed the medical officers. In the end, all he had to promise was not to apply for the cavalry.

It has been said that troop leadership consists largely of many small things. If so, Eisenhower put this wisdom into practice in his first assign-

Official U.S. Army photograph. Courtesy U.S. Army Military History Institute.
17. General of the Army Dwight D. Eisenhower. Eisenhower's dominant and endearing attribute was his genuine humility, notwithstanding his famed temper. This attribute enabled him to learn from his mistakes perhaps better than any other man who ever wore a general's stars.

ment at Fort Sam Houston, Texas. He volunteered for the enlisted cooks and bakers school so that he could better oversee mess halls and the preparation of food, a prime source of morale as well as nourishment. He also tried for aviation training but backed off when the father of his fiancée balked.

A year later, when the United States entered World War I, he tried so many times to get transferred to France that he was officially reprimanded for it, and had to settle for training duty at Camp Meade, Maryland. There he rose quickly to the temporary rank of lieutenant colonel and was in line for promotion to colonel. After the war, he led the first attempt to drive a motor convoy across the country—a feat that later inspired him, as President, to initiate the interstate highway program. Later he served with George Patton in an experimental tank unit. Once, a towing cable under tension snapped and missed severing both of them by inches. And both got into trouble with their respective branch chiefs for writing articles on tank warfare contrary to established doctrine.

It was also during this period that Mamie gave birth to their first son, Doud Dwight, whom they nicknamed Icky and who subsequently died of scarlet fever. It was a loss from which the future general never fully recovered, but at least he and his wife were able to have another child, John, who survived the medical traumas of childhood, graduated from West Point, and rose to the rank of brigadier general in the army reserve.[1]

Shortly afterward, Eisenhower was transferred to Panama and served under Brigadier General Fox Conner,[2] who had been a principal staff officer on Pershing's staff in the AEF. Conner saw the potential in Eisenhower, and led him through a tailor-made, one-on-one, comprehensive course in military history and strategy. Conner also pulled strings to ensure that his protégé had a chance to attend the staff college at Fort Leavenworth.[3] The Chief of Infantry was opposed to it and even predicted failure; but like Marshall much earlier, Eisenhower out-persevered himself and graduated first in his class. That marked him for some choice assignments.

After a brief sojourn at Fort Benning to coach football, Eisenhower became aide to General Pershing when the latter was director of the American Battle Monuments Commission. He served in this capacity for five years, except for a nine-month break at the Army War College. Pershing was not an active mentor to Eisenhower; but in the process of working for him and compiling materials for the general's war memoirs, the old stalwart's ways must have rubbed off. Ike later admitted that he owed much of his success in the second world war to adhering closely to the lessons Pershing learned in the first. He also had his only significant contact with Marshall until just before the outbreak of World War II. Ike had redrafted Pershing's accounts of the final phase of World War I in narrative rather than journal form. Pershing was intrigued with this, but Marshall stopped by one day and advised against it.

In 1930, Eisenhower was selected for general staff duty in the War Department, coinciding with MacArthur's appointment as Chief of Staff. Within two years MacArthur picked Eisenhower as his aide, a rather remarkable choice given the general's preference for subservience within his immediate staff. Eisenhower wasn't the subservient type: for example, he tried hard to dissuade MacArthur from personal involvement in the bonus narchers incident in 1932. Nevertheless, when MacArthur's tenure drew to a close and he headed back to the Philippines, he prevailed on Eisenhower to come along with him. They continued to get along reasonably well until the general attempted to organize a grand military demonstration in Manila, drawing on representative units from all over the country. When the Philippine president, Manuel Quezon, heard about the demonstration, he called MacArthur in and told him to cancel it because of the expense. MacArthur responded by putting the blame on Eisenhower, an act that Eisenhower could not abide. Eisenhower thus sought a reason to leave as soon as possible.[4]

That reason was evident by 1939 as the global war clouds formed. Ike insisted on returning to the states to get involved with troops. In quick succession, he served as a regimental commander, then as chief of staff for the 3rd Infantry Division, next the IX Corps, and the Third Army, accompanied by promotions to colonel and brigadier general. He greatly impressed fellow staff officer Mark Clark, who recommended him to General Marshall for senior staff duty in the War Department. Later he caught Marshall's eye during maneuvers in a way that was similar to Arnold's impression of Marshall twenty-five years earlier in the Philippines.

Now in physics there is a phenomenon known as the *tunnel effect,* whereby electrons shoot through material that normally imposes enough resistance to stop them (the basis for transistors). Eisenhower was about to demonstrate the military parallel to this; and while the story has been retold many times, the accounts all seem to misgauge the critical moment, including Ike himself. With the outbreak of the war, Marshall summoned Eisenhower to the War Department as a senior planning staff officer, primarily to deal with the Pacific theater (read *MacArthur*).

A few months later, Marshall pulled him aside and preached one of his infrequent homilies, in this case, that promotions would be going to field commanders not staff officers. Then he told Eisenhower, in rather harsh terms, that he was in the latter category. Eisenhower responded: "General, I'm interested in what you say, but I want you to know that I don't give a damn about your promotion plans. I came into this office from the field and I am trying to do my duty. I expect to do so as long as you want me here. If that locks me to a desk for the rest of the war, so be it."[5]

For Ike it was very dramatic, but for Marshall that scene was premeditated. The Chief of Staff did not know Eisenhower very well, and worse—from Marshall's viewpoint—Eisenhower had spent nine years serving under MacArthur. Yet after observing Eisenhower for several months, Marshall, like Pershing and MacArthur before him, undoubtedly recognized that Eisenhower had talents that transcended staff work. Marshall was also aware of Eisenhower's frustration about not getting to the battlefront in World War I. Consequently, Eisenhower was put through the aforementioned test.[6] There is no other explanation. Marshall was austere, but he never harassed subordinates, especially competent subordinates. Thus, unwittingly, Ike pulled the plug on his own rowboat—but in the process, he passed the fortitude test. It must have been with flying colors, too, because Marshall recommended him for promotion to major general the next day.

General Marshall now had a subordinate who could fill any of several roles when, as anticipated, Marshall took command of the cross-channel invasion of Europe. Eisenhower could serve as an army commander or principal staff officer, or he could succeed Marshall as Chief of Staff. Marshall wanted no repetition of Peyton March's insidious behavior when Pershing was the commander in France during the previous war. Unknown to Marshall, however, other events would accelerate Eisenhower through the "tunnel" faster than the planned velocity. The first whoosh began with Eisenhower's assignment to Great Britain as theater army commander pro tem to prepare for the invasion of Europe and possibly to command the American ground forces therein.

But Marshall had underestimated Churchill's ability to persuade Roosevelt to change the venue of war in Europe to the Mediterranean. That sideshow was too small for Marshall to assume; and, thus, the task fell to Eisenhower. All things considered, the Mediterranean operation proved to be more trying than OVERLORD a year and a half later.

The problem was that Vichy France occupied much of northwest Africa and had become a de facto Nazi ally. If it were not pacified, the invasion forces would have two wars to fight. Moreover, the Germans, who were located further to the east, would have more time to dig in and, perhaps, stymie the whole operation.[7] Eisenhower let this diplomatic problem, as well as the need to improve cooperation with the British, distract him from the pressing needs of the battlefield, a situation exacerbated by the greenness of the American commanders and troops. In short, he was on the verge of failure.

Marshall grew acutely aware of the constriction, flew to North Africa, and recommended that Eisenhower take on a general-officer field representative—his "eyes and ears," as he put it—and started reeling off a list of names. Eisenhower stopped him when he came to Bradley. The significance of that choice is covered in the next chapter. In the meantime, the British high command also grew weary of the situation and succeeded in elevating Eisenhower to the stratosphere of Supreme Commander in order to leave them free to run the war itself. In a way, the plan backfired. By this time Marshall had become the indispensable man in Washington, while Eisenhower's new stature made him the fallback candidate for the command of OVERLORD.

The difficulty of launching an amphibious operation against an entire continent cannot be underestimated. Great Britain had foiled Napoleon's and then Hitler's plans to invade their homeland from the continent—a much easier task—and now it was Eisenhower's job to ensure that it worked in the harder reverse direction. Although initially delegating command of invasion ground troops to Montgomery, Eisenhower took firm control of the preparations,[8] which included the masterful deception plan (FORTITUDE) that created an imaginary army group under Patton, coupled with the intentional leak that the main attack would come at Calais (the shortest cross-channel distance between England and France). He also insisted that independent British strategic bombing operations under Air Marshal "Bomber" Harris be placed under his direction so that they could be used for tactical interdiction missions when necessary. Eisenhower (and Bradley) also took with a grain of salt Air Marshal Trafford Leigh-Mallory's warning that the airborne tactical envelopment would suffer seventy percent casualties.

In all, OVERLORD was the most thoroughly planned military operation in history, extending to such details as sending reconnaissance parties ashore to measure the thickness of bunkers in order to determine the best fuzes to use for each target that would come under naval and air bombardment. The one thing that would not submit to this kind of rigorous planning was the weather. Eisenhower knew it could defeat the operation on the beaches. And because he knew little about meteorology, he spent a great deal of time with the chief meteorologist, Group Captain J. M. Stagg, to determine just how reliable he was. As it was, bad weather postponed the landings by twenty-four hours, forcing Eisenhower to make the tough decision whether to go ahead on the following day under still unfavorable conditions.

Thus began the restoration of Western Europe. It came to be known by many names and generated hundreds of books. It meant many things to many people, but to Eisenhower it became the battle of Montgomery—Field Marshal Bernard Law Montgomery. From the beginning, the Supreme Allied Commander envisioned the war with a broad-front strategy—which, as developed in Chapter 12, was a euphemism for attrition warfare. Such a strategy meant Eisenhower had no illusions about a dramatic envelopment of the German forces. The space and time factors were just too big for that; the Germans could easily cut off any Allied thrust in the absence of infinite resources and troops to sustain it. But Montgomery saw things differently.

The field marshal bragged that he would break out of the lodgment

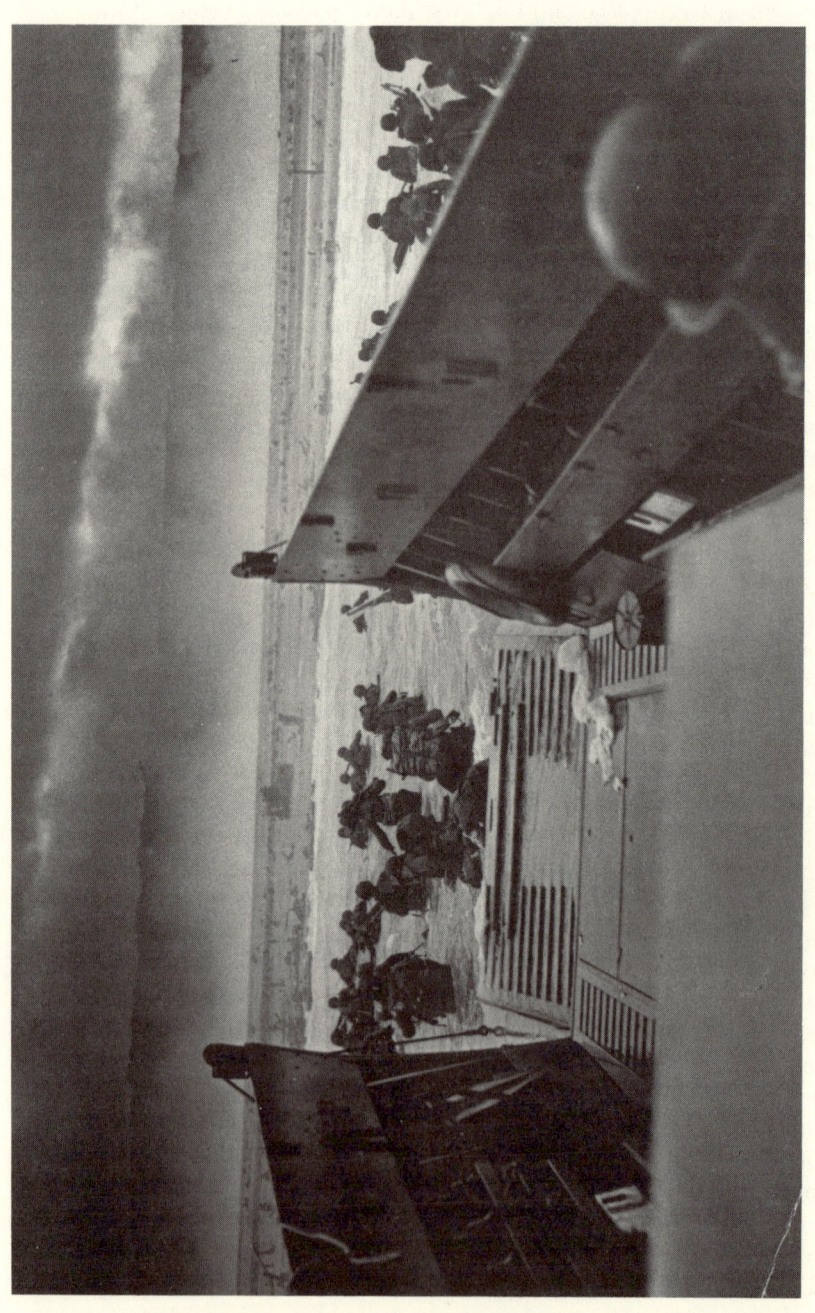

Official U.S. Army photograph. Courtesy U.S. Army Military History Institute.

18. Normandy Beach on D-Day. Eisenhower was often indecisive; but when it came to critical decisions he held on tenaciously and went to every conceivable length to prevent failure. The success of the landings on June 6, 1944, belongs primarily to him.

area and perhaps make it as far as Caen, a distance of eleven miles from the beaches, all in twenty-four hours. That didn't pan out. Later, Montgomery conceived of the thrust towards Nijmegen, known as *Operation Marketgarden,* popularized in the film *The Bridge Too Far.* That didn't work either. Then, in the defense against the German counteroffensive through the Ardennes (the so-called Battle of the Bulge), Montgomery insisted on taking semipermanent command of the American forces north of the salient and making a final enveloping rush to force Germany to surrender. Eisenhower really dug his heels in that time and arranged to have Montgomery put in his place.

About the only time that Montgomery gave even the appearance of cooperating voluntarily in the broad-front approach was when the American First Army, under Courtney Hodges, unexpectedly secured the bridgehead at Ramagen. Some of the lower ranking British generals opposed exploiting this opportunity because it wasn't in the plan, but Montgomery turned enthusiastic. The reason, however, was that he presumed it would draw German forces away from his front and thus give him an opportunity for a final glorious dash into the heartland of Germany. Once more, he was wrong.

Montgomery's problem was twofold. First, he had an inflated opinion of himself (even more than Patton's). Churchill later said that in defeat, Montgomery was unbeatable, but in victory, he became unbearable. Second, his verbal daring was not matched by his methods. As at El Alamein, he seldom commenced an offensive unless he had overwhelming superiority and could not fail. *Marketgarden* was the exception, and the failure stung him badly.[9] Moreover, the Chief of the Imperial General Staff, Field Marshal Alan Brooke, had minimum admiration for Eisenhower and kept feeding his angst privately to Montgomery. Warren Harding once said that his enemies were no problem; he could take care of them: "It's my goddamn friends that keep me awake at nights."

In spite of all this, Eisenhower retained his equanimity. He understood the importance of Allied cooperation: without it the consequences would be heavier casualties and a longer war attributable to squabbling factions. On one occasion, he said, "I don't mind if someone calls another a son of a bitch, but I'll be goddamned if he will call him an American son of a bitch or a British son of a bitch." He meant it; several staff officers were sent packing when they violated the rule. He made only one exception, and that occurred when his chief of staff Lieutenant General Walter Bedell Smith made a minor slip under extreme duress.

This is not to say that Eisenhower couldn't make battlefield decisions. By the time of the Ardennes counteroffensive, he was, in fact, the ground commander and immediately recognized the German move for what it was.[10] He then made the necessary decisions to contain it, to include ordering Patton to make a ninety-degree turn with part of his Third Army (a major feat anytime, especially in the dead of winter) to relieve the 101st Airborne Division at Bastogne. This maneuver enabled the Allied forces to close the gap, thus forcing the Germans to retreat or face annihilation much faster than would otherwise have been the case.

At any rate, when the war drew to a close in early May, Eisenhower's staff officers were understandably beside themselves as they drafted increasingly glorious messages to send to Washington. Eisenhower bore with this contest for a while and then told his staff to get some sleep. At that point he sat down at a field desk and wrote the simple message that was sent: "The mission of this Allied force was fulfilled at 0241 local time, May 7, 1945."

A few months later, Eisenhower was selected to follow General Marshall as Chief of Staff. Although this was the highest post in the army, Eisenhower (unlike Nimitz) did not want it. He had little patience with administration and recognized that the Pentagon was a sort of merry-go-round, except that instead of the building rotating, it was the occupants who spent most of their time going around in circles. Compromising, he agreed with Truman to take the position for just two years, with the understanding that Bradley would succeed him. He was also reluctant to publish his war memoirs. However, as retirement neared, he accepted the argument from Doubleday that he owed it to his country, an argument sweetened with a lump-sum payment of $635,000, subject only to a capital gains tax of twenty-five percent.[11] About the same time he also accepted Nicholas Murray Butler's offer of the presidency of Columbia University.

Unfortunately, the university environment was not Eisenhower's forte. He was not a scholar and did not fully appreciate the role of professors and academic freedom. Thus, when the opportunity came to return to active duty as the first Supreme Commander of NATO, Eisenhower gladly took a leave of absence from Columbia and then let it lapse. As to why Dr. Butler picked Eisenhower in the first place, one can refer to the former's concept of an educated man:

> As a fifth evidence of an education I name efficiency, the power to do. The time has long since gone by, if ever it was, when contemplation pure and simple . . . was a defensible ideal of education. Today the truly educated man must be, in some sense, efficient . . . Indefinite absorption without production is fatal both to character and to the highest intellectual power. Do something and be able to do it well; express what you know in some helpful and substantial form; produce.[12]

Eisenhower knew how to produce, so the rest of his career bears little comment here. He was sought by Democrats and Republicans to run for

President and, in fact, shortly after World War II, Truman offered to help him get the 1948 Democratic nomination if he wanted it. In the intervening years between 1948 and 1952, he grew tired of Democratic activism and leaned toward the Republicans. They, in turn, helped him into the White House for eight years. Mamie later remarked that this was the longest time that she and her husband had ever spent in one house; and for Ike, like Yogi Berra, it must have been "déjà vu all over again." By all accounts he was passive for most of his two terms. Only in the last eighteen months did he exert himself as a distinctive leader, much as he had done in the closing months of the European campaign.

In summary, then, genuinely humble men seldom have major character flaws; and Eisenhower was no exception. He is often faulted for being indecisive and for trying to please too many people too much of the time; but that is hardly a defect in character and in the event he overcame it when the chips were down. However, he can be faulted for his blind spot when it came to keeping loyalties in good repair. The most serious incident occurred when he failed to defend General Marshall against Senator McCarthy's vitriol by deleting some minor praise of his former boss in a prepared speech. His later explanation falls flat.[13] In a similar vein, he never understood why Allied soldiers taken prisoner in Africa saluted Field Marshal Erwin Rommel, even though Churchill himself had praised the Desert Fox in 1942—in Parliament, no less. He was also tight with money. Shortly after he collected the after-tax $476,250 from the sale of all rights to *Crusade in Europe,* he balked at paying for a cutaway coat and other formal wear that would be required in his role as president at Columbia, leaving it to one of the trustees to pick up the $1,550 tab.

Fortunately, small stuff of this nature does not detract from Eisenhower's stature as a great and good man. One is reminded of Emerson's tribute to Abraham Lincoln written a few days after the tragic assassination:

In a host of young men that start together and promise so many brilliant leaders for the next age, each fails on trial; one by bad health, one by conceit, or by love of pleasure, or lethargy, or an ugly temper—each has some disqualifying fault that throws him out of the career. But this man was sound to the core, cheerful, persistent, all right for labor, and liked nothing so well.[14]

11

OMAR NELSON BRADLEY

Even while men teach, they learn.

—Seneca

The life of General Omar Bradley is a study in quiet perseverance and good judgment. In the twenty-five years between graduation from West Point and 1940, he never left the United States and its territories on duty, rose only to the rank of lieutenant colonel, and spent the majority of that time as an instructor or in school. For the most part, his few troop unit assignments were easygoing and seldom required him to work in the afternoon. Yet from this seemingly laid-back development, he rose to become the senior American ground forces commander in Europe and the first formal chairman of the Joint Chiefs of Staff, between which roles his remarkable achievements as chief of the Veterans Administration have been all but forgotten.

Like Admiral Leahy, Bradley was a steady rider, rarely if ever colorful, yet dependable and competent to a degree that makes individuals of his caliber increasingly valuable as the level of warfare rises to higher levels of perspective. In moments of extraordinary crisis, generals like Bradley may not respond with the ruthless alacrity of an Alexander or a Nelson, but they more than make up for this lack with a sustained solid performance in the face of continued adversity.

Omar Bradley was born on February 12, 1893, on a farm near Clark, Missouri. The family lived in genteel poverty and had one other son who died from scarlet fever, although two orphaned first cousins were raised with Omar as if they were his sisters. In high school he did very well in math and science, so much so that his class (which bestowed a descriptive one-word nickname on everyone) marked him as "calculative." He also grew fond of one classmate in particular, Mary Quayle, whom he married seven years later. They had a daughter, Elizabeth, who married the son of one of Bradley's classmates.[1]

Unwittingly following in the path of fellow Missourian John J. Pershing, Bradley wanted to become a lawyer and sought West Point as an educational means to reach that goal. He competed for an appointment by examination and won it, to his disbelief. There he continued to do reasonably well in academics, very well in military discipline, and exceptionally well in athletics, (especially baseball, batting .383). In the yearbook, the *Howitzer,* his classmate Eisenhower wrote of him: "If he keeps up the clip he's started, some of us someday will be bragging to our grandchildren that 'sure, General Bradley was a classmate of mine.' " Ike then inserted the quotation: "True merit is like a river, the deeper it is, the less noise it makes."

Bradley's first assignment was with troops in Spokane, Washington, and later near the Mexican border at Yuma, Arizona. When the first world war broke out, he tried, like Arnold and Eisenhower, to get to France; but, instead, he was stuck stateside with training duty and with guarding the copper mines in Montana against a minuscule threat of sabotage. After the war, he requested duty in the Pacific Northwest but left out the word *Pacific.* At the time *Northwest* by itself meant the north central states, and thus he ended up on ROTC duty in South Dakota.

A year later the Military Academy accepted a large class to compensate for the drain that the war had made on the Corps of Cadets. Given his ability in mathematics, Bradley was reassigned to West Point as an instructor; and during that tour he honed his calculative skills to near perfection, especially at poker. He would not take a risk unless the odds were in his favor—usually seven out of ten—and that outlook began to permeate his life. For example, one summer he tried to augment his income by working on the Bear Mountain suspension bridge about five miles south of the academy. During the first week, a cable snapped and sheared off his watch. Calculating that the next one would likely slice him in two, he quit.

It is not that Bradley was the forerunner of the *Star Trek* character Mr. Spock; but he did say of mathematics that it was "a study of logic" that stimulates thinking and sharpens the "power of reasoning," adding that when complex incidents later imposed life-and-death decisions on him, he was sure that his "immersion in mathematics" helped him "think more clearly and logically." He was a rare exception to Plato's lament that mathematicians never made any sense.

From the West Point faculty Bradley went to the advanced infantry officer's course at Fort Benning, Georgia; then to the 27th Infantry Regiment in Hawaii as a battalion commander; then to Fort Leavenworth for the staff college; again to Fort Benning as an instructor; then to West Point

Official U.S. Army photograph. Courtesy U.S. Army Military History Institute.
19. Omar Bradley as a Lieutenant General. This is the photograph by which General Bradley wanted to be remembered. He cared for his men and demonstrated that as the scope of operations in war climbs to a theater level of perspective, the steady hand contributes more than the strutting boot.

as a tactical officer; and, finally, to service on the general staff in the War Department as a member of the Secretary, General Staff. Through all of this he was promoted only once, from major to lieutenant colonel.

The school at Fort Benning was his favorite. It taught maneuver warfare in complete contrast to the trench tactics of the previous war, and the field-oriented environment seemed to bring out the best in him. He graduated second in his class, just a fraction of a point below Gee Gerow (who then went to Leavenworth and graduated just a fraction of a point below Eisenhower). When Bradley returned to Benning as an instructor, it was under George C. Marshall, who made him chief of the weapons section. Funds were tight, but Bradley impressed the faculty and student officers alike on just how effective combined weapons fire could be when optimally employed. He was also pleased with Marshall's rule that whenever a student produced a workable answer different from the "school solution," it would be published locally for other students and faculty to read.

When he later reported to the general staff in Washington, Bradley found that Marshall had transferred his emphasis on simplicity in infantry tactics and manuals to the organization of the entire War Department. Marshall also demanded that his staff act on their own initiative and was disappointed if a week went by without at least one of his staff strongly disagreeing with a position that he had taken.

Still, Bradley yearned to be back with troops in some form. When the position of Commandant of Cadets at West Point opened, he requested it. This was a lateral rather than an upward move, but it did have advantages. At any rate, when Marshall heard of it by way of the Superintendent (who approved), he asked Bradley if that was what he really wanted. When Bradley said yes, Marshall offered him command of the infantry school. As that was a brigadier general's billet, Bradley did not hesitate: it meant immediate promotion to colonel and perhaps general officer rank in the not too distant future. Not very distant at all, as it turned out, because Marshall had an aversion to unnecessary paperwork. He had Bradley promoted directly to brigadier general, the first man in his class to wear a star.

Bradley didn't get to wear it for long. Within six months, Marshall paid a visit and asked him if he had given any thought to his replacement when he took command of the 82nd Division (before it was designated airborne). That was a two-star position, which Bradley took over a few days after Pearl Harbor. He made Matthew Ridgway his deputy commander and invited the 82d's most famous veteran—Sergeant Alvin York, who won the Medal of Honor in World War I—as the guest of honor during a demonstration weekend. As York was leaving, he commented to Bradley that the latter probably would not go much higher because he was "too nice a guy." The general took the point to heart.

Bradley continued to do so well that Marshall gave him a more difficult assignment—command of the recently activated 28th Division of the National Guard—holding out the promise of a corps command in the European theater if he mastered the situation. Bradley's main problem was the grip that states maintained over their units, even when called to active duty, restrictions that were written into statutes. As a result there was so much "hometownism" in various units that it was impossible to get the division to conduct itself as a unit. Bradley took the tack, if not the Solomonic wisdom, of *asking* the officers and noncommissioned officers if they would consent to a division-wide rotation plan. Surprisingly they agreed, and things worked out. At the end of the training cycle, Bradley put the entire division on a twenty-five-mile trek at night, marching along with them with a common pack. He overheard one soldier ask, "Who the hell ordered this march?" To which Bradley replied, "I don't know, but they ought to hang the S.O.B."

Marshall then ordered Bradley to go alone to North Africa to serve as Eisenhower's "eyes and ears," an assignment which he dreaded. Those whom he observed would quickly come to regard him as a commissar. However, the battlefield was at a considerable distance from the Allied headquarters in Casablanca, and the American troops were not doing well at all, having just suffered defeat at Kasserine Pass. This situation was analogous to the campaign in the Solomons when Halsey relieved Ghormley. Eisenhower had just about decided to relieve the corps commander Major General Lloyd Fredendall. Bradley's opinion confirmed that decision.

Eisenhower then gave Patton command of II Corps with Bradley as deputy, with the plan of pulling Patton back within a short time to command the newly formed Seventh Army for the invasion of Sicily. This meant that Bradley would move up. The drawback was that the overall ground commander, British General H. L. G. Alexander, a distinguished battlefield leader with eight years of combat experience, did not have a high opinion of American forces and, therefore, assigned them only a minor role in the final drive to clear Tunisia. Bradley balked at this, to which Alexander was at least sympathetic.

When Bradley went to Eisenhower with the request for a larger role, Eisenhower dropped his normal tendency to go along with the British and got it for him. General Bradley also exercised his newfound decisiveness by relieving commanders who failed to maintain discipline in their units, even those commanders who could win battles. In the long run, undisciplined units will do more damage than good, especially in the face of superior force, vaguely reminiscent of the Bill Mauldin cartoon "He's right, Joe, when we ain't fighting, we should act like soldiers."

Bradley continued in command of II Corps in the Sicily campaign under Patton. It was a tougher battle, and Bradley learned the price of sacrificing unity of command to discordant expediencies. As mentioned earlier, when the British generals maneuvered Eisenhower into the exalted position of

Supreme Commander, they were free to run the campaign in any way they saw fit. The flaw in their scheme was that there was no longer a single individual to integrate the various initiatives into a coherent, efficient battle plan. This led to three major problems.

First, the British Eighth Army (under Montgomery) and the American Seventh Army were allowed so much independence that the campaign reduced itself to an egotistical contest between the two commanders to see who could reach Messina first, which was the town on the narrow strait that separated Sicily from Italy. Second, had these forces been fully coordinated, they could have seized Messina early in the campaign by enveloping it from sea rather than by racing for it. This would have blocked the escape of the German forces on the island. Third, Eisenhower was nearly reduced to a visiting fireman who pestered his subordinate commanders with on-site visits and reporting requirements. Bradley made his displeasure known while carrying out Eisenhower's orders as best as possible. He must have done it well, for Eisenhower recommended him as the senior American field commander for the cross-channel invasion before he was himself selected as its overall commander.

Bradley's role in Europe has often been overshadowed by Patton's theatrics, and there is no doubt that the latter was more aggressive when it came to battle. But the European campaign was not a battle; it was a sustained war over a broad front that required a higher perspective to balance logistical reality with tactical or strategic daring; to throttle lieutenants that were too aggressive; and to boost, or sack, those that were too cautious.[2]

Furthermore, many authors emphasize Bradley's lack of initiative in failing to close the Falaise-Argentan pocket. This situation arose when the Germans attempted to cut off the Third Army's sweep toward the Seine by a westward thrust of their own across the Allied line of communications. This thrust failed because by that time the Allies' increasing mass nearly surrounded the German force. This situation reduced the task to closing the narrow gap between Falaise and Argentan in order to bag more than a hundred thousand Germans trapped in the pocket.

The idea was simple enough; and by this time Bradley had moved up to command the American Twelfth Army Group, located to the south of the pocket, and reported directly to Eisenhower, while Montgomery commanded the ground forces to the north. However, Eisenhower had not yet taken active control of the war on the battlefield. In the absence of a firm overall commander, and because Montgomery failed to ensure that his half of the gap was crimped, Bradley decided against closing the gap from the south. He believed it to be too risky. Nineteen German divisions intent on escaping annihilation could mount a formidable attack on a weakly held shoulder.

With the benefit of hindsight, this was not necessarily the case; there wasn't sufficient time for the Germans to organize that kind of threat, and, therefore, a bold commander would have probably taken the risk because of the immense potential gain. In *A General's Life,* Bradley admits that his timidity was in part to blame.[3] However, the consequences were not as serious as commonly perceived. First, the retreating German units were forced to leave much of their heavy artillery and equipment behind. Second, many of the Germans fell to Allied artillery and air strikes during their retreat. Third, some were cut off further to the east.

This is a good example of the human tendency to emphasize exceptions. Being the one sour note in an otherwise optimistic picture, historians have spent an untoward amount of ink on it. Moreover, any careful review of the facts reveals that the blame should fall more heavily on Eisenhower, and the balance must be placed equally on Montgomery.[4] That, of course, requires the analyst to consider the higher perspective imposed on theater commanders, a perspective that all too often enables those commanders, perhaps unwittingly, to let responsibility slide down to the shoulders of their lieutenants.

At any rate, when the war in Europe ended, Bradley was given a new one to "fight"—this one at the Veterans Administration (VA). The VA had sixty-five thousand employees, ninety-seven hospitals, and an organizational structure that had grown moribund. The battle was joined when World War II generated twelve million new veterans, tens of thousands of casualties that would require long term rehabilitative care, and the need to administer the generous package of benefits that Congress had voted for these new veterans. Clearly the role demanded a leader who was decisive, careful of numbers, and benevolent. Bradley met those criteria, and Truman personally asked him to take the job, with the promise of appointing him Chief of Staff at the end of two years. He accepted and turned in so remarkable a performance that it would take a separate book to do it justice.[5]

At the end of the two years, Truman kept his promise, and more, by later elevating him to Chairman of the Joint Chiefs of Staff. As Chief of Staff, Bradley's main responsibility was to make the best of the skeleton of an army. Most of the troops were in reality performing administrative tasks in their capacity as occupation forces in Germany and Japan; and even that manpower faced a steady drain as the navy and the air force fought for an ever larger share of the defense budget in order to fund new ships and aircraft. Only one division, the 82nd Airborne—his former command—was in any way combat ready.

Of more immediate significance was the brew in the new Department of Defense cauldron. The second echelon of senior military leaders in World War II had risen to the top posts, and most of them were intent on advancing the cause of their own service. In the absence of any major war,

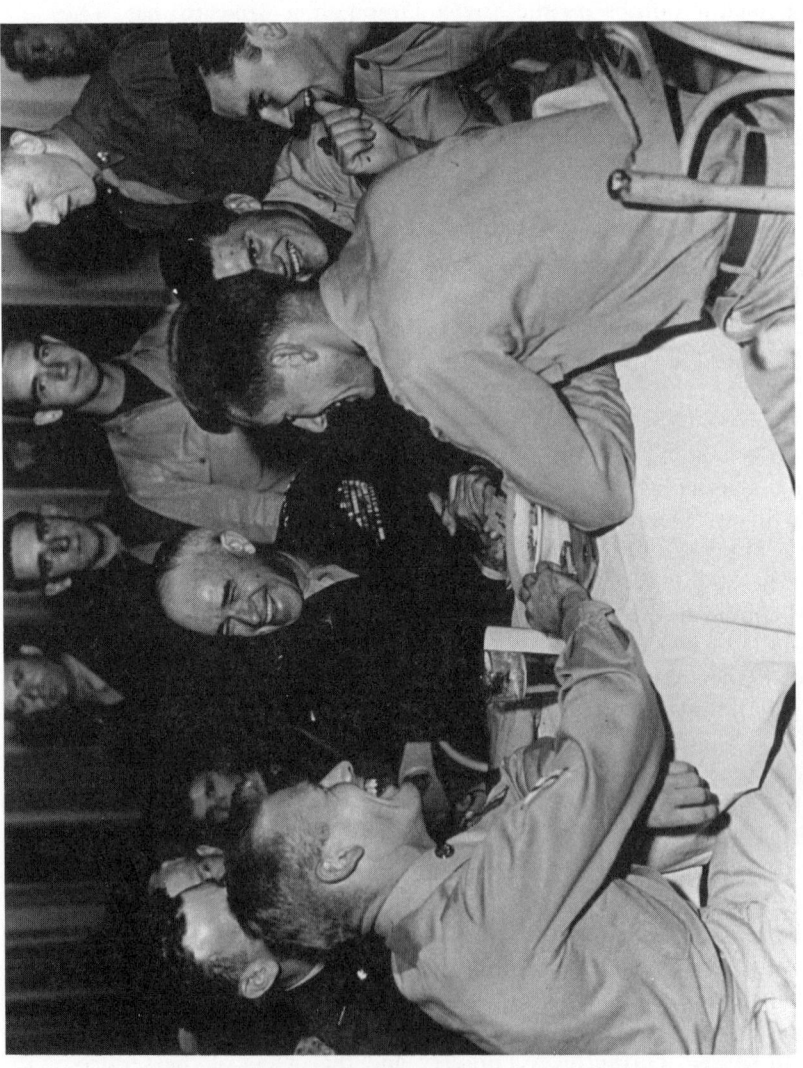

Official U.S. Army photograph. Courtesy U.S. Army Military History Institute.

20. General Bradley as Chief of the Veterans Administration. Bradley's magnificent role in preparing the VA hospitals for returning wounded servicemen, and for administration of veterans benefits, has been overshadowed by his role as a senior field commander.

the intramural squabbling consumed one hundred percent of their time, not the mere ninety percent that prevailed during World War II. The most noted campaign in this "war" came to be known as the "Admirals' revolt," led by Admiral Arthur Radford. This mutiny of sorts centered on the air force's demand for the new B-36 bomber, which had the capability of raining nuclear bombs on the Soviet Union, if it came to that. The navy wanted a new supercarrier, the *United States,* because it believed its future depended on sophisticated naval aviation, including nuclear delivery capability on a global basis. Secretary of Defense Louis Johnson opted for the bomber and arbitrarily canceled the carrier project. The navy then tried to impugn the integrity of Johnson and others in an attempt to restore the carrier.[6]

Later, as chairman of the joint chiefs, Bradley surprised everyone by his forceful testimony before the Senate Armed Services Committee. His remarks bear repeating even today, except that they apply to all the services, not just the navy, witness the sacking of air force Chief of Staff General Michael Dugan during Operation Desert Shield for intemperate remarks about the role of his service at the expense of the others:

> Many in the navy are completely against unity of command and planning as established in the laws passed by the Congress of the United States. Despite protestations to the contrary, I believe the navy has opposed unification from the beginning, and they have not, in spirit as well as deed, accepted it completely to date . . . [World War II] should have taught all military men that our forces are one team—in the game to win regardless who carries the ball. This is no time for "fancy Dans" who won't hit the line with all they have on every play unless they can call the signals.[7]

Still, Bradley was dignified about the entire matter and later recommended Radford to succeed him as chairman of the joint chiefs. Moreover, when the Korean conflict broke out, it would be MacArthur that became the more apt target of Bradley's criticism.

The key events in the Korean War are well known. Briefly, as Chairman of the Joint Chiefs of Staff, it was Bradley's job to mastermind the conduct of that war, despite the embryonic state of the formal joint chiefs. The problem was that the joint chiefs were faced with an individual who had been a general officer for thirty-two years and wore one more star than any of them.[8] Furthermore, Bradley and the chiefs of the services were opposed to MacArthur's plan to envelop the North Koreans at Inchon, believing it to be scatterbrained. When MacArthur's plan succeeded brilliantly, they were no longer in a position—politically speaking—to throttle MacArthur.

Thus, as the war progressed into North Korea *at the recommendation of the joint chiefs,* and the Chinese massively counterinvaded, the chiefs had to feed Truman's well-known, long-term disgust of MacArthur to the point where the President would fire him.[9] Even at that, it took the concurrence of Secretary of Defense George C. Marshall. At any rate, Bradley clearly recognized the futility of MacArthur's position, which he summed up before Congress in one oft-quoted sentence: "[It] would [be] the wrong war at the wrong place at the wrong time with the wrong enemy."

Bradley retired from the military in 1953 and lived for another twenty-eight years. For the first twenty of those years, he was the director of the research and development division of the Bulova Watch Company and later was its board chairman. He also tried to write his memoirs; but if mathematics was his strength, writing was not.[10] Nevertheless, he seems to have enjoyed his retirement more than any of the other principals, at least until 1965 when his wife Mary died from leukemia as they approached their forty-ninth wedding anniversary. Despondent with grief, he married twice-divorced Kitty Buhler less than a year later. She had acquired the rights to his memoirs and planned to have them written by way of a contributing author. In July 1973, Bradley suffered a heart attack that marked the beginning of increasing physical disability. He died on April 8, 1981, at the age of eighty-eight.

Bradley was supposedly the least colorful of the principals, and it is perhaps no coincidence that the literature lacks a significant biography on him beyond the contribution by Clay Blair in the autobiographical *A General's Story.* On the other hand, his integrity and character equaled Marshall's. His only flaw seems to have been the unwarranted slighting of two or three senior general officers who served with him in World War II, and part of that slighting can be attributed to the physical suffering of his last years.[11]

So the hell with color. The quality that caused Eisenhower to praise him unreservedly and that caused Truman to come to regard him with the same respect was his utter reliability without a trace of sycophancy. Senior commanders suffer their worst headaches from personnel problems that develop among their subordinates. When one of them proves unfailingly dependable and never causes any trouble, he is regarded as a godsend. True, as mentioned at the beginning of this chapter, a general like Bradley will rarely impose his will with the daring that returns great dividends in crises, but in the long run he will achieve more with less effort. As the level of perspective rises, that is what counts. This is the central theme of the analysis that follows in the second part of this book.

PART II

PERSPECTIVE

Any perspective that focuses on the main figures of an era begs a comparison of them. There are several ways to go about this. One way is to compare two leaders in "sets," a practice that Plutarch mastered nearly two thousand years ago. Unfortunately, that approach doesn't work well with ten principals who were contemporaries. A second way is to select a nearly ideal leader from history—if one can be found—whose performance synthesized all the tasks faced by the group under study. That failing, and it is sure to do so, a third way would alloy the best features of each member of a group and use that paragon as a standard or norm. That's a neat idea, but it runs headlong into contradictory attributes. General Marshall once told a portraitist that the canvas gave him too much the look of a MacArthur, adding that he was a much plainer man than that.

A fourth alternative would compare leaders on the basis of accomplishments, and this has some obvious merit. The flaw, however, is that not every leader has equivalent opportunity to compile them; and even if they did, the tendency would be to value the accomplishments rather than the comparative difficulties of achieving them. In short, a good comparison, at least for military personages, demands a more comprehensive, if pragmatic, approach that takes into account: (1) the level or levels of perspective in which a commander operated, (2) the individual's character and other attributes, (3) the extent to which the person's leadership skills had matured at the time, and (4) the difficulties that the individual had to confront.

Such a comparison is not easy; and to the extent that it is possible, it can be done only by first reviewing the key factors. Accordingly, this part of the book comprises four chapters and a summary. Chapter 12 examines the levels of perspective that operate in war, formalizing what was implied throughout the biographical sketches of the principals. Chapter 13 then posits a model of leadership that seems flexible enough to cover each leader in a framework built from those levels of perspective.

Chapters 12 and 13 are followed by what may seem—at first glance—to be a tangential matter, namely, the entanglements that result when different levels of perspective conflict and require an almost impossible mix of attributes in any one individual to resolve. This criterion seldom being met, these conflicts are seldom resolved, at least not with any degree of efficiency. The relevancy to the overall perspective stems from the ancient advice to avoid judging a man until you have walked in his shoes for a mile. The principals had to walk in very uncomfortable shoes many times.

With chapters 12, 13, and 14 as a reference, then, chapter 15 compares the ten principals. This was by far the most difficult chapter to write, and it ends by reminding both the writer and the reader that these generals and admirals were men of very great character and ability, and that therefore any comparison should seek an understanding of the many lessons to be learned, and not be a judgment of them.

This matter can be expressed in more colloquial terms, by recalling the anecdote about the navy commander transferred from the base at Charleston to San Diego. Upon arriving, he took his son to Point Loma, where he pointed out that the ocean that lay before them was more than twice as large as the one by which they formerly lived. The lad pondered this for a moment and then replied, "Perhaps so, Father, but it doesn't look a whit bigger to me." That is to say, no man should be pilloried because he bases his actions on his experience and education to that point. With that caveat, let us proceed.

12

LEVELS OF PERSPECTIVE

Eagerness for battle becomes soldiers, but generals better serve the cause by fore-thought, by counsel, and by timing rather than temerity.

—Tacitus

The *Iliad* makes two points about war clear. The first is that war combines different levels of perspective, including heroics, operations, and persever-ance at the theater level. Without perseverance, the heroics are in vain and even with it, a ruse may be required. According to Virgil's *Aeneid,* Troy fell only after the inhabitants accepted a giant gift horse concealing Greek soldiers. In the two major wars of the twentieth century, the Allied forces combined personal heroics, collective national perseverance, and a great deal of operational strategy in between.

True, the prosecution of those wars might have been more efficient, especially the first. Then, too, the squabbling among the parties often rose to ludicrous heights. Yet the fact remains that the Allies won tremendous victories. In other words, the heroics of battle, the stratagems of opera-tions, and the perseverance of a nation must align favorably on the path to victory: failure beckons when they don't, which is the essence of the second point.

That point warns that different levels of perspective often conflict with unfortunate, if not deadly, consequences. Before leaving for war, Aga-memnon propitiated the gods for a previous sin by sacrificing his daughter Iphigenia. Upon his return, he forfeited his life at the hands of his wife Clytemnestra, making the victory seem hollow indeed. Less tragically, he could have easily shortened the Trojan War by keeping the objective more clearly in mind rather than entertaining Achilles' emotional hang-ups for years on end.

In modern times, some of the same forces under some of the same leaders that prevailed in World War II had to settle for a draw in Korea five years later. Because the inherent capabilities and attributes of senior commanders do not change that radically in that short a period, it is obvious that at least a few of them failed to realign the various levels of perspective.

This failure to realign is not a point to take lightly, for war imposes five distinct levels: (1) heroism, (2) tactics, (3) operations or campaigns (4) theaters, and (5) national purpose and resources. These levels give the lie to the theory that a war equals the sum of its battles. That sum, if not greater than its parts, may wring out quite differently than the wash on the battlefield. However, all five levels are subject to a singular base of reference, and that reference is *time*. Correctly managed, time is a weapon, especially in the hands of a individual endowed with perseverance, patience, and a clear perception of what needs to be done and how to do it.

A leader should understand, if not practice, the virtues and attributes necessary to succeed at lower level commands; but a leader should also clamp down on the excesses when they operate to the detriment of a higher level. Thus Eisenhower had to defuse Montgomery's repeated attempts to envelop the German defenders because the effort could not be sustained long enough to ensure a victory. When Eisenhower did give in, as in Operation Marketgarden, the outcome was a failure. The Germans had sufficient time and maneuver room to parry the thrust. Thus with time as a reference, each level can be distinguished by different aspects of common factors. These factors are:

- *Purpose or objective.* To have meaning, every action or related set of actions requires a purpose or an objective. The action may be concrete, like taking a hill or sinking a ship, or it may be abstract, like restoring the global balance of power. Because objectives at higher levels tend to be abstract, the issue becomes whether the more concrete objectives of lower levels will satisfy a higher-level purpose. If that purpose is survival by way of expelling an evader, then the goal will be reached ipso facto. By contrast, when the objective is to stem the flow of a certain ideology, then the relation between lower-level tactical objectives and higher-level purpose is tenuous. Because time is on the side of ideas, they rarely succumb to military force, though many a head of state has beat his head against a wall trying.

- *Ways and means.* As the level of perspective rises, so too does the time required to achieve success. And because time consumes matériel, logistics takes on increasing importance. Even in the relatively small-scale Punitive Expedition, Pershing discovered that it was not so much a battle as a theater of operations in which he needed roughly ten thousand troops to support the one thousand that were prepared to fight. However, the same is not quite true for strategy. When space and time are tight, the lack of maneuver room precludes strategy. Then, as available space and time increase, so too does the opportunity to exercise strategy—read *maneuver*—up to a point. Above that point, the stage grows too vast and thus the fallback is to attrition warfare. This is the story of the two world wars writ large. More on this discontinuity between logistical clout and strategic prowess later.

- *Consequences of failure.* Bad decisions at higher levels can easily negate extensive success at lower levels. Napoleon in Russia was an example. By contrast, good decisions at higher levels can sometimes overcome a string of bad performances in the field, especially if a conflict is large enough to depend primarily on attrition and the logistical ability to persevere. The Civil War comes easily to mind. The South fought brilliantly time and time again, but they sadly misjudged the strength of the Union and the resolve of its eminent commander in chief. In short, the consequences of a mistake increase exponentially as the level of perspective to which it pertains rises.

To get on with it, then, the first or heroic level has the most appeal. At this level success depends on the actions of an individual, and the heroic nature of the deed can even take precedence over a failure. Rudyard Kipling noted: "But there is neither East nor West, border, nor breed, nor birth, when two strong men stand face to face, though they come from the ends of the earth." This was borne out when a squad of Australian commandos were caught within Japanese lines in civilian clothes. At the trial, which resulted in death sentences, the prosecutor said:

> With such fine determination they infiltrated into the Japanese area. We do not hesitate to call them real heroes . . . The valorous spirit of these men reminds us of the daring enterprise of our own men of the Naval Special Attack Corps. The respect the Australian people showed them we must return to those in our presence. When the deed is so heroic, its sublime spirit must be respected and its success or failure becomes a secondary matter.[1]

Still, in the context of war, most situations that call for extended heroism are anomalies. The tactical flow of battle depends on discipline and teamwork. Tactical briefings (the poets excepted) do not ad-lib: "Now at this point, Jones, you will charge up Hill so-and-so and win yourself a

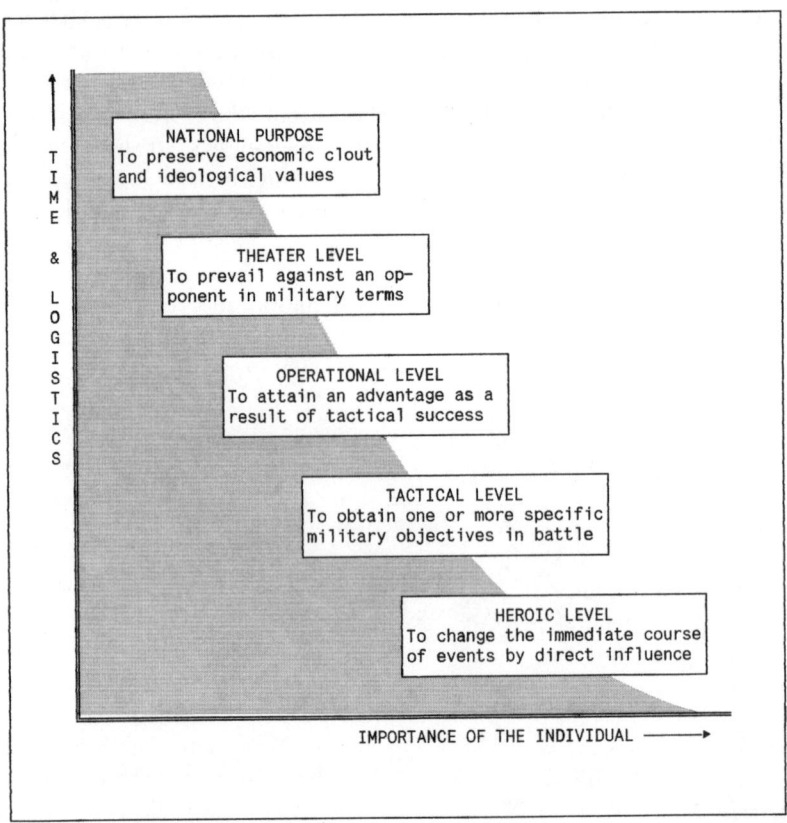

Figure 3. Levels of Perspective in War. War is not the sum of its battles. Many factors intrude at higher levels of perspective that can enhance or denigrate battlefield success. Most of these factors derive from the amount of time available.

such-and-such medal." But plans go awry. Troops suddenly confront momentous choices; or alternatively, the rescue of a fellow soldier or sailor demands extraordinary bravery. In these situations the objective is immediate and within the grasp of one or a handful of individuals even if it means instant death. Time is of the essence and logistics are meaningless. On the other hand, in these situations the consequences of failure are rarely significant in the overall course of a war. World War II produced approximately five hundred Medal of Honor recipients; yet had not a single individual acted above and beyond the call of duty, it would not have changed the outcome. On the other hand, this does not mean that cowardice can carry the day; but *extraordinary* heroism, which may sometimes decide a battle, will rarely, if ever, determine the outcome of war.

Heroism is also the stuff of prophets, military and otherwise. Billy

Mitchell, with whom Arnold shared a friendship, was court-martialed for carrying his prophecy on airpower to an extreme (and twenty years later was awarded the Medal of Honor posthumously).[2] MacArthur was a member of that court-martial and would himself evolve into something of a prophet and be relieved of command for his troubles. In short, heroism above and beyond a genuine call for it is seductive and has lured more men to destruction than ever did the sirens in the *Odyssey*. Liddell Hart put the matter this way:

> The prophets must be stoned; that is their lot, and the test of their self-fulfillment. But a leader who is stoned may merely prove that he has failed in his function through a deficiency in wisdom, or through confusing his function with that of a prophet. Time alone can tell whether the effect of such a sacrifice redeems the apparent failure as a leader that does honour to him as a man.[3]

The next two levels, that is, the tactical and operational, are related, in the sense that operations—or campaigns, as they are sometimes called—comprise a sequence or related set of tactical encounters. The typical aim of a battle is a specific objective: for example, capturing a terrain feature or rendering an opposing unit ineffective—war at the retail level. By contrast, the objective of an operation may be the last objective in a tactical sequence, or it may have a more abstract purpose. Thus, the operational purpose of a blockade is denial of ingress or egress, whereas this denial is achieved tactically by sinking ships or downing aircraft, or at least by the deterrent ability to do so. Whatever the case, tactics and operations are not normally seeded with heroism. Said one observer of the famed Charge of the Light Brigade: "It was magnificent, but it was not war."

Admittedly, the dividing line between a battle and an operation is sometimes hazy. The battle of Midway—coincidentally, midway between the two levels—comprised two distinct battle areas under different task force commanders, Rear Admirals Jack Fletcher and Raymond Spruance, under the operational command of Fletcher, the senior of the two. However, Fletcher's single carrier, the *Yorktown*, was sunk. Of necessity, Spruance assumed operational control; but he clearly understood the difference between the two levels of perspective. The operational objective was to repel the Japanese fleet before it could destroy the American counterpart or take Midway Island. This was accomplished tactically by sinking the four Japanese carriers, which made continuation of the attack untenable for Admiral Yamamoto.

On the other hand, Spruance chose *not* to pursue the retreating Japanese fleet because he would then be at a disadvantage. He did not have the wherewithal to take on that many ships; besides, the Japanese might lay a trap for him, which is what Yamamoto would have done, by using land-based aircraft positioned on Japanese-held islands to the west. Thus,

Spruance envisioned the defeat of Japan as a theater-level goal, that is, it would take many operations and battles to achieve the goal. Midway was the time and place to make a stand against a pending Japanese invasion; it was neither the time nor the place for Spruance to *unnecessarily* risk his still outgunned American fleet.

This difference was more sharply demonstrated in the battle of the Coral Sea, less than a month earlier. In that battle, the American fleet, admittedly not very strong at the time, was outfought by the Japanese; the U.S. fleet lost one carrier (the *Lexington*) and sustained serious damage to another (the *Yorktown*).[4] Yet because the navy fought so bravely and intensely, sinking at least one escort carrier, Japan ceased offensive operations directed at Australia and New Zealand, or at least directed toward severing the U.S. line of communications to those countries. Accordingly, historians commonly accept the conclusion that the battle of the Coral Sea was a strategic if not a tactical victory.

A more complex operation took place in Leyte Gulf, this time with Admiral Halsey in command of the main naval fleet. Halsey abandoned his operational mission of protecting the amphibious assault on Leyte in order to pursue the tactical objective of sinking a Japanese carrier task force steaming in from the north. It was not a prudent trade-off; and, as mentioned in previous chapters, the Japanese carriers were a decoy: they had no planes and were intended only to draw Halsey's fleet away from Leyte Gulf so that other Japanese task forces could wreak havoc on the U.S. operation. Halsey was a first-class fighter and leader of men, but he was not always able to make the transition from the tactical to the operational level of perspective.

The remaining two levels are theater and national purpose. They overlap considerably for the obvious reason that a wartime national purpose is fully dependent on success in the theater, or theaters, of war. The difference, which is analogous to the difference between a battle and an operation, is that the national objective may be more abstract: for example, restoration of the balance of power; whereas to achieve balance, a theater commander must still aim at concrete military objectives. These commanders don't have magic wands. Whether attaining those objectives will restore a balance of power is problematic; and, in theory, it is not the commander's problem. In practice, senior commanders exert an enormous, if subtle, influence on national decisions: witness Admiral Leahy's role as Roosevelt's chief of staff.

At any rate, as posited at the beginning of this chapter, the emphasis at these higher levels is normally on attrition warfare inflicted against the opponent by way of sustaining military force long enough to prevail without permanently damaging the economy. Pyrrhus, after the battle on the river Siris at Tarentum, said: "One more such victory and we are done for." A modern case in point was General Marshall's recommendation in World War II to field no more than ninety divisions.[5] The population could have been taxed for more, and perhaps the defeat of Germany might have come sooner; but such added pressure would have also hampered the civil sector, which was already manufacturing half the armaments used by the Allied nations. Incidentally, Marshall was quite successful in this matter. By the end of war, the United States had eighty-nine active divisions and one more forming.

Another facet here is the comparative weight of the opposing forces. If these forces are roughly balanced, as in World War I, then in the absence of a rare opportunity to exercise a strategic envelopment, the side that holds out longest will usually prevail. If the opponent has numerical superiority, at least in what that nation is willing to expend, then some form of a strategic envelopment is essential to win, as with the German conquest of France in 1940. By contrast, when military forces overwhelmingly outgun the opponent, then the outcome is assured, provided that high-level decision making is not fatally flawed. The method of choice in this favorable situation is a more efficient prosecution of the war. This was the Allied emphasis after the first eighteen months of World War II.

So much for dissection. In practice, the various levels of perspective tend to mesh together in unforeseeable ways and can lay waste to the august principle of unity of command. This principle advocates placing responsibility on one individual and vesting him with adequate control over the resources required to meet all objectives. It's a worthy goal and relatively easy to implement at lower levels of command. The same is not true at the theater and national levels. Nevertheless, the absence or degradation of this principle begs inefficiency. This is especially true in coalition warfare, as evidenced by the large number of conferences that were held during World War II. After that war, Admiral King started to write a book on the subject while Commander Walter Muir Whitehill wrote his biography. In the process, their efforts merged, resulting in a long autobiography that obscured King's original intent.

Closely associated with differences among levels of perspective are those among the services beyond the obvious. For example, until recent times the army emphasized tactics and battles while giving short shrift to operations, except on matters of logistics. As a result, many of the operations within the European theater, and in the Pacific theater for that matter, were lackluster and sometimes missed opportunities for inflicting more casualties. An example was Bradley's decision to refrain from closing the gap at Argentan, which allowed a good part of the hundred thousand entrapped Germans to escape from the pocket.

By contrast, the navy paid more attention to operations and less to logistics and some key aspects of battle. The result was that during the early campaign in the Solomons, namely, the fight for Guadalcanal, Admiral

ARGENTIA Newfoundland Aug 9 - Aug 13 1941	This conference produced the *Atlantic Charter*, in effect a mutual defense treaty between the United States and Great Britain without the U.S. formally declaring war on Germany.
ARCADIA Washington, D.C. Dec 22 - Jan 14 1941 1942	The highlight was the *Declaration of the United Nations*, which aligned most of the free world in an informal treaty of mutual support and defense against the Axis powers.
ANFA Casablanca, Jan 12 - Jan 23 1943	The key agreements were to delay the counter-invasion of Europe until 1944 and to mount an invasion against Sicily. The "unconditional surrender" policy was an unplanned aftermath.
TRIDENT Washington, D.C. May 12 - May 24 1943	This was the most important conference from a military viewpoint. Operation OVERLORD was agreed upon and the war in the Pacific theater upgraded in spite of requirements in Europe.
QUADRANT First Quebec Aug 14 - Aug 24 1943	OVERLORD was confirmed notwithstanding the collapse of Italy. A secondary attack through southern France was added, and a Southeast Pacific theater under Mountbatten created.
SEXTANT Cairo Nov 23-26, 1943 Dec 2- 6, 1943	China was brought into the picture but the main thrust in the Pacific theater remained the ocean route to Japan. Chiang Kai-shek was mollified by a planned campaign in Burma.
EUREKA Tehran Nov 28 - Dec 1 1943	This sidetrip within Sextant accommodated Stalin, who wanted to stay near Russia. He pressed for a second European front, which resulted in Eisenhower being named commander.
OCTAGON Second Quebec Sep 11 - Sep 16 1944	The players recognized that complete victory was inevitable. The political leaders pushed to start converting resources to peacetime rehabilitation; the military wanted to wait.
ARGONAUT Yalta Feb 2 - Feb 11 1945	The key agreement formalized the entry of the Soviet Union into the war against Japan. Both Roosevelt and Churchill made concessions that only with hindsight proved unnecessary.
TERMINAL Potsdam (Berlin) Jul 16 - Aug 1 1945	The agreements addressed political problems in post-war Europe; few of which had lasting effect. The surrender ultimatum to Japan was also ignored, leading to use of the A-bomb.

Figure 4. The Major Allied Conferences in World War II. There were ten of these conferences; but the first one, named Argentia, was not counted in the numerical-based naming plan, while the missing "Quintain" was the conference of foreign ministers in Moscow in the fall of 1943.

Halsey succeeded, but only with an untoward loss of ships in various tactical encounters. And the air force often ignored the synergism of combined arms. During World War II, its senior officers advocated strategic bombing even at the cost of supporting critical tactical operations. More than once, army and navy commanders in both theaters had to order the air force to provide that support, even at the Normandy landings.

This brings the discussion to what might be called the mechanics, or the physics, of war. Although this subject is arcane, it explains, in part, the success or failure of many military decisions. The common theme is that the conduct of battle and war, as differentiated from leadership, consists of placing the various implements in various arrangements headed in various directions at various speeds. War is not purely linear, like dominoes or a track meet. Efficiency depends more on arrangements and timing, like billiards or football. Subordinate commanders can and often must make adjustments; but, in general, the initial arrangements and quantities foreshadow the outcome. In military parlance, these arrangements are better known as tactics and strategy.

To restate this point in reverse, tactics and strategy are variations on efficiency. In battle, when the field is small and the available time short, strategy is often reduced to a handful of "formulas" or "plays" that can be used in various combinations or sequences. This codified strategy is called *tactics*. At the operational level, when the field of battle is larger and more time is available, the opportunities and alternatives for maneuvering increase markedly and thus lend themselves to ingenuity. This is called *strategy*.

There are at least four keys to tactics and strategy. The first key, as mentioned earlier, depends on the amount of maneuver room available. If it is too constricted, the geometry of the situation may force a commander to rely on tactics and local attrition. Similarly, if the space is vast and time is of little consequence, a commander may again be forced to depend on attrition, although at this level it is often called a broad-front strategy and is typical in a major theater of war. However, when an entire theater is severely constrained by geography—as, for example, in Korea—then strategic envelopment can be employed, which is exactly what MacArthur did at Inchon. By contrast, when Churchill tried envelopment in World War I at Gallipoli, the strategy failed. Even if it had succeeded tactically, it would have had little effect on the war on the Western front or in Russia.[6]

The second key is the high ratio of force that it takes to dislodge a determined defender, especially when the terrain or geography (for example, mountains) favor defensive tactics. Under the best of circumstances, the offensive typically requires three times the firepower exercised by the defender. That ratio can increase to ten-to-one or even twenty-to-one under less than ideal circumstances. The reason is that the defender is stationary (and, thus, rocks, for example, become the equivalent of armor plate, as it were). The defender also has what are called *interior lines*, which means that he can quickly reallocate their resources to counter an attack anywhere along his boundary. Thus, efficient warfare seeks to envelop the defender and cut his umbilical supply tether, usually called a line of communication. When this succeeds, the defender is placed in an untenable position. But not every theater or battlefield lends itself to that strategy; and even when it does, not every commander is up to it.

The third key occurs when reach exceeds grasp. This happens when a nation attempts to conquer its neighbors without having the strength to sustain that conquest. In *The Rise and Fall of the Great Powers,* Paul Kennedy called it "imperial overstretch." At the tactical level, this national or strategic-level "overstretch" has a counterpart which Clausewitz, in his book *On War,* called the "culminating point." Clausewitz wrote: "An attacker may take on more than he can manage and, as it were, get into debt."[7] In practical terms, this means that a commander in battle may continue an attack past the point of his ability to sustain it, but in so doing he has "shot his bolt." This makes him especially vulnerable to counterattack because he might not be able to reverse his forward momentum in time to defend himself.

This phenomenon works the same way at the national level. Obviously, both Germany and Japan expanded their empires far beyond their ability to maintain them, once the full weight of the massive Allied resources were brought to bear. But what if Japan had neither invaded China nor attacked Pearl Harbor? With that plan, they could have secured their hold on the Pacific basin and effectively cut off the lines of communication to Australia and New Zealand from both directions. Furthermore, the three-fourths of the Japanese army that was deployed in China could instead have been pumped into the defense of Japan's Pacific strongholds. And what if Germany had not invaded Russia but, instead, had invested her armed resources in the conquest of Great Britain, Spain, Portugal, and the entire Mediterranean basin? In that event, the United States would have had to persuade the Soviet Union to declare war against Germany and then figure some way to get there in support. This may be speculation, but it makes a point.

The fourth and sometimes most spectacular key gives the appearance of contradicting everything that is known about science, at least until recent times. This occurs when a single, sometimes minor event triggers a radical change. In physics this is called *critical mass* or, alternatively, *catastrophe theory.* The latter purports to explain sudden disasters, like earthquakes, as well as radical but constructive change, for example, genetics.

Why does it happen? Simply because some arrangements are more favorable than others: witness any sporting event, board game, bridge hand, traffic pattern, or airline schedule. Even the simple attrition-tactics game

	LOGISTICAL CONSIDERATIONS	STRATEGY AND TACTICS	OVERSTRETCH
HEROIC LEVEL	Logistics are rarely of any consequence in acts of heroism; the act speaks for itself. Exception: in heroic one-man campaigns, e.g., T.E. Lawrence in Arabia in W.W. I; strategy, if not logistics, may be critical.	These are seldom relevant. Time and space are too limited to significantly affect maneuver.	Heroism exerts enormous force, witness the Battle of Britain, but not always in sufficient measure to overcome potential failure, no matter how much praise the act elicits.
TACTICAL (BATTLE) LEVEL	Supply is the common name used for logistics at the retail level. And wherewithal must be carried by the troops doing the fighting or be *dependably* available on short notice.	By definition, tactics are the essence of the tactical level. Space and time factors are limited to the point where strategy must be codified into a slate of tactical procedures.	At these levels, the line at which reach exceeds grasp is the *culminating point*. It is passed when the attacker no longer possesses the force to sustain his advance, and thus any further attack is merely
OPERATIONAL (CAMPAIGN) LEVEL	This is the transition zone of logistics. Smaller operations require only retail battlefield supply. But campaigns demand wholesale planning. Without it they will sputter, if not fail.	Operations present the optimum range of time and space to employ strategy, and as such are the focal point of military history. Still, success often depends on logistical factors.	forward motion on the road to perdition. Even when the attack is reined in, the defender will inflict severe casualties and send his opponent reeling back to a less favorable position.
THEATER LEVEL	A theater usually encompasses too much time and space to affect strategic maneuver; the opponent just sidesteps it. As a result logistical capability becomes the dominant factor, which means the outcome of war depends on attrition. This was the essence of the Western front in World War I, in all theaters in World War II, and in Korea once U.N. forces crossed the 38th Parallel.		Paul Kennedy's term *historical overstretch* aptly describes the consequences for a nation when it reaches for more than its resources can manage. In war, those consequences arise from passing the culminating point inherent in the theater or by insufficient strategic clout to hold that which was taken. This is the story of World War II writ large.
NATIONAL LEVEL	Here, logistics extends back into the means of production and the long-term effects on the economy. A nation can destroy itself winning a war.	Strategy at this level focuses on priorities and schedules. Leahy, Marshall, King, and Arnold devoted most of their time to problems of this kind.	

Figure 5. The Parameters of War. Success in battle and war depends on the correct mix of logistic capability, of tactics and strategy, and in arrangement and timing. Unfortunately, these parameters defy easy alignment.

of checkers can end dramatically in one catastrophic play. On a much larger scale, the Japanese attack on Pearl Harbor galvanized American opinion to a degree that surprised everyone. On a more concrete level, the battle of Midway terminated abruptly when dive bombers attacked the Japanese carriers just as they were rearming their planes on deck for another sortie. This brought an end to Japanese hopes and is said to have marked the turning point of the war. True, the overwhelming resources of the United States would have reached that point sooner or later; but in this case, the unwitting operation of catastrophe theory made it occur earlier.

It would be good if all of the above points could be neatly packaged into a simple table, thus permitting the conduct of war to be reduced to a computer program. Unfortunately, the elements don't cooperate that much. It takes a certain amount of mental prowess as well as leadership skill to weave these various threads into ad hoc paradigms that fit the circumstances of each battle or war to be fought or analyzed. The only simplification available is to keep the different levels of perspective foremost in mind and then err on the side of favoring the higher level when the perspectives conflict. As the history of this era clearly indicates, that simple concept is exceptionally difficult to put into practice.

13

Facets of Leadership

A man's character is his fate.

—Heraclitus

There are as many schools and models of leadership as there are writers and practitioners of the subject. The model offered in this chapter makes no pretense at synthesizing this mass of opinion. Nevertheless, no comparison of leaders is possible without a base of reference, preferably one that takes into account the levels of perspective that a commander must deal with, the difficulties facing him, the commander's character and other attributes, and the extent to which his leadership skills have matured at the time.

Accordingly, this model is derived from the levels of perspective outlined in the previous chapter and extended to cover management and politics in a democracy. Wars, no matter how intense, are fought within the context of a national ethos and purpose. In a democracy, that purpose is often to preserve individual rights. Hence, the importance of the individual prevails at the lower levels in both military and civil environments. At the military end, this translates into the heroics of a few individuals. At the other end, it is the collective exercise of individual freedom that eschews standouts.

Similarly, organization more than concern for individuals per force dominates the thinking of higher levels of military and civil concerns, although the difference between them is not as pronounced. When a government must act in a crisis, the exact nature of that crisis—military, economic, or political—matters less than the need to exert some form of control over otherwise democratic processes: for example, price controls during World War II. They were invoked again for a short time in 1972 to head off a problem that had little to do with war.

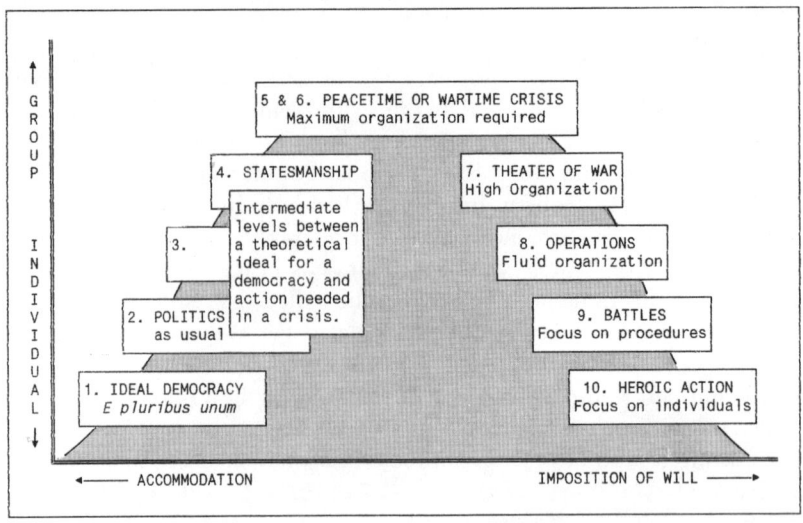

Figure 6. Scale of Leadership Requirements. Leadership is generic only in the abstract. In practice, different forms of it are required for each level of perspective. Few individuals operate well at all of these levels.

The key to this extended scale of leadership is the proportion of initiative versus a willingness to accommodate, as may be appropriate for each level. At the heroic pole, the emphasis is entirely on initiative and imposing one's will on circumstances. At the opposite pole, the abiding principle is accommodation and compromise. Neither is all good or bad, and there are times when something of a heroic performance is needed in the middle of the range: Lincoln and Churchill are examples. Unfortunately, power corrupts; and many individuals who ascend the scale fail to keep the heroics in check, and, consequently, degenerate into louts or dictators.

This is why Franklin D. Roosevelt had a difficult role to play in World War II. The United States was not in an immediate survival situation; and several times earlier, he was stung trying to impose drastic solutions to ameliorate social problems generated by harsh economic times. And he did not have the luxury enjoyed by George Washington, namely, freedom from partisan politics (at first), nor the unique situation handed to Lincoln of limited but nearly absolute power.

Furthermore, Roosevelt never understood the lack of interest in politics on the part of his senior military advisors, and vice versa. When his reelection in 1944 seemed secure, he turned to his bored chief of staff and said, "Bill, you don't understand a thing about politics, do you?" Leahy replied, "Mr. President, that's the nicest compliment you paid me." When General Marshall was asked about his politics, he replied, "My mother was a republican, my father was a democrat, and I am an episcopalian."

Churchill had it somewhat easier. First, he was not head of state. King George VI was, which meant that the Prime Minister had a freer hand. Second, Churchill was not *directly* elected to his office.[1] Third, he had wartime experience and was easily the most popular figure in the United Kingdom at the time. Fourth, his country had been in extremis during the Battle of Britain. As such, he wielded considerably more authority, even though his sense of strategy was off-kilter. His nearly insatiable desire to attack Europe through the Alps—which he called the "soft underbelly of Europe"—finally lost out; but he was able to get Roosevelt to go along with the invasion of North Africa, partly on the grounds that the invasion would begin before the 1942 midterm elections in the United States.

Thus, the great challenge for a democracy in war is to preserve itself while shifting temporarily to a semidictatorial state in order to accomplish ends that are beyond democratic means. Admiral King addressed this issue in far more harsh terms while a student at the Naval War College. He wrote:

> It is traditional for us to be inadequately prepared. This is the combined result of a number of factors . . . democracy, which tends to make everyone believe he knows it all; the preponderance of people whose real interest is their own welfare as individuals; the glorification of our victories in war and the corresponding ignorance of our defeats and disgraces and of their basic causes; the inability of the average individual to understand the interplay of cause and effect not only in foreign but in domestic affairs, as well as his lack of interest in such matters.[2]

This is *not* the kind of essay that gives voters warm fuzzy feelings. It *was* a logic that Germany and Japan depended on to expand their empires without interference from the United States. Had Germany and Japan been more prudent in their choice of conquests—a point discussed briefly in the previous chapter—they might have gotten away with it.

The fortunate thing about assessing leaders and leadership is that despite an infinite variety of styles and personalities, at least some common ground abides. In 1967, the Department of Defense asked the Franklin Research Institute to perform that kind of a study.[3] Moreover, to keep the study from becoming too academic, the institute employed two retired four-star generals to do most of the interviewing and analysis, namely, the army's General Bruce Clark and the air force's General I. D. White. The common trait that the researchers found among senior officers was the ability to accept information, process it intelligently, and then disseminate the results in the form of orders, directives, and suggestions.

It is easy to understand why this is so. The essence of leadership and command is to make decisions and then motivate subordinates—and sometimes superiors—to carry them out. The process of motivation varies, but decision making requires input, processing, and output. That may sound more like a computer program than leadership, but the process of winning a war depends on moving the right mix of resources to the right place in the right quantity at the right time; and when things don't go as planned, to reshuffle as necessary. This ties in with the discussion on the mechanics of war in the previous chapter.

True, this common trait of leadership must be considered in context. Are the decisions and directives appropriate for the circumstances and the level of perspective under consideration? In the absence of complete information—which is usually the case—what role does intuition and calculated risk play? Does ego get in the way of information that merits consideration? Can the leader accept blunt criticism from subordinates when the leader is wrong?

One thing is certain, information processing depends on intelligence *up to a point*. If intelligence, in part, is the capacity to sift through material and find meaningful relations or their lack, then extreme intelligence has the tendency to go beyond and to dwell on secondary or immaterial points or, alternatively, to discourse on windy analogous matters, often theatrically. MacArthur was undoubtedly a genius, and when Eisenhower was once asked if he knew him, Ike replied, "Know him! Why I studied dramatics under him for nine years." In short, although MacArthur's high intelligence contributed to his many successes, it also led to dramatic but imprudent initiatives that eventually did him in.

Actually, for military commanders the capacity for perception and vision may be more important than raw intelligence—the ability to visualize the way things ought to be and how those things can be achieved. The end result may be entirely practical and perhaps nothing more than the *status quo ante bellum*. The means to achieve it might be nothing more than motivating subordinates to perform better. Freud supposedly said that sometimes a cigar is just a cigar. Put another way, useful intelligence does not seek brilliant solutions for the sake of being brilliant.

Now how much of this mental filter for leadership ability is due to preparation? Does it require a lifetime of extensive reading? Or writing, for that matter? Or a sharpening of the mind by extensive teaching or instructing? With the possible exception of Admiral Halsey, all of the principals were voracious readers; and without exception, all were instructors, writers, or both, though what they wrote about varied considerably. MacArthur's mind, in particular, was a giant maw that fed insatiably on the written word. It is fair to conclude, therefore, that extensive preparation counts for something. A "conversation" with other minds, past and present, is often a commander's inoculation against an overreaction when the opponent bites especially hard. This abstraction was brought to the fore in the film *Patton,* when, just before a battle in North Africa is to be joined, the general says, "Rommel, you magnificent bastard, I read your book!"

So much for attributes of the mind. Edison once said that genius was one-percent inspiration and ninety-nine percent perspiration, implying that the character of an individual was more important than intellect. But what is character? Is it a collection of attributes, or is it something singular with many facets? Is it the essence of one's psyche, or something imposed on it? What is the proper role of ambition?

All of the principals were ambitious, even General Marshall; and few tried to quash it. When they did, the resolution didn't last long. In 1916, in order to gain Mamie's hand in marriage, Eisenhower gave up his plans to transfer to army aviation—more at the insistence at Mamie's father than her own. Consequently he vowed always to do the best with whatever lot the army handed him. A year later he was officially reprimanded for repeatedly hounding the War Department to send him overseas in battle in World War I. Without a doubt, then, the general question of character is shrouded in academic difficulty.

This book assumes that character is an entity, and that what are sometimes called the elements of character are in reality facets or effects that surface when leadership is exercised. This may be wrong—and it is certainly unprovable—but at least it yields a focal point. However, it is important not to confuse character and ability. Men of great character can lack ability and vice versa. Think of character, then, as the strength to do what seems right under the circumstances and as the strength to refrain from or resist doing what seems wrong. That implies a steady hand and perseverance when the going gets rough.

Furthermore, one can easily surmise that perseverance is the most crucial facet for military success. Reminiscent of Edison's observation, the old saw puts it that perseverance will win every time. That's not quite true, but it's true more often than not, especially as the level of perspective climbs from the heroic to the national purpose. There, time and space stretch, which means that the massing of resources, often at the expense of competing claims, takes precedence. All of the principals were marked by perseverance, and each opted to stay in the service during the darkest days between the wars, despite lucrative offers from civilian industry.

Another word for this kind of perseverance is willpower. Willpower can come from an outer or inner source. If it is from an outer source, then the individual serves primarily to implement plans that have little to do with his own initiative, and he gains satisfaction only by doing those tasks well. By contrast, if willpower is from an inner source, the exercise of it springs from ideas formulated in one's own mind. These extremes may be rare in practice, but some individuals hove close to one or the other. To illustrate the inner source variety, it's hard to find a stronger example than Hitler's depravity; indeed that was the whole theory behind his *führer prinzip*. For the outer source kind, General Marshall's character set a standard—or at least renewed the one laid down by Washington and by Lee in previous centuries.

This discussion leads directly to the issue of integrity. Some of the most effective leaders in history had notoriously lax moral standards, especially in matters of the bedroom. As a corollary, many honest men proved inept when it came to exerting leadership. *But if character is a singular entity, then it follows that a lack of integrity will eventually seep into the encompassing character like a slow-acting poison.* One need only consider the eventual fate of Napoleon, or General Patton for that matter. Patton had a twelve-year–long affair with his wife's niece, Jean Gordon, whom he had brought over to Europe during the war in order to continue the affair, bragging that he bedded her seventy-one times.[4] This conduct was clearly immoral; and had Jean been his own niece, it's a sure bet he would have been sent packing in disgrace.

Patton also evinced despicable character flaws on the battlefield, especially when he sacrificed the lives of troops for his own glory or other personal reasons. The best known example was his race to Messina in the Sicily campaign in order to show up Montgomery. His lack of ethics was brought out quite clearly in the film *Patton,* primarily by way of a comment made by Major General Lucien K. Truscott. Another case was Patton's unauthorized and unsuccessful raid behind German lines in an attempt to rescue his son-in-law, Lieutenant Colonel John K. Waters (later General), from a prisoner-of-war camp. More than one soldier lost his life in that raid. To this writer, such action constitutes manslaughter, be it intentional or by wanton disregard for the consequences of one's actions. Both Eisenhower and Bradley were furious and came very close to relieving Patton of command on the spot.

This brings up another aspect of Patton's conduct. He was also on the carpet for the well-known "slapping" incidents; but contrary to the popular view, they may not have stemmed from a character flaw. Arguably, they were tantamount to his saving grace. For when General Patton put his entire mind and soul into winning a battle, he was all but unstoppable. In this, his character became his personality and could tolerate no shirkers. The same was true of his distant mentor, General of the Armies John J. Pershing, who once decked a soldier for merely goldbricking at a river crossing in peacetime. In short, while the slapping may have shown an intolerable lack of judgment, it also demonstrated the man's character at its strongest, and it was this trait that caused Eisenhower to spare Patton time after time.

Among the principals, there is only one similar case. MacArthur's character flaws more than once led him to engage in battles or to extend war for which he had little authority. This included operations against lesser Philippine islands in World War II and, more seriously, operations in Korea six years later. All of the other principals may have made mistakes in judgment—and sometimes the consequences were disastrous—but there is just no other instance among them of human life being sacrificed to sate inner desire. And the saving grace for MacArthur was that his decisions were based on a cause that in his mind went beyond purely personal reasons. His paramount aim was to lay waste to any enemy that stood defiantly before him. One of his biographers put the case this way:

> In the Attic tragedies of Aeschylus, Euripides, and Sophocles, the hero is a figure of massive integrity and powerful will, a paradox of outer poise and inner passion who recognizes the inevitability of evil, despair, suffering and loss. Choosing a perilous course of action despite the counsel of the Greek chorus, he struggles nobly but vainly against the enduring cruelty and ultimately, defeat, his downfall being revealed as the consequence of a fatal defect in his character which, deepened by tumultuous events, eventually shatters him.[5]

Sometimes character flaws are the product of the excess of one's virtues, sometimes they are separate, and sometimes they are a combination. Thus, for example, a battlefield commander can fight too aggressively and incur higher casualties than would a more self-controlled commander. At the other extreme, cowardice is generally considered to be an outright flaw in character if not an absence of it. The difference? The excess aggressiveness is dealt with—if at all—by admonishments or by keeping closer tabs on the individual. Nimitz dreaded the thought of Halsey succeeding him as theater commander, even temporarily, and went out of his way to ensure that it didn't happen.[6] By contrast, cowardice has more than once been cured by a firing squad. Fortunately, among the principals only two or three had serious flaws in their character; and in each case, these flaws seem to have arisen largely from an excess of their virtues.

This doesn't mean the principals were without faults. For example, Pershing, despite his extraordinary self-discipline, was late for just about everything to the point of rudeness. Admiral Nimitz, by contrast, became unbearable when anyone, including members of his immediate family was late for an appointment. And many of the principals were guilty of puffery and distortion in their memoirs: MacArthur the most, Leahy the least. Nimitz and Marshall avoided that problem altogether by not writing any.

On the other hand, faults are not the same thing as incompatibilities or insufficient training. A senior officer whose blood boils away from action will make a poor logistics staff officer. Admiral King had a rough time in that regard. Or if a lieutenant colonel is whooshed to three-star rank in the same number of years and is then placed in a complex political and military situation where not even his superiors can fully agree on the objectives, the general's performance is bound to fall short of expectations. Eisenhower came close to being sacked in North Africa, but it had little to do with any personal shortcomings. Rather, the onus was attributable to what Patton admitted after the war: "It is sad to remember that, when anyone has fairly mastered the art of command, the necessity for that art usually expires—either through the termination of the war or through the advanced age of the commander."[7]

Any discussion of faults inevitably leads to the question of arrogance. Is arrogance a flaw in character or just an unfortunate side effect of being placed in a difficult situation? Because all of the principals were arrogant at times, some more so than others, perhaps the answer depends on the severity of the arrogance. Momentary impatience that flakes off within hours is hardly a flaw, and at times it may be a virtue. But a studied and practiced arrogance exercised against those who disagree or fail to perform up to standards may very well be a defect in character.

Admiral King seems to have been plagued by this flaw more than the others to the point of deserving a black belt in pugnacity. Still, his arrogance was never as bad as the op-ed piece that appeared recently in the *Mensa Bulletin*. The writer lamented that the world failed to appreciate the "gifted" and that geniuses often have to retreat behind various cloaks of trivia in order to insulate themselves from a world that it is their birthright to lead, concluding that "we"—apparently meaning he and his fellow geniuses—were "not equals" but "the best."[8] Oh, my.

The remaining aspects of character to consider are courage, risk taking, and decision making. The exercise of courage always entails risk taking, else there would be no need for courage, and all such acts stem from a decision. Another way of expressing these three aspects is *judgment* in the largest sense of that word. However, courages takes different forms depending on the level of perspective. Courage on the battlefield usually means disregard for personal safety in the face of potential danger. At higher levels, the risk is not so much the grim reaper but perseverance in the face of potential disgrace. Pershing accepted the risk of humiliation and condemnation by refusing to let the French and British use American troops as cannon fodder for their depleted ranks at a time when victory seemed elusive.

This, then, brings us to the matter of personality and style. Few, if any, military leaders in history had similar personalities; and among the ten principals, no two came close. King was caustic; Marshall, austere (on duty); Pershing, a martinet; and so forth. What *is* important is the influence that personality and style evoke. An outgoing or charismatic personality will encourage others to volunteer crucial information, while an austere individual has to work harder to obtain it. In this regard, General Arnold was a curious mixture of both. At times he confronted subordinates as caustically as Admiral King did, but he also possessed an almost childlike innocence. His nickname "Hap" was short for "happy." As a result, he was sacked more times than he liked to admit but was always brought back to the fore with greater responsibilities.

One more point. The need for leadership is as common to political and corporate environments as it is to military command, but the military has always demanded an additional measure from its practitioners—namely, to take care of the troops. This is especially true in wartime. The reason is that commanders are obliged to send men to their deaths. This means leaving children without both parents—or, in some cases, without the only parent they have. As such and like it or not, a commander is temporarily forced to assume the role of God. In a just war, men understand this. What they cannot understand and will not tolerate is when their lives are expended uselessly. The dead cannot speak out, but the survivors will. Shortly before Pershing arrived in Europe, the French army mutinied en masse. The way that troops tell the difference in motive is by how well their commanders take care of them. If this is clear, they will forgive the honest errors of judgment that are bound to occur.

Ernie Pyle said that he was bent on tracking down and stamping out everybody in the world who failed to appreciate the lot of the common soldier. When World War II ended, Admiral Halsey's first spoken thought was that he would no longer have to send men to their graves. And Eisenhower put the matter this way:

> Humility must always be the portion of any man who receives acclaim earned in the blood of his followers and sacrifices of his friends. Conceivably a commander may have been professionally superior. He may have given everything of his heart and mind to meet the spiritual and physical needs of his comrades. He may have written a chapter that will glow forever in the pages of military history. Still, even such a man—if he existed—would sadly face the fact that his honors cannot hide the crosses marking the resting places of the dead in his memories.[9]

All of these issues and items may be combined into a model that is both attribute- and situation-oriented:

- *Character and flaws.* Character may be considered to be the font or driving force of leadership; and the effect of character is the trident

	HEROIC LEVEL	TACTICAL & OPERATIONAL LEVELS	THEATER AND NATIONAL LEVELS
CHARACTER Perseverance Integrity Courage Judgment Decisions	Character is everything at this level; heroism is synonymous with courage. Heroic acts are almost spiritual in nature and earn respect regardless of the outcome.	The character appropriate for these levels varies. Battle leans to heroism; operations depend more on perseverance. Few men possess the range to do equally well on all counts.	Perseverance marks character here, but a lack of integrity will eventually weaken it. As such, heroism appropriate for this level tends to risk reputation more so than life.
THE MIND AS A FILTER Intelligence Perception Instructing Processing	Intelligence is not especially correlated with heroism in battle. Both geniuses and men of plain mind have shown great courage under fire, often at the cost of their lives.	Success in intense situations often depends on rapid processing and dissemination of information and decisions. Equally intense preparation can really count.	Because logistical factors play a dominant role at these levels and typically generate many conflicting priorities, the attributes of the mind are especially critical.
STYLE and PERSONALITY Polemics of austerity versus amiability	Style has little to do with heroism, but it might in some circumstances indicate the motive for exercising courage, e.g., to save life versus to effect a goal.	Here, amiability is a better asset than austerity. Men must be led, and they will more readily follow if they can readily perceive humanity in their leaders.	By contrast, austerity seems essential at this level. It enables a leader to take a stand in the quicksand of politics, witness Pershing, Marshall, and King.
CONCERN FOR THE TROOPS Extent to which this is put into practice	If the motive is to save life at the risk of one's own, then the expression "greater love hath no man" applies. But if it is to sate ego, failure can be tantamount to manslaughter.	This attribute is crucial at these levels. Lacking it, an officer may still succeed on occasion, but as a result he will likely encounter the intense hatred of his men.	Concern for the troops is equally critical here, but in concert with austerity, it is sometimes best exercised by decisions that result in the least cost in human life.

Figure 7. Leadership versus Levels of Perspective. Character is the font of leadership percolating through the filter of the mind and manifesting itself in a wide range of styles. The mind affects the level of perspective at which a leader best operates, but it is no substitute for character.

of courage, risk taking, and decision making. Closely associated with this generalization is the extent of the leader's concern for his subordinates, as well as the extent to which he manifests this concern.

- *Information processing, intelligence, and perception.* This is the filter through which character manifests itself, almost always by exercise of the ability to process information into directives, as factored by intelligence and perception or vision.

- *Personality or style.* Anything is possible here, but the important point is the effect that style has on efficiency in decision making and in the motivation of subordinates.

- *Capability of the leader.* This results from the combination of the above factors, and means the level or levels of perspective at which a leader is proficient or capable of dealing with at the time he confronts a task.

- *Level(s) of perspective required in a situation.* This is the mix of heroism, tactical ability, operational strategy, theater acumen, and/or sensitivity to national concerns; necessary to accomplish a task, mission, or obligation. In extreme cases, a task may require consideration of three, four or five levels concurrently, but one is usually dominant. When this isn't the case, the conflicts may be irreconcilable.

Additionally, one other aspect of leadership rates mention. This is the so-called *Nelson touch,* named after (and by) Admiral Lord Horatio Nelson. Although this idea has never been precisely defined, it describes a commander who predisposes his resources to favor a striking victory (the mechanics of war) and then inspires his subordinates to act as if they were an extension of himself while still exercising their own initiative to deal with circumstances as need be (leadership). That's a mouthful, and a tall order, to boot; but when a commander pulls it off, the result is happy catastrophe theory at work. For in this situation, it is the opponent who experiences the catastrophe. Thus, Halsey was sometimes considered the equivalent of several aircraft carriers. At the Chief of Staff level, General Marshall raised the Nelson touch to an art form.

14

ENTANGLEMENTS

Chaos is indigestible mass.

—Ovid

Prometheus, so legend claims, was for eons chained by Zeus to a rock as punishment for showing too much initiative—especially for revealing some of the secrets of the gods to mere mortals. Yet over the centuries, mortals unraveled some of those "secrets" by sheer dint of analysis. In the process, they often entangled if not bound themselves in a web of their own spinning. Hence, in an era of global war fought under complex alliances, these entanglements were destined to frustrate leaders, even those with a high degree of initiative and authority.

The seven cases included in this chapter were selected for two reasons. First, collectively they involved all of the principals. Second, the cases remain controversial to one degree or another. This suggests that the underlying complexities should be studied in their own right instead of seeking resolution, especially if the leaders involved are to be compared. A better understanding of the circumstance guards against unfair judgment.

Fortunately, at least for the purpose of analysis, most of these entanglements arose from a threefold generic problem: *conflicting levels of perspective in the absence of sufficient unity of command compounded by the inability of most decision makers to adapt to rapidly changing circumstances.* Because the human mind has a limited ability to digest conflicting priorities and information—especially when they pour in relentlessly—each situation demanded a degree of leadership and ability that was beyond reality in all but one instance. Of the remaining six cases, four generated major problems. The other two seemed to work out for the best because the priorities were more favorably aligned than was commonly believed at the time.

The first of the cases addresses the utilization of American forces in France during the last year of World War I. The central problem, as discussed in Chapter 2, was that the war appeared to be going against the Allied forces; hence the proposal to infuse American soldiers into French and British units as replacements had Voltaire's justification, namely, that God is ordinarily on the side of the heavier battalions. In other words, the tactical level of perspective demanded that American troops be used as cannon fodder to stem potential defeat. Furthermore, from the viewpoint of France and Great Britain, that cannon-fodder justification had the endorsement of the higher levels of perspective.

Different factors prevailed for the United States. The United States had entered the war for a higher moral purpose, not to enthrone the futility of trench warfare. Wilson's desire "to make the world safe for democracy" may have been ridiculed by some historians, yet the fact remains that for the Allies the hope eventually became reality. It just took longer. Accordingly, Pershing weighed in on the side of the higher U.S. perspective and then stood his ground against the pressures imploding on that decision.

First, Pershing's battle experience was lightweight compared to that of the Allied generals. Second, the Germans were mounting new offensives strengthened with troops brought back from the victorious Eastern front. Third, France and Great Britain were draining themselves of everything they had. Fourth, the Allied powers were going behind Pershing's back to American political leaders. Fifth, French battlefield veterans temporarily imported to the United States insisted on teaching trench warfare to American recruits. Sixth, the Chief of Staff, General Peyton March, was leading a cabal to displace or at least reduce his authority.

On the other hand, Pershing had five reasons for holding out: (1) a fear of feeding men into a machine that had slaughtered millions with little to show for it—a hundred Vietnams rolled into one, (2) a belief in maneuver as an efficient and decisive alternative to static trench warfare, (3) the language problem between American and French soldiers, (4) an implied obligation to make the American contribution more distinct, and (5) his escape clause—namely, that if the situation became desperate enough, he agreed in advance to recant and put Americans into the line wherever they were most needed.

In short, Pershing took a calculated risk, persevered in it by sheer willpower—and, in the end, prevailed. As a result, Pershing became the most well-remembered senior American military figure of that war, perhaps the only one. Yet it should be noted that he had both a free hand and the confidence of President Wilson. Further, his emphasis on maneuver went flat. The battle of the St. Mihiel salient was an isolated offensive against opponents who had decided beforehand to withdraw from it, and the Meuse-Argonne offensive was only part of a broad-front, attrition-based final campaign. Hence, even when an extraordinary leader makes the right decision in a situation that threatens entanglements at every turn, that leader may escape the snare of ignominy by mere inches.

The second case concerns the lack of preparedness at Pearl Harbor, namely, the inability to repel, or at least inflict punishing damage on, Japanese forces during the sneak attack. Whether a totally alert state of readiness would have *deterred* Japan from attacking in the first place is problematic; but it's a safe bet that if the senior commanders on the scene—Admiral Kimmel and General Short—had thrown everything they had at the Japanese, they would not have been relieved of command. Thus, the issue becomes: could exceptional commanders have made a difference?

Arguably, the only way to have succeeded would have been to place military forces on around-the-clock alert seven days a week, combined with 360-degree reconnaissance at a radius of at least 250 nautical miles (knots). Alternatively, the reconnaissance could have been limited to daytime if it covered one night's sailing, that is, the entire donut from two hundred to five hundred knots out. Hence, with a warning of at least an hour, every plane could have been put in the air to meet the attacker before he reached Oahu, and most ships positioned to good advantage and brought to battle stations.

The factors operating against this approach were: (1) the available aircraft and patrol ships were limited in both quantity and capability, (2) the cost in dollars and the effect on morale of *continuous* alert status in peacetime would have been too high, (3) the army and navy commands in Hawaii were independent of each other, (4) Washington kept sending mixed signals, (5) few people thought that Japan would be so foolish as to mount an unprovoked attack on the most powerful nation in the world, and (6) in the event, Japan could afford to wait until the United States grew tired of staying on alert.

It is true that a single radar installation was by then in operation, but it was experimental. Commanders had little reason to rely on it and even if they had, a continuous alert posture would still have been required. Still, at least one of the principals might have made a difference. Admiral King had twice before demonstrated the vulnerability of Pearl Harbor during fleet exercises using precisely the tactics that the Japanese carrier fleet employed in 1941. In his own words, he could be "a son of a bitch" and therefore might well have imposed the necessary alert status had he been in command.[1]

Restated, it would have taken exceptional willpower to ensure preparedness on a peacetime military establishment in a country that had not been attacked since 1812, discounting Pancho Villa's raid on the border town of Columbus, New Mexico, in 1916. Kimmel did send out two carriers on screening duty (in conjunction with a mission to Wake Island), but it wasn't enough. Thus, Kimmel's (and Short's) lack of *extraordinary* willpower at the tactical level was suddenly transformed into a national level trauma.[2] The American ethos was deeply shocked and roused to a fever pitch. Ironically, however, had the Japanese attack been deterred, the United States would have waited longer to enter the fray, which would have resulted in an even longer and bloodier conflagration.

The third case—antisubmarine warfare in the Atlantic—is the most complex of the seven cases. And it was *not* a failure. On the contrary, the solution imposed eventually proved to be an outstanding, if unsung, success. Yet given the experience of World War I and the fact that this type of warfare had been going on in the Atlantic for a year before Pearl Harbor, the question must be asked: Could more have been done earlier to reduce the high shipping losses? And if so, would it have made any difference in the overall war effort? The second answer is important because if it is negative, then a higher priority for this theater of war could have jeopardized the other theaters. The immediate factors were these:

- First, much of the shipping to Europe and to the Soviet Union *was* convoyed and, hence, sustained *comparatively* fewer losses than it otherwise would have. What was being sunk at will were ships carrying raw materials, especially those sailing the Atlantic seaboard.

- Second, the implements of antisubmarine warfare were scarce and did not have a high priority. This was symptomatic of the navy's lower regard for wholesale logistics at that time. Of necessity, capital warships, carriers, and submarines took first priority, while landing craft and retail fleet supply ships competed for the balance of resources.

- Third, the navy saw the Pacific as the primary theater of operations, at least for their service.

- Fourth, the United States underestimated the German intent, which intensified during 1942, even though the United States intended to use the same strategy against Japanese shipping and fleet vessels.

- Fifth, some practical ad hoc solutions were initially dismissed out of hand—for example, using the civil air patrol to spot submarines along the coast.

- Sixth, civilian shippers were not enamored of convoys, which meant shipping delays and reduced profits.

- Seventh, for a while it appeared that new ship production would exceed losses and perhaps cost less than the price of a massive antisubmarine theater of war.

- Eighth, the initial emphasis was on offensive tactics—for example, sinking U-boats rather than defending convoys. Unfortunately, the guerrilla nature of submarine warfare rendered this offensive strategy ineffective. If the United States had possessed a thousand sub-chasers, each would have had to patrol twenty thousand square miles of ocean.

- Ninth, Admiral King did not assume the position of Commander in Chief, U.S. Fleet until after Pearl Harbor, and he did not gain the concurrent job of Chief of Naval Operations until March 1942. Further, there was no unified command in the Atlantic, neither between Great Britain and the United States nor within the American navy. Finally, King was immediately saddled with the higher priorities of the war in the Pacific.

Cohen and Gooch's superb study on this aspect of World War II bears careful reading.[3] These authors attribute the inability to respond faster to slowness of learning. Thus, given the complex array of factors operating in the Atlantic theater, it is possible that a Bradley in a navy uniform, imbued incongruously with Arnold's vast energy, might have turned in a better performance, provided (1) he could have gotten King's ear long enough and persuaded him that this part of the war was crucial, and (2) he had been given the necessary command structure to make it work.

The fourth case was the decision to launch an invasion of North Africa (TORCH) in late 1942 instead of a cross-channel invasion of Europe earlier than OVERLORD.[4] This was probably the most momentous decision in World War II, and it illustrates what happens when an external influence operates in an environment that lacks unity of command, or at least agreement on purpose and method. Briefly, and as mentioned in several previous chapters, the United States wanted to counterinvade Europe directly across the English Channel, whereas Great Britain wanted to fight the war in the Mediterranean and then attack north from there if it proved necessary. Five factors dominated the situation:

- First, Great Britain had major interests in the Mediterranean, whereas the United States did not.
- Second, Churchill had a poor sense of global strategy, especially in his opinion that the Alps were the "soft underbelly" of Europe.
- Third, Great Britain did have a much more realistic view of what it would take to mount a successful invasion of the European continent.
- Fourth, it was imperative to keep the Soviet Union in the war and on the offensive past the Polish border, or else the full weight of

the German army would be brought to bear in Western Europe and the Mediterranean—which would have increased the Axis strength in those theaters at least fourfold.

• Fifth, the United States and Great Britain agreed that Europe and not the Pacific basin was the priority theater of war.

As Churchill embodied these factors, he was able to prevail upon Roosevelt to overrule his military chiefs—fortunately as it turned out. When the cross-channel invasion was launched in June 1944, the Allies had accrued the following advantages, directly or indirectly, as a result of TORCH: (1) the Soviet Union had the bulk of the German army in full retreat, and the latter would not likely shift many troops back to the western front; (2) the Allies had absolute air supremacy, except for fighter resistance over some strategic targets; (3) the logistical output of the United States had reached so feverish a pitch that it was about to be scaled back; (4) the United States had gained valuable combat experience, and (5) the war was going well on all fronts and had immense popular support. Yet, despite these massive advantages, it still took the Allies eight weeks to break out of the Normandy lodgment area, the boundary of which was never more than fifteen miles inland.[5]

Had TORCH not been mounted and the cross-channel invasion launched in 1943, these advantages would not have accrued and therefore, in all probability the invasion would have been defeated. As mentioned in chapter 12, it takes at least a three-to-one ratio to eject a defender; and in an amphibious operation, the ratio can reach ten-to-one or higher. Alternatively, had OVERLORD been launched in 1944 without TORCH, the British still would have been heavily committed in the Mediterranean, and the United States would have had no significant combat experience.

All things considered, then, no military figure could have changed this decision or, having changed it, prevailed any earlier than what actually occurred (and probably would have done so much later).[6] Worse, given the resulting inactivity in Europe, the Pacific would have drawn off more resources and delayed the restoration of Europe even further. Put another way, this was an unusual case of a decision by default, in the absence of any real unity of command, that turned out for the best. However, it might have been better if the plans for the Italian campaign had been scrapped and those resources devoted to the cross-channel operation.

The fifth case was Admiral Halsey's decision to abandon *direct and immediate* protection of the Allied amphibious operation at Leyte Gulf in order to pursue Vice Admiral Jisaburo Ozawa's carrier task force steaming in from the north. As mentioned in several previous chapters, by this time the two theaters in the Pacific had more or less merged without the two theater commanders—General MacArthur and Admiral Nimitz—taking the necessary steps to more closely coordinate or consolidate operations. As a result, Halsey was operating under two conflicting directives: one under MacArthur, which concentrated on support of amphibious and other land operations, and the other under Nimitz, which perforce emphasized the defeat of the Japanese navy. In this conflict, MacArthur defended Halsey's actions but more as a rub against Nimitz for not letting him control the entire Pacific theater. Nimitz himself realized that Halsey was only following his orders, a point which Nimitz's own son, then a lieutenant commander, pointed out to his father in front of some more senior staff officers.

By his own admission, Halsey had three choices: (1) to ignore Ozawa, unless and until he became an intolerable threat, and concentrate on protecting the Leyte operational site instead; (2) to split his forces and perform both missions; or (3) to go after Ozawa with virtually his entire fleet, which was the course of action he chose.[7] Even if his decision had been the right one, Halsey should have ensured that the other two Japanese task forces already operating in the general area had retreated beyond the distance that would permit them to return to the battle area while he went after the carriers. *He did not do this, and that was the failing.* Nor would he admit that Ozawa's task force was a decoy, even after the war when the evidence became incontrovertible. Worse, he blamed Kinkaid, who commanded the smaller Seventh Fleet at Leyte, for not taking sufficient measures to protect himself.

Fortunately for Halsey, Kinkaid's men fought with incredible bravery. When pilots expended their torpedoes and ammunition, they continued to attack the Japanese fleet with "dry runs." Against such fury, even when the numbers indicate that the battle is winnable—attackers will sometimes back off. That is how the Japanese responded in this case (and how Germany eventually responded to the Anglo-Saxon backbone exhibited during the Battle of Britain). These were rare cases when sustained heroism really did make a difference in war.

Unfortunately, the tendency is to blame the man on the spot—for example, Kimmel as the scapegoat for Pearl Harbor. Halsey was acting as he best understood war. It is just that his actions at the tactical level suddenly had adverse effects at the operational and theater levels. Undoubtedly a more prudent commander—for example, Admiral Spruance—would have acted differently; but then, Spruance was cut from a different cloth, possessed perhaps the strongest intellect in the navy, and had spent several years as Nimitz's chief of staff.

The sixth case links two events that are not always fully considered in tandem: (1) the decision to bring the Soviet Union into the war against

Japan, and (2) the decision to employ the atomic bomb. Briefly the facts were:

- First, roughly three-fourths of the Japanese army was stationed in China. The United States did not want those forces brought back to Japan to defend against the planned invasion.

- Second, the Soviet Union had its hands full on *its* western front but promised to put thirty divisions into Manchuria a mere ninety days after the war in Europe ended. *The Soviet Union kept that promise.*

- Third, there was no guarantee that Japan would surrender before being annihilated.[8] On the contrary, almost everything, including kamikazes and children trained to crawl under tanks as human suicide bombs, suggested the opposite.

- Fourth, the unwelcome political leverage that the Soviet Union might gain from participation in the war did not outweigh the potential reduction in casualties.

- Fifth, the destructive power of the atomic bomb was minor *at the time*. There were only two of them in the arsenal and their combined firepower was small compared to the collective destruction that was being unleashed daily on Japan.

- Sixth, Truman did not *decide* to use the atomic bomb so much as he *did not veto* its use. The United States had not spent a large fortune to develop it as an exercise in pure research; and moreover, Truman came to regard it as essentially another weapon in the arsenal, not as the herald for Doomsday.

Afterward, the United States was accused of coddling the Soviet Union at Yalta and Potsdam and was criticized for ending the war by using the A-bomb rather than relying on a conventional blockade of Japan. The first allegation doesn't stand up under the facts as they were known and understood at the time. The second has more validity, and it was the position of the navy from Admiral Leahy on down. The Japanese surrender mooted the case; but as the blockade would have been absolute, Japanese civilians would have sustained far higher casualty rates over a period of time than they did at Hiroshima and Nagasaki. Arguably, then, the decisions made were the best possible under the circumstances.

The last case—the Korean conflict—concerns the largely U.S. decision to pursue the retreating North Korean forces into North Korea, following MacArthur's successful envelopment at Inchon. The immediate issue was whether the Chinese—and, possibly, the Soviet Union—would intervene.

As such, there were three options: (1) to stop at the 38th parallel or, alternatively, along a line in that vicinity that had slightly better defensive characteristics; (2) to counterinvade as far as Pyongyang (which is located along the narrowest part of the peninsula); or (3) to counterinvade the entire country, at least until the North Korean army could be soundly defeated and the two countries reunified.[9]

The first option was the default—for example, to do nothing further. The second option made little sense: the North Korean army would have retreated farther north, and the attempt at reunification would have been downgraded to an expansion of South Korea at the price of a smaller North Korea. The third option did make sense, but the price tag was a de facto declaration of absolute war against North Korea, that is, the total defeat of their army and the subjugation of their country under South Korea. If the Chinese and Soviets stayed out, the South Koreans, backed by the United Nations forces, had the clout to prevail. But if either China or the Soviet Union intervened in force, the U.N. forces did not have the resources to win, at least when one considers what the United States and her allies were willing to expend.

It is true that the political situation was anything but clear, which made prognosis difficult. John Gunther said that a former ally—the Soviet Union—backed its satellite North Korea in a war that was fought from Japan by the United States in the name of the United Nations, while this same Soviet Union insisted on its prerogative to sit in on treaty negotiations with its enemy Japan, the success of which would have brought peace between Japan and its other enemy the United States.[10] Even this can of worms omits the fact that China was sitting on the other side of the Yalu and would not tolerate anything that threatened the power dams along that river.

Unfortunately, all of this was ignored. The euphoria over the success of the Inchon envelopment blinded most decision makers to the risk (Secretary of State Dean Acheson was the notable exception); and thus the United States, as the leader of the U.N. forces, jumped into a new war with new parameters and yet a familiar outcome. Invasions, no matter how righteous, don't work unless the attacker has overwhelming resources and armed superiority. The United States realized this when China intervened, and decided that she did want to try, MacArthur excepted. But could another commander have prevented the failure of this "new" war?

Given the fact that it was the President and the Joint Chiefs of Staff who recommended pursuit into North Korea, the answer is probably no. The only possible compromise would have been to conduct the counterinvasion with maximum reconnaissance of Korea north of the line of battle, accompanied with standing orders to retreat to the 38th parallel in the event of intervention. This caution might have saved some lives, but the

	PRINCIPALS INVOLVED	LEVEL-OF-PERSPECTIVE ENTANGLEMENT	RESOLUTION (Planned or by Default)
EMPLOYMENT OF U.S. FORCES IN WORLD WAR I	· Pershing	The U.S. was intent on a distinct contribution to the war. France and Great Britain wanted to use U.S. troops as cannon fodder to stem the tide of battle.	Pershing held out for American interests, saving men from needless slaughter in the process. It was a high risk decision that might have cost the victory.
DEFENSE AGAINST THE JAPANESE ATTACK OF PEARL HARBOR	· Marshall · King · Arnold	The national aim sought to protect military resources as a deterrent. The tactical mission was to defeat if not deter a sneak attack by Japanese forces.	As Japan intended to neutralize the U.S. in the Pacific, local commanders couldn't deter it. Tactical defeat was inevitable, even if they had fought better.
ANTI-SUBMARINE WARFARE IN THE ATLANTIC	· King	The conflict was on priorities for the many theaters in the war. Naval battles in the Pacific and land warfare in Europe demanded and got higher priority.	With hindsight, the defeat of German submarine warfare might have proceeded more rapidly, but there is no assurance it would have had a major impact on the war.
OPERATION TORCH The decision to invade North Africa	· Leahy · Marshall · King · Arnold · Eisenhower	Arguably, this was the most momentous decision in World War II. U.S. military figures sought a direct military counterinvasion of Europe. Churchill had other ideas and persuaded Roosevelt to his point of view. Nevertheless, the decision was correct because resources were insufficient to have done otherwise. Roosevelt understood this.	
BATTLE OF LEYTE GULF	· MacArthur · Nimitz · Halsey	The conflict was Halsey's highest priority under Nimitz to inflict damage on Japanese forces, vs. the mission under MacArthur to protect the Leyte operation.	Halsey favored his tactical mission, without first ensuring the Japanese could not disrupt the operation. Only the extreme heroism of the defenders saved the day.
BRINGING THE U.S.S.R. INTO THE WAR IN THE PACIFIC, and USE OF THE A-BOMB	· Leahy · Marshall · King · Arnold · Nimitz	Because Japan did not seem to believe in surrender, the goal was to defeat her at the least possible cost in human life. The A-bomb was really a tactical sideshow.	The bomb merely coincided with Japan's realization that further war was futile but because there was no way of knowing this, the decisions made were optimal.
EXTENDING THE KOREAN CONFLICT INTO NORTH KOREA October 1950	· Marshall, as Secretary of Defense · MacArthur · Bradley	The national goal was to restore South Korea to its citizens, but this changed radically after MacArthur's masterful envelopment at Inchon.	The U.S. slowly recognized that it did not want a war with China and thus settled for a draw, but not before MacArthur's decisions and acts embroiled her in one.

Figure 8. Command Entanglements in War. This era of history generated many situations that defied resolution, except perhaps with the benefit of hindsight. Accordingly, some of its leaders have been criticized by historians when perhaps admiration would have been more appropriate.

whole idea is ludicrous. Armies don't cross the Rubicon on a tether. And it certainly wouldn't have deterred the intervention. In sum, the decision makers failed to take the radical change to national perspective into account when they crossed the 38th parallel, and hence in this situation any commander would have been doomed to failure.

To review the bidding, then, wars often lead to complex decisions when the various levels of perspective interleave, and no single decision can possibly satisfy the conflicting demands of these different levels. The tendency is to favor the lower level because of the heroics and "honor," whereas wars and the fate of nations usually depend on a higher level of perspective. In World War I, Pershing understood that higher level, stuck to his guns, and won, aided by exercising unity of command over all U.S. forces in an environment where the political and military situations were more or less constant.

In the case of Pearl Harbor and Leyte Gulf, the local commanders were acting as best they could, but owing to traumatic encompassing circumstances, the strategic inadequacies of their reasonably good tactical-level decisions have been magnified out of proportion, in both cases exacerbated by a lack of unity of command and rapidly changing conditions. More fundamental blame can be laid at higher levels for failing to sharpen and coordinate directives: President Roosevelt, General Marshall, and Admiral Stark in the case of Pearl Harbor; and Admiral Nimitz and General MacArthur for Leyte Gulf.

Regarding the antisubmarine warfare problem, that was not so much a failure as a matter of taking more time than perhaps necessary, notwithstanding the initial absence of unity of command and bona fide higher priorities. Yet once the logistical consequences were recognized, priorities were revised, a more unified command structure imposed, and the problem resolved.

When it comes to operation TORCH and the final subjugation of Japan, both were situations where prevailing national interests and the theater actions taken coincided; yet in the absence of unity of command—especially for TORCH—operational priorities and other considerations were allowed to obfuscate the issues. A direct counterinvasion of Europe may have made immediate military sense, but the logistics and the global force ratios worked against it. As for the Pacific theater, the national objective was to force an enemy to surrender in the absence of any apparent willingness to do so. One may argue the merits of various alternatives, but all of them would have served that national purpose.

This leaves Korea, which marked the end of both MacArthur's career and Anglo-Saxon dominance of the globe. Actually, that dominance existed only by exerting leverage from geographical islands of safety, and in this case there wasn't much to leverage once the Chinese counterinvaded. When the troops crossed the 38th parallel, the national level of perspective changed radically. If MacArthur couldn't see it, the President and the Joint Chiefs of Staff did, but not until it was too late.

15

COMPARISONS

The judgment of mankind is as relentless to the weaknesses that fall short of what is required as it is antagonistic of arrogance that exceeds necessity.
—Thucydides

Drawing on the previous three chapters as a combined base of reference, this chapter compares the ten principals. It does so by first contrasting the various levels of perspective *imposed* on them with the levels of perspective at which they best operated or at least were prepared to operate at the time. Within that framework, their attributes of mind, character and style, and concern for the welfare of subordinates are then considered.

However, before launching into this comparison, several points common to all or most of the principals can be noted. First, they were all raised in farms, small towns, or isolated army posts, and developed the greatest respect for their parents. Second, they were all graduates of their respective service academies, except General Marshall, who graduated from the equivalent Virginia Military Institute (and he had wanted to go to West Point). Hence, they all went through the same leveling process that weeded out the weak of character and then challenged each survivor to develop and prove his mettle. This process has never worked with perfection, but apparently it worked well enough.

Third, with the exception of Admiral Halsey, all the principals had been, were, or would become chief of their respective services, although only three (Marshall, King, and Arnold) held that post in time of war. Fourth, none of them emerged from the woodwork, as it were, like Grant's sudden rise from near-derelict to famous general during the Civil War. It is true that Pershing, Arnold, Eisenhower, and Bradley leap-frogged in rank to one degree or another; but their reputations and abilities had been established over many years of earlier service. It was only the pattern of slow, lower-grade promotions, more prevalent in the army than in the navy, that whipsawed them into senior rank.

Fifth, eight of the ten had no *significant* experience in combat prior to achieving senior rank; and only two more gained it afterwards. Pershing and MacArthur were the two exceptions, with Halsey and Bradley joining those ranks after earning their third stars. Earlier, Halsey had sunk one German submarine in World War I, Marshall had served in a high-level staff capacity in the same war, and Leahy commanded a gun turret for a few hours in the Spanish-American War. This is another proof that the attributes essential for higher levels of perspective are different than those for the battlefield.

To begin, then, consider the matrix on levels of perspective compared with the principals, as depicted in the accompanying chart. Although not explicitly delineated in that chart, the principals can be subdivided into a number of subgroups. The first subgroup consists of the two that came closest to operating at the national level: Admiral Leahy and General Bradley (in his later service), both of whom served as chairmen of the Joint Chiefs of Staff and in that capacity were presidential advisors beyond the continuing influence of the respective services. Leahy was ideal for the role, having gained three years' experience first as governor of Puerto Rico and then as ambassador to Vichy France (following his first retirement from the navy). Further, military considerations were the dominant national concern during Leahy's tenure; and he had a breadth of perception that lent itself to keeping the national perspective in mind. Bradley, who succeeded Leahy, was also a steady rider and thoroughly understood the changing situation in Korea when China entered the war en masse. However, he had to contend with MacArthur, whom not even Truman could handle, short of relieving him of command. Both chairmen had the complete confidence of their presidents, and both were strong humanitarians.

The second subgroup comprises the wartime chiefs of staff—Marshall, King, and Arnold—who during their tenure struck a delicate balance between the national perspective of the president and the theater perspective of their chief subordinates.[1] Marshall probably came closest to the national perspective and won almost universal respect from civil officials and from Congress while never losing sight of military necessity. By contrast, King's perspective stressed military affairs—and usually the navy's, at that—although he also understood, perhaps better than anyone else, the need to keep the Soviet Union and China in the war at full tilt. Arnold was somewhere between Marshall and King. He was the restless advocate of airpower, of course, but had a fine understanding of national priorities,

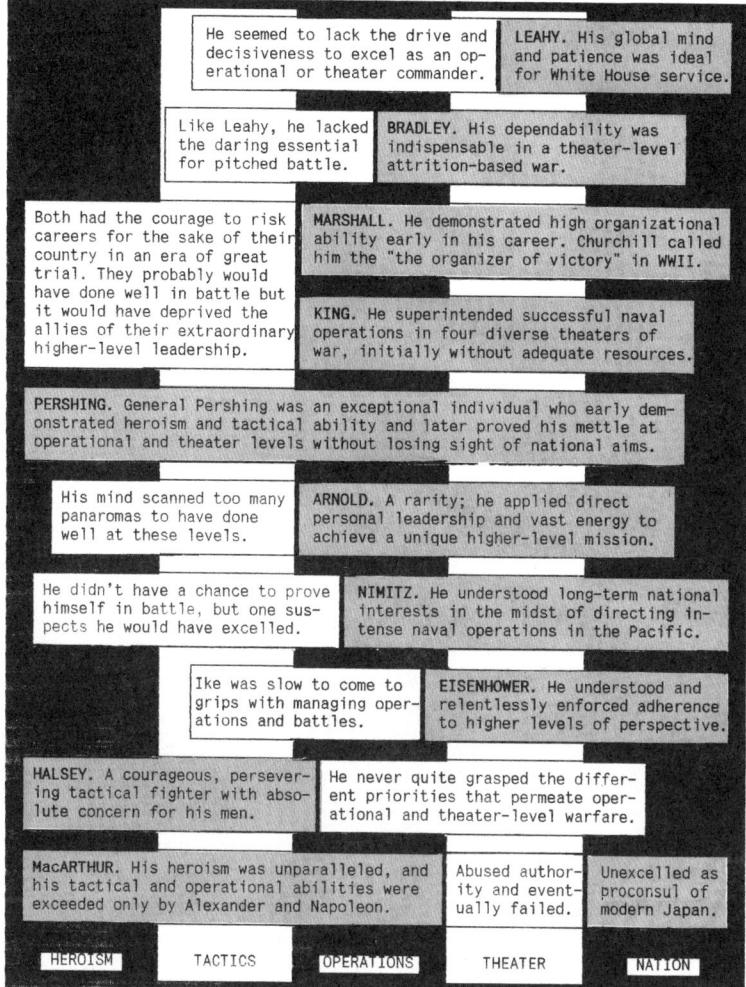

Figure 9. Comparative Leadership. Comparing ten senior military and naval leaders is no easy task. Reference to the various levels of perspective in the conduct of war helps.

perhaps because he spent much of his time with the civil sector in order to bring that form of warfare to realization.

The third subgroup focuses on theater-level command. In addition to MacArthur, three of the principals served at this level: Pershing, Nimitz, and Eisenhower. True, Pershing commanded only a fraction of the Allied troops fighting in France during World War I, but by the same token he had a tougher job exercising his will regarding the utilization of those troops while successfully keeping the national long-term view in mind. At any rate, all three grew into their jobs and each earned laurels that have stood the test of time. Furthermore, each understood the need for an attrition-based strategy at the theater level while encouraging the exercise of strategic leverage at the operational level, Pershing and Nimitz more so than Eisenhower.

The fourth subgroup covers the two operational-level commanders: Bradley (earlier) and Halsey. Bradley, once he left the Mediterranean, had to think like a theater commander because he commanded most of the American troops on a broad-front strategy from Normandy to VE Day. Yet when he found himself in command of a tactical challenge, he lacked the willful decisiveness that often spells the difference between stirring success and mediocrity in tight situations. By contrast, Halsey possessed that decisiveness so strongly that it interfered with his performance at the operational level, witness his carelessness at Leyte Gulf.

This leaves MacArthur, who, so to speak, could hum a tune in five octaves. In World War I, he exemplified the heroic and tactical levels of perspective. In World War II, he was a theater commander; but during the first two years of the war the nature of the Papua–New Guinea campaign allowed him to function more at the operational level. Here he performed exceptionally well, almost flawlessly. The same was not necessarily true when his theater expanded to the Philippines, witness his childish squabbling with the navy, his much higher casualty rates, and his unauthorized counterinvasions of lesser Philippine islands. Later, as proconsul of Japan, he *was* the national level of perspective—at least for the Japanese. Then in Korea he reverted to theater command where the peninsular geography at first permitted him to treat it as an operation. Again, a sterling performance, followed by misery when the situation escalated to a true theater of war subsumed by a wavering national purpose.

MacArthur's great problem was separating the various levels of perspective; and when these levels conflicted, he favored lower rather than higher-level priorities. Thus, he was a remarkable success as proconsul precisely because that role demanded the quiet heroism and detachment of an individual whom the Japanese perceived as a true samurai; whereas in Korea he never seemed to grasp the disadvantages of taking on China in an all-out war that his country did not want. In fine, his unexcelled bravery—there is no comparable example in history—combined with his genius, places him in the ranks of those on whom history dotes but democratic nations shun, except in times of great crisis.

The inquiry next turns to the fonts of leadership. The first item to consider is information processing. Here, Marshall, Arnold, and Nimitz were masters. Each made an exceptional effort to gain access to a wide range of information by immersing themselves at the focal points of its flow. At the opposite end, MacArthur, and Halsey to a lesser extent, sometimes ignored the information that did flow past them, resulting in serious mistakes that cost the lives of men.

Between these poles, Pershing, Leahy, Eisenhower, and Bradley regarded information processing as an adjunct of duty more than as a primary resource of command leadership. Each relied on information germane to the problems at hand, which is as it should be, but often missed opportunities that are less apparent without a ruthless pursuit of intelligence. This leaves King, who at one moment was the epitome of information processing and at another didn't want to hear much of it. However, in this case, his high intelligence and intense concentration on his work often provided the answers before anyone brought the questions to his attention. This trait is not uncommon among dynamic leaders in all walks of life.

Turning next to intelligence, perception, and vision, we find that with the possible except of Admiral Halsey, the principals were all voracious readers, a practice which honed their powers of reason in proportion to their native intelligence. As a result, MacArthur's genius was capable of remarkable, perhaps excessive vision. Below the genius level, King, Nimitz, Marshall, and Bradley probably had the strongest intelligence *and* they employed it to the maximum extent, as evidenced by their writings and their roles in military education. Arnold, Leahy, and Pershing also had strong intelligence but were indifferent to their studies at West Point or Annapolis; and except for writing wartime memoirs, they were not inclined to exercise their intelligence to any great degree beyond the immediate call of duty. At that, Leahy did not care to teach or write even when placed in assignments of that genre, while Arnold wrote his memoir primarily to supplement his income after retirement.

One other point. For the principals, at least, both genius *and* a comparative lack of high intelligence seems to correlate with trouble, for example, for MacArthur and Halsey. Both of them rated fighting ability higher and became good friends on that account. And at times, King, who may have bordered on genius, also fits here because of his arrogance.

As for character and style, it is obvious that each of these senior officers exemplified perseverance, some to a fault. However, we also see a distinct division. Four of them *routinely* persevered by imposing their will on events—Pershing, Marshall, King, and MacArthur—albeit with varying degrees of selflessness or its lack. These four were also the most austere or imperious.

At the other end, Leahy, Eisenhower, Nimitz, and Bradley were noted for their willingness to accommodate. Not surprisingly, they were the most likable of the ten. However, Nimitz and Bradley, more than the other two in this subgroup, learned by necessity to impose their will on events. This aspect in Nimitz bothered some of his wartime staff; while Bradley came to relieve commanders who could not discipline their units, even when they were tigers on the battlefield.

The remaining two principals operated between these poles. At one moment, Arnold played the part of a human teddy bear; the next, a ruthless commander who was his own hatchet man. Halsey, too, was affable but more as a devoted, selfless leader than an inherently amiable individual.

In turn, all of the principals showed great concern for the welfare of their subordinates, although there was considerable divergence in methods and a few notable lapses. The three who were truly outstanding in this regard were Marshall, Bradley, and Halsey. Bradley's and Halsey's benevolence grew legendary; Marshall's benevolence was disguised by his austere mein; but it was, nonetheless, just as pervasive. Truman insisted that the European economic aid plan be named for him, which in turn led to Marshall's being awarded the Nobel peace prize.

Eisenhower, Nimitz, and Leahy were not far behind. Eisenhower had a tendency to rely excessively on the written word to express his concern for troops, and he did have his blind spots in this department. Yet his empathy for subordinates was genuine. By contrast, Leahy and Nimitz made a point of practicing their concern on a personal basis. Arnold, Pershing, and King also endeavored to care for their men; but their concern seems to have been more an outgrowth of duty than an intrinsic propensity. Arnold, in particular, had to concentrate on a massively complex task and often ran roughshod over his subordinates. Yet when an opportunity arose to see how low-ranking airmen were doing, especially in isolated posts, his concern may have exceeded even Bradley's. As for King, because he hated anything that appeared sentimental, he relied on frequent praise of subordinates while declining credit for himself.

This leaves MacArthur, whose conduct again runs the gamut. His respect for his men at Fort Leavenworth and during World War I was pervasive; and they in turn, almost loved him for it. This changed during the intervening years, witness his treatment of the bonus marchers and his cavalier, if not disgraceful, attitude toward his troops in the Philippines after the outbreak of World War II. Yet once on the battlefield, he again exercised concern by inflicting the most damage with the fewest casualties, at least during the Papua-New Guinea campaign. In Japan, his concern for his "subjects" still reads like magic; yet in Korea he didn't seem to care how many casualties it would cost to extend the war beyond the sanction of the president.

Arguably, concern for subordinates extends to family life, and here the record is even more remarkable. There were thirteen marriages in all: ten first marriages, two more as widowers, and one after the single divorce among the ten. That divorce was filed by MacArthur's first wife, who had been divorced once before and went on to try two more husbands.

Furthermore, eight of the thirteen marriages seemed idyllic or close to it: Pershing's, Leahy's, both of Marshall's, Nimitz's, both of Bradley's, and MacArthur's second.[2] Eisenhower's and Arnold's marriages were also solid, but they were marred by periods of high strain, especially Arnold's. Only King's and Halsey's went sour, yet both still cared for their families. Moreover, in the case of Halsey the difficulty was in part attributable to his wife's acerbic personality that grew progressively worse.

This leads to the question: To what degree did the principals' flaws detract from conduct and performance of duty? Remarkably, all but three of the ten principals demonstrated nearly flawless character. For them, one must dig deep to uncover any kind of psychical decay, even though they all had their share of peccadilloes and understandably many of them stumbled when first confronted with tasks for which they were not adequately prepared. The three exceptions were Halsey, King, and MacArthur. At that, Halsey's flaws were confined to his strained justification for honest mistakes, which he carried to the point of making a fool of himself after the war. This is especially painful because his mistakes themselves stemmed less from any deficiency in character than from his dominant tactical perspective.

Unfortunately, the other two—King and MacArthur—do not get off the hook so easily. King's arrogance was deep-seated enough to be considered a major character flaw, although he managed to keep it from destroying his effectiveness most of the time.[3] MacArthur, by contrast, displayed his arrogance in a more polished format, exuding a genuine charm and charisma that won over many, if not most, of his enemies. Further, although this egotism may have been more than offset by his enormous talents and contributions, it still brought him to an unfortunate end.

This leaves the issue of development—whether leaders are born or trained. Here we find an unusually specific correlation. The four who imposed their will as a way of life were all marked from youth. Each was the ranking cadet at his respective service academy: Marshall at VMI, King at Annapolis, and Pershing and MacArthur at West Point. Moreover, each one demonstrated exceptional ability early in his career, even though King and MacArthur got off to rough starts.

Of the four who were inherently accommodating, Bradley and Nimitz learned of necessity to impose their wills. Both of them graduated high in their classes—Nimitz slightly higher than Bradley—and both had high cadet or midshipman rank in their final year. By contrast, Leahy and Eisenhower finished much lower then they were capable of, and neither had any significant cadet rank. Moreover, Eisenhower was busted of that which he did have—color sergeant (flag bearer). Of the remaining two, Arnold gave little evidence of later success while at West Point, except what may be inferred from his mischievous audacity; while Halsey excelled in sports and was at least a lower-ranking midshipman officer in his last year at Annapolis.

Fortunately, and irrespective of the degree of willpower exercised, all but one of the principals benefited from one or more senior officers serving as mentors. In the case of Pershing, it was Theodore Roosevelt who advanced his career. For MacArthur, it was the example of his father and the constant prodding—some would say meddling—of his mother. Pershing also had a great deal of respect for MacArthur and helped his career along, even if he did not care for him personally. Once, during a dark moment in World War I, Pershing pulled MacArthur aside and said, "We First Captains must never flinch." For Leahy and King, the mentor was Vice Admiral Henry T. Mayo. Leahy also benefited from his long-term friendship with Franklin D. Roosevelt. Nimitz's mentor was Rear Admiral Samuel S. Robison.

Marshall's mentor was Pershing. Eisenhower had four (a combination that is hard to beat): two passive, Pershing and MacArthur, and two active, Conner and Marshall. Bradley had Marshall and Eisenhower, while Arnold also had Marshall, and Malin Craig as well. Only Halsey seems to have lacked a mentor, although Leahy, King, and Nimitz watched over him as if he were a younger brother (and leaned in his favor when it came time to make the last of the navy's five-star promotions). That lack perhaps contributed to Halsey's inability to recognize the higher perspective of operations as well as the other principals could.

One last item here. Most of the principals experienced one or more traumatic moments that were turning points in their careers, some more dramatic than others. Pershing was "silenced" as a tactical officer by the cadets at West Point. MacArthur had two such moments: first, the close call when as First Captain he engineered an unauthorized visit to an officer's quarters; and second, the deservedly stinging efficiency report that he received at the hands of the district engineer in Milwaukee. Leahy's traumatic moment was observing maimed soldiers after his one-day "turkey shoot" in the Spanish-American War.

The turning point in King's life occurred when he received the last of his four "black marks" as an ensign. That reprimand was undeserved, but it made him realize that if he did not change his ways, his superiors would make his life miserable. He also gained some insight when he lost his original bid to become Chief of Naval Operations. He dug his heels in, went back to work, won the respect of the man who did get the job (Admiral Stark), and then made it on the second try.

For Nimitz, his court-martial for running a ship aground seemed to steel his resolve, even though his performance to that point was already first-rate. For Halsey, witnessing the turret explosion that killed thirty-one men shaped his outlook for life. Bradley's turning point appears to have occurred when Sergeant York commented that he was too nice a

Official U.S. Navy photograph.

21. The Culminating Moment of World War II. The phalanx of senior officers that observed this scene is impressive; but let us not overlook the greatness of the principal leaders, represented here by MacArthur, Nimitz, and Halsey, yet symbolic of all of them.

person to advance any further in the army. And for Eisenhower, the turning point was probably the time in the Philippines when MacArthur tried to blame him for his own error of judgment. From that moment forward, Eisenhower became his own man and set out on a path that impressed virtually all of his seniors. The incident perhaps explains the one great inconsistency in this remarkable individual. He was truly humble; but at the same time, he was intent on carrying out his duties, come hell or high water. As such, he often vacillated between imposing his will and seeking genuine cooperation by persuasion.

This leaves Arnold and Marshall. Arnold may have had a lot of close calls, but he never stopped to learn as much from them as he might have, not even from his series of heart attacks during the war. As for Marshall, his character, integrity, and genuine humility were so strong that he didn't seem to need any wake-up call. Indeed, the one time he was taken aback occurred at the end of the war when Secretary of War Henry Stimson effusively commended him in front of his staff. He was unaware of his own greatness.

Interestingly, the friendship between Arnold and Marshall ripened during the course of the war. Who else but Arnold could get away with outlandish pranks in which his distinguished mentor was the sole victim? And when the war was over, Marshall made a point of walking over to Arnold's quarters and quietly thanked him for his role in winning it.

In conclusion on this matter, then, it may be said that leaders with the potential for high command are born with the strength of character and the raw attributes for it. Although it takes considerable and diffuse development to hone those attributes, it does not seem to be a process that lends itself to a formal training program. Perhaps a more detailed study would refute this; but if so, it would mean that great men could be turned out in droves. That's not likely to happen. What does stand out in the biographies of these men is that mentorship, both as providers and beneficiaries, combined with turning points, played a more crucial role than the schoolhouse, at least after graduation from the service academies.

In sum, the principals of what is perhaps the last profound tale to emerge from this era may have had flaws and they certainly committed their share of mistakes and blunders. Yet when great men are compared, the unfortunate tendency is to lose sight of their caliber and, instead, nitpick at their reputations. When this temptation grows too strong, one would do well to step back and remember the culminating scene of World War II. That will put everything in perspective.

16

SUMMING UP

It is no doubt a good thing to conquer on the field of battle, but it needs greater wisdom and greater skill to make use of the victory.

—Polybius

In his memoirs, Sir Winston Churchill posited that World War II was the most preventable war in history.[1] Perhaps so, but that view presumes a collective wisdom within mankind unwarranted by millennia of facts to the contrary. Hence, the global wars ushered in at the turn of this century were likely the crescendo of an epic struggle that had been brewing piecemeal for hundreds of years and which took half of this century to resolve.

Yet man was not an unwilling slave to fate. A handful of individuals imposed their will on their countries to fuel that crescendo to a magnitude of destructiveness hitherto unwitnessed by history. Upwards of a hundred million people fell victim to this relentless slaughter. Another handful imposed the same degree of willpower to bring that era of destructiveness to an end. Dominant among the latter were President Roosevelt and Prime Minister Churchill. Both had grown with the era that would elevate them to positions of unparalleled responsibility. And in their wake each brought to the fore a few dominant military leaders that would give life and purpose to the task at hand.

Clearly, Great Britain had the tougher time of it, suffering casualties and destruction of property at a *proportional* rate at least six times greater than borne by the United States. Nonetheless, the Anglo-Saxons got off easy. Combined, China and the Soviet Union sustained twenty-six times the number of fatalities. Yet, if America did not suffer as badly as her allies, she did act with a more global view. Great Britain, Russia, and

China were all fighting for survival; and each, therefore, had to keep their respective national interests foremost in view.

Put another way, the United States could afford a larger perspective. The balance of power had to be restored, and the injured—ally and former enemy alike—restored to health. That role called for a different type of command and leadership. In the absence of a compelling and immediate threat to survival, competing interests, priorities, and opinions hounded the principals to death; while the multiple theaters with distinctly different geographic characteristics permitted a larger number of senior level leaders to arise than normal in most crises—each leader with a different perspective that fueled the arguments. As such, they fought amongst themselves no less than did the gods on Mount Olympus.

Insufficient time has passed for history to sort out what this era can teach, but several lessons are fairly obvious. The dominant three are: (1) war operates at several levels of perspective, (2) each level has its own set of rules, and (3) any attempt to apply the rules of one to another risks failure. Moreover, when a situation superimposes conflicting levels at the same time on one decision, only exceptional leaders with sufficient authority over resources can hope to emerge a success.

As might be expected, when these conflicts do occur, it is the factors operating at the higher level that carry the day. Extraordinary heroism and sustained tactical success at lower levels cannot compensate for bad decisions and poor leadership at the top. In other words, when it comes to war, it is geopolitical clout, or at least the amount of it that a nation is willing to expend in its prosecution, that determines the outcome.

Unfortunately, it is often the heroic perspective that captures the imagination; it touches upon the spirit of man far more than a treatise on logistics. Thus sets in the myth that war is the sum of its battles; if a country fights long and hard enough it is bound to win, or so goes the theory. As a corollary, when a country begins to lose a war—or even when a major battle is lost within a war it is otherwise winning, the blame is placed on the battlefield leaders or, alternatively, on the unwillingness of the press and the public to support them adequately.

Hence, this era of greatness ended on the sour note of Korea. To the soldier on the battlefield, the perspective was the same as in the world wars; but at the higher level of national interest, the perspective had changed radically. Worse, this inability to differentiate at the national plateau carried over into Vietnam with even more disastrous results. Therefore, as harped on by Clausewitz, every nation that chooses or is forced to engage in war ought to consider the consequences of that war and the way it conducts it.

This is no different from ancient times. Homer appeals to us as much as his first readers, but it is easy to forget that generations of hero worship

practiced by the even more ancient Greeks eventually led to the Peloponnesian War, in which Pericles tried to conquer Sparta far past the point of
being able to sustain that conquest. When that truth began to seep in,
Thucydides records Pericles as saying to his countrymen: "What we took
we did so in tyranny and it was wrong, but to let it go would be unsafe."[2]
Twenty-five years later, Athens lay in ruins.

Still, whether or not a nation is willing to learn from its past, when that
past exemplifies the best in human nature, it will be remembered for all
times. Churchill said that "if the British Empire should last a thousand
years, men will say this was her finest hour." And George C. Marshall
put the case this way:

> It is morale that wins the war. It is not enough to fight. It is the
> spirit which we bring to the fight that decides the issue. The soldier's
> heart, the soldier's spirit, the soldier's soul are everything. It is what
> men believe that makes them invincible.

Those who fought in the two world wars did so for an invincible—and
immortal—right, despite the endless and often colorful disagreements
among the more senior of them. The denizens of Mount Olympus had
more than met their match.

NOTES

PART I

1. The act specified the title "General of the *Army* of the United States," even though it referred to the 1799 act that created the title "General of the *Armies* of the United States" and stated explicitly that it was the older title that was being reactivated. Whether this was a typographical error or an intentional obfuscation is unknown.

2. Actually, British general officer rank is inflated. Colonels are promoted directly to major general. There is no one-star rank, except in the limited sense of designating some colonels as *brigadiers*.

3. The opening section of the act specified the title *Fleet Admiral of the United States Navy* for the naval recipients, but thereafter shortened it to *Fleet Admiral*.

4. That law is still in effect, but in practice most three and four-star officers are retired in their highest grade upon Senate confirmation.

5. When this practice was instituted around 1980, the lower-half rear admirals were at first designated *commodores*. In 1985, the title reverted to *rear admiral* (lower half), ostensibly because the title of "Commodore" was regarded as something less than flag rank in diplomatic circles. Also, during World War II the rank of commodore was reactivated temporarily as a kind of recognition for captains who did not have a record to warrant promotion to rear admiral. Only one of the recipients bucked the rule, Admiral Arleigh "30-Knot" Burke. Those commodores received the pay of a navy captain and were not considered to be flag officers, although they could fly a one-star flag from their flagship.

6. Many years later, the navy did build a few "command ships," but they are used primarily in amphibious operations.

CHAPTER 1

1. Bob Woodward, *The Commanders* (New York: Simon & Schuster, 1991), pp. 158–161. The officer was navy Lieutenant Adam J. Curtis. His wife's name

was Bonnie. The apparent reason why they were abducted was that they had witnessed the shooting of another American officer fleeing—in a confused situation—from a Panamanian Defense Forces checkpoint.

2. Winston S. Churchill, *A History of the English-Speaking Peoples,* vol. 1 *(The Birth of Britain)* (New York: Dodd, Mead & Company, 1962), 60. For another example of this, consider the late Barbara Tuchman's *The March of Folly: From Troy to Vietnam.* She drew on Homer's *Iliad,* as written, as one of four case studies to illustrate pig-headedness in government.

3. MacArthur did receive two minor wounds in the first world war, but nothing in subsequent wars.

4. Manchester, *American Caesar,* p. 17.

5. *Works of Theodore Roosevelt,* vol. 18, p. 411.

6. Mahan's book nearly missed being published. Although he had written a previous book *(The Gulf and Inland Waters),* this one started with a highly abstract chapter on national power, followed by a long discourse on sailing ship battles, the last of which was more than a century old and not particularly applicable to steam-powered iron ships. Nine publishers turned it down. Then, at the intervention of Assistant Secretary of the Navy James R. Soley (who had been in the publishing business), Little, Brown and Company agreed to publish it. One hundred and three years later, it is still in print.

7. The cause of the explosion has never been resolved. It could have resulted from mechanical problems that had nothing to do with Spanish sabotage.

8. In January 1903, Secretary of State John Hay negotiated a treaty with Columbia, which at the time had sovereignty over what is now Panama. But since the proposed treaty gave the United States de facto sovereignty over the canal zone, Columbia did not ratify it. Roosevelt then encouraged a Panamanian revolution for independence—some historians say he fomented it—signing virtually the same treaty with the new state of Panama on November 18, 1903.

9. Manchester, *American Caesar,* p. 33.

10. The air force remained part of the army until 1947; and, therefore, Arnold technically remained Marshall's subordinate. In practice, Arnold worked with Marshall as a partner. See also chap. 6, n. 2.

11. Manchester, *American Caesar,* p. 154. Secretary of War George Dern was a witness to this outburst and congratulated MacArthur. Yet MacArthur, so the accounts read, was so upset that he vomited afterwards. This may be true. He did suffer a permanent queasiness in his stomach that erupted many times during World War II, especially during his escape from Corregidor in a PT boat.

12. See *Encyclopaedia Britannica,* vol. 23, 1973, p. 802J, "World wars." For Chinese civilian fatalities (see Ruth Leger Sivard, *World Military and Social Expenditures, 1987–1988,* World Priorities, 1987), p. 30. The data is rounded to the nearest one thousand.

13. For many years before the war, the respective chiefs and a few senior staff officers met as a congressionally mandated Joint Board, but it had no real authority. The first Joint Chiefs of Staff were an outgrowth of that board and used the board's existence as a legal basis for their new mantle. In time the Joint Board faded out of existence.

14. The Chief of the Imperial General Staff was Field Marshal Alan Brooke, and his representative on the Combined Chiefs of Staff in Washington was Field

Marshal Sir John Dill (who died in 1944). The senior naval officer (the First Lord of the Admiralty) was Admiral of the Fleet Sir Dudley Pound, who died of a brain tumor in 1943 and was succeeded by Admiral of the Fleet Sir Andrew Brown Cunningham. The representative on the Combined Chiefs was Admiral Sir Percy Noble. The senior air officer was Air Chief Marshal Sir Charles Portal, and his representative on the Combined Chiefs was Air Marshal D. C. S. Evill.

In addition, Admiral Leahy had two counterparts in Great Britain. General Sir Hastings Ismay was Churchill's equivalent of chief of staff and Lieutenant General G. N. Macready was Churchill's aide in the latter's dual role as Minister of Defense. General Eisenhower's staff also included senior British officers, who are sometimes confused with the representatives on the Combined Chiefs.

15. In one instance, Arnold had an actor, disguised as a foreign manufacturing agent, crash into Marshall's office and offer to pay for influence with vast sums of cash spilling out of his briefcase. Marshall boiled over, at which point Arnold walked in to reveal the script.

16. The act did not specify Spruance by name but merely gave the Navy Department permission to provide the benefit to an officer of its own choosing. However, it stipulated criteria that only the existing fleet admirals and Spruance met. See also chap. 8, n. 4.

17. Some military writers have already assessed the Persian Gulf conflict as an anomaly in that an aggressor rarely gives his opponent the advantages that Saddam Hussein did.

18. Napoleon's approach to Moscow required that he first defeat General Count Mikhail Kutusov at the battle of Borodino. He did, but with such losses that Kutusov knew Napoleon had passed his culminating point, which Kutusov then accelerated by letting Napoleon occupy Moscow without resistance. Thus, Kutusov conserved his own forces until Napoleon realized his predicament and started to retreat, whereupon Kutusov set upon him so vigorously that only a few thousand French (and allied) troops escaped. For saving Russia, Czar Alexander promoted Kutusov to field marshal. Tolstoy's *War and Peace* (bks. 8 and 9) provides an excellent account of the battle of Borodino and of Kutusov's strategy, completely apart from the encompassing novel.

19. Summers, *On Strategy*, p. 1.

CHAPTER 2

1. Pershing's "official" birthdate is September 13, not January 13, 1860. However, the mass of evidence points to the earlier date. The reason for the discrepancy was that the law stipulated a cadet must not have reached his twenty-second birthday by the first day of the month that he entered the Military Academy. Pershing had passed his twenty-second birthday by July 1882 (Smythe, *Guerrilla Warrior*, pp. 283–84). This rule is still in effect.

2. At the time, the Corps of Cadets consisted of four companies. Each company was commanded by a cadet captain. The captain that was rated highest in military leadership was designed #1; the second, #2; and so forth: hence, the name First Captain. Some years later, a separate position was created for the First Captain as the cadet commander of the Corps of Cadets.

3. Dawes was an unusually capable individual, having at one time or other

served as president of corporations and banks, Comptroller of the Currency, director of the Bureau of the Budget, Vice President of the United States (1925–1929), ambassador to Great Britain, and for a short time director of the Reconstruction Finance Corporation. In World War I, Dawes was initially commissioned as a lieutenant colonel and then was immediately promoted to colonel.

4. This statistic has never been officially documented. For the period 1954 to 1958, the author calculated the percentage of those officers who served in the tactical department between 1954 and 1958 as roughly thirty-five percent for all positions, a figure that increases to fifty percent when the period of consideration is 1954 to 1956, excluding staff positions. The names were drawn from the yearbooks for those years and checked against the current *Register of Graduates*. Most tactical officers report to West Point in the grade of captain. The general officer batting average for all captains is less than five percent, which means that if these findings can be extrapolated for a longer period, tactical officers reach general-officer rank seven times more frequently than junior officers as a whole.

5. When the intended victim was officer of the day and entered the cadet mess hall, the entire Corps of Cadets would sit at attention and neither speak nor eat another bite. The demonstration was never repeated for the same officer, yet virtually all of the officers on post were graduates themselves and understood the meaning of being silenced. Thus in the eyes of his peers, the officer had been labeled as an intolerable martinet. Accordingly, the story would always spread, thus ruining his career.

This silencing was infrequent, occurring perhaps once every two or three years, although it was practiced at both West Point and VMI (where in 1901, cadet First Captain George C. Marshall quelled one attempt). Apparently, the last occurrence at West Point was in 1910. That time, the tactical department brought it to an end by severely punishing the ringleaders, one of whom was the great grandson of General "Stonewall" Jackson. They were confined to barracks for six months, except to attend classes and perform official duties, and had to walk punishment tours on the area during that time. Further, the cadet First Captain was reduced to cadet private. While walking off those punishment tours, one of the cadets, Paul Sorg Reinecke, composed the words to West Point's *alma mater*. (The research on this was completed by the author in 1956 by correspondence with surviving members of the class of 1911. The results were published in the cadet magazine, *The Pointer*, around 1956.)

6. Captain Adolphus W. Greely was promoted to brigadier general, with the title Chief Signal Officer, on March 3, 1887. Captain Leonard Wood, medical corps, was promoted on February 4, 1901 (to a general officer of the line, not Army Surgeon General); and Captain Franklin J. Bell, on February 19, 1901. There may have been two others.

7. Vandiver, *Black Jack,* vol. 1, p. 571. The awards board at the War Department had already turned the recommendation down, but Pershing did not know that.

8. Instead, the job went to Clarence P. Townsley, who was given the temporary rank of major general.

9. MacArthur, *Reminiscences,* p. 48.

CHAPTER 3

1. At first, Leahy called Hopkins a "Pinko," referring to the latter's earlier role in the New Deal administration; but in time Leahy came to admire Hopkins's absolute dedication and selflessness, especially as Hopkins was often in great pain, slowly dying of cancer (which would take his life in January 1946).

2. The term comes from Gilbert and Sullivan's *Mikado* where the character *Pooh Bah* has a number of titles, including Lord High Everything Else, in order to handle any situation that might arise. Hence, the navy uses the term somewhat differently from the original meaning. At any rate, the term is not from *Winnie the Pooh,* although Field Marshal Sir Alan Brooke, Chief of the Imperial General Staff during World War II, sometimes privately referred to Sir Winston Churchill as "Pooh Bear."

3. Japan used the Chinese raid on Japanese forces near Mukden as the pretext for the invasion of Manchuria, where the Japanese installed the former and last Manchu emperor of China (P'u-i) as the figurehead monarch. This was depicted in the popular film *The Last Emperor.*

4. On December 12, 1937, the Japanese without provocation attacked and sank the U.S. gunboat *Panay* (and three U.S. commercial oil-supply ships), on the Yangste river twenty-seven miles above Nanking, and later strafed the survivors. The United States put up a stiff protest, as a result of which Japan apologized and paid an indemnity of $2,214,007. However, it should be noted that Japanese diplomatic apologies are often perfunctory. Arguably, the purpose of this attack was to test U.S. resolve.

5. Marshall's biographer, Forrest Pogue, has indicated that Marshall advocated making Leahy an informal chairman of the joint chiefs but has overlooked Roosevelt's earlier intimation to Leahy. It may be that both are correct, in that when Marshall made his recommendation he was unaware of Roosevelt's existing commitment.

CHAPTER 4

1. Judge Roy Bean was not the "hanging judge"; that reputation belonged to Judge Isaac Charles Parker (1838–1896) of Arkansas, who in his day sent eighty-eight men to the gallows. Bean was only a justice of the peace, but in that humble capacity he was a character. Once, when he came across a dead man in the street, rolled him over, and found a revolver and two $20 gold coins, he fined the deceased $40 for carrying a concealed weapon. His brother said of him, "You may have graduated at Yale or Harvard and carry a number of diplomas, but if you have not seen or heard of Judge Roy Bean of Texas you are groping in darkness and there yet remains a large space to be filled in your classical head." The Jersey Lily, where Bean held court in a manner of speaking, is now a Texas state park.

2. During the period, the school at Leavenworth changed names several times: the School of the Line, the Infantry and Cavalry School, and finally the Command & General Staff College. The idea was to train officers, both as commanders and staff, to think in terms of combined arms rather than just their branch of service.

3. Part of the letter stated: "I am determined not to exert political influence in my effort to be recognized, and I do not want to follow the usual course of writing

to a number of senior officers soliciting letters from them, though a number have offered their services without solicitation by me. . . . I am prepared to gamble on my written record in the War Department before, during, and since the war, for I have been told no one else in the list of colonels can match mine" (*Papers of G. C. Marshall,* vol. 1, pp. 446–47).

4. Early plans were code-named by colors to symbolize different countries against which the United States might have to fight. When it became apparent that the potential for war would likely involve several concurrent enemies, the older color-coded plans were merged and renamed *Rainbow* for the obvious reason.

5. It is rare for the Medal of Honor to be awarded for anything other than distinguished heroism above and beyond the call of duty except for the symbolic awards given to the remains of the four unknown soldiers buried at Arlington National Cemetery (and to the unknown soldiers of several other countries). The case most comparable to MacArthur's was the posthumous award to Rear Admiral Isaac Kidd, who perished aboard his flagship *Arizona* at Pearl Harbor on December 7, 1941. The difference, of course, is that MacArthur survived while many of those he left behind did not. On the other hand, it should be remembered that twice before he had been recommended for the Medal of Honor (at Vera Cruz and later in France during World War I). Furthermore, in the campaign to retake the Philippines, his personal bravery earned him a third Distinguished Service Cross.

6. Marshall tried to "pull the plug" once again after the war. He, as secretary of state, and Clark Clifford were arguing with President Truman over whether to recognize the pending creation of the state of Israel in 1947. Marshall was against it, at least for the immediate future, on the grounds that it might drag the United States into another war. When it became obvious that Truman saw the matter otherwise, Marshall said, "Mr. President, if you do this, I won't vote for you in the next election." Normally, Truman would have laughed off such a remark; but his respect for Marshall was so great by this point—and Marshall was, as always, speaking from the depths of his integrity—that it did bother him.

7. Jefferson to Dr. Walter Jones, January 2, 1841, *The Life and Selected Writings of Thomas Jefferson,* Adrienne Koch and William Peden, eds. New York: Random House, 1944, pp. 173–76.

CHAPTER 5

1. Although some writers refer to the earlier Naval Academy cadet organization in army terms, it consisted of four divisions of four crews each when King was there. In 1903 to 1904, it changed to a brigade with two battalions of six companies each. In 1914 to 1915, this organization was realigned to a regiment of four battalions with three companies each—the same number of companies but an increased number of cadet-officer positions.

2. In the fourth instance, King had the watch when a signalman acknowledged a garbled message from another ship before giving it to King. The signalman should not have done this, but King as the officer on watch was responsible. So when King asked that the message be repeated, it was he and not the signalman who was nailed. Obviously, the admiral that inflicted the reprimand was harboring a grudge; the mistake was trivial.

3. Sims was the only American officer in modern history to have permanent command of a battleship before reaching the grade of captain.

4. The Naval Post Graduate School subsequently became a degree-granting institution and is presently located in Monterey, California.

5. As King himself was quick to note, he did not take the final examination and, therefore, never formally qualified. He never offered any explanation, but it would be naive to conclude that he could not have passed. The most reasonable speculation is that he wanted to stay in aviation.

6. Although the Medal of Honor is normally awarded only in time of war, the Department of the Navy also gave it for acts of extraordinary heroism between the two world wars. There were twelve such awards, most of them involving rescue operations; but they were also given to Admiral Richard Byrd and Machinist Floyd Bennett for their flight over the North Pole. Congress also made two such awards on behalf of the army: the first was given to Charles Lindbergh for his solo flight over the Atlantic, and the second (largely at the behest of William "Billy" Mitchell) to the Arctic explorer Major General Adolphus W. Greely, on his ninety-first birthday, "for a life of splendid public service."

7. In his autobiography, King drew a parallel with Marshall, in that Marshall and Stark should have borne equally any responsibility for the unpreparedness at Pearl Harbor; yet Marshall was absolved of any blame. However, King was not trying to hurt Marshall's reputation, only trying to salvage Stark's. Moreover, when Stark was relieved, King did not at first support him, recommending to Roosevelt that he be given only an inconsequential post.

Another possible explanation for Marshall's getting off the hook is simply that the navy (as a result of Japanese targeting) sustained more than ninety percent of the fatalities and damage. Further, it was damage that was photographically dramatic, inflicted on capital ships that would take two years to replace. Also, Marshall at least sent a warning message (however late it might have arrived) to General Short, whereas Stark took no action to inform Admiral Kimmel of the latest intelligence. This may appear to be a minor consideration, but as cited and discussed in chapter 13, the one common trait among great leaders seems to be their ability to process information and disseminate the resulting intelligence.

8. When Nimitz visited Ghormley, he found that whenever a crucial message came in, Ghormley would say, "My God, what are we going to do about this?" Interestingly, when Ghormley reported to CINCPAC on his way to take command of the Fourteenth Naval District (headquartered on Oahu), he complained to Nimitz about his being relieved. Admiral Nimitz then looked at him in a kindly way and asked, "Were you the best man for the job?" Ghormley replied, "No," and went on to his new job with his pride restored.

9. As it turned out, and unlike the battle of Midway, the Japanese no longer had the capability to lay a trap for Spruance. In other words, Spruance could have pursued the Japanese and inflicted even more damage. That is the nature of calculated risk. In battle, one can take higher risks because those risks will average out over the span of operations in a theater of war. By contrast, calculated risks at higher levels are more carefully weighed because the losses tend to be much higher and might not wash out so easily in relation to the overall war effort. See also chap. 12.

10. This includes both the current (15th) edition and the final issue of the 14th

edition (1973). Brief articles on King did appear in the 1965 edition and previous issues and may have appeared as late as 1972.

CHAPTER 6

1. At the time, newly graduated cadets from West Point were not required to accept commissions, and Arnold had not yet accepted his, indicating to the Adjutant General, Major General Fred C. Ainsworth, that he might not do so.

2. The air force went through many name changes between 1911 and 1947, of which the three most prominent were (1) Air Section of the Signal Corps, (2) Army Air Corps, and (3) Army Air Force(s). Many writers use a later name when referring to an earlier period, and the word *Army* is often omitted from the last.

3. The author previously corresponded with General Ira Eaker on this and several other points. At the time of the court-martial, Eaker was stationed in Washington, as were Arnold and Spaatz. Eaker did not think the Scopes trial had any influence on Mitchell's decision (Hall to Eaker, May 11, 1979; and Eaker to Hall, May 24, 1979).

CHAPTER 7

1. Truman's intent was to have the message delivered privately to MacArthur, but the plan went awry and hence, the knowledge of it came over the radio. Sidney Huff heard it first and then told Mrs. MacArthur. The accounts of what happened next are not consistent, but they all seem to agree that MacArthur's first reaction was as quoted and that there was at least one witness.

2. It was not awarded until twenty years later.

3. Arthur MacArthur commanded the cruiser *Chattanooga* during World War I and was awarded the Navy Cross. His son Douglas MacArthur II was a career diplomat and was assigned to the consulate at Vichy France, when Leahy was the ambassador. Douglas MacArthur claims that he was also awarded the Distinguished Service Medal (*Reminiscences,* p. 17), but the archivist at the U.S. Naval Academy says that this was a Letter of Commendation.

4. Some writers have claimed that MacArthur, as a plebe, was asked to share a room with a first classman, Arthur P. Stanley Hyde, who became an episcopal minister after retirement from the army. Given the rigid class distinction between plebes and upperclassmen, this seems improbable; but Hyde himself (Hyde, "Douglas MacArthur," p. 3) said that it happened. If so, this may explain why other upper classman nearly killed him in a hazing incident.

5. His average was 98.14. His weak subjects, in a manner of speaking, were engineering and drafting. The only higher average in comparable terms was earned by Irving Hale, class of 1884, who compiled an almost unbelievable 99.78. Shortly after graduation, Hale resigned his commission but fought in the Spanish-American War, rising to the rank of brigadier general in the volunteers.

6. During his second (yearling) year, MacArthur was initially designated as the second-ranking cadet corporal. Ulysses S. Grant III was first. At the end of summer camp, the precedence was reversed.

7. The incident occurred in March, 1903, during his first-class (senior) year. He was originally cited for obtaining permission to attend an indoor track meet as

a subterfuge for stopping by the instructor's quarters on the way back. This was a serious charge; but MacArthur had, in fact, attended the event, and, therefore, the implication was subjective, at best. The report was then reworded to state simply that MacArthur made an unauthorized visit to an officer's quarters, for which he was given five demerits (the most he had ever received for any offense during his four years there). The source of this information is the archivist's office at the U.S. Military Academy, specifically, correspondence with the archivist in June and July 1992, followed by two extended telephone conversations on July 13 and 15, 1992.

8. James, *Years of MacArthur,* vol. 1, pp. 169–72. The letter was sent to Pershing on June 12, 1918; but since MacArthur was promoted on June 18 and there was no airmail in those days, it is highly unlikely that it influenced Pershing. However, James speculates that Pinky must have badgered Secretary of War Baker earlier and that Baker, in turn, leaned on Pershing.

9. Pershing paid the same *summa cum laude* compliment to Patton, who had served as his aide during the punitive expedition and later distinguished himself in combat during World War I. Patton was severely wounded in that war and initially left for dead.

10. Manchester, *American Caesar,* p. 85.

11. A newspaper reporter (apparently this author's father) rummaged through the waste can in the deliberations room and found a slip of paper with the words "not guilty" in MacArthur's handwriting. And according to General Ira Eaker, Billy Mitchell said to him after the trial that he believed MacArthur had voted for acquittal. Eaker further stated that in 1943, MacArthur told him privately that he had so voted (Eaker to Hall, April 27, 1979). MacArthur had known the Mitchell family from childhood when they were neighbors in Milwaukee. He tried to date Mitchell's sister, but she was not interested. However, when MacArthur became superintendent at the Military Academy, Mitchell's sister visited him there at least once, commenting that he had "lost his boyish charm."

12. Although it has never been proved that the tents were fired by MacArthur's order, there is no question that he used force to drive the bonus marchers out. In his *Reminiscences* (pp. 92–94), MacArthur reaffirmed his belief that the marchers were radicals rather veterans; but the facts do not sustain this assumption.

13. MacArthur elected to make his escape from the Philippines by PT boats. The small flotilla was commanded by Lt. John Buckeley (later Vice Admiral and a Medal of Honor recipient). Buckeley thought it was a stroke of genius because the Japanese would have expected a submarine to be used. On the other hand, they would not have expected a man whom they regarded as a samurai to leave the field of battle in the first place. Moreover, the use of PT boats was extremely dangerous, arguably with a less than ten-percent chance of success. As it was, one of the four boats did not make it. Given the fact that his wife and child were with him, and three weeks earlier he had sent Manuel Quezon out on a submarine, his decision defies logic. That is, while he had no concept of fear, it is not likely that he would have risked the death of his wife and son without a compelling reason.

There are two possible explanations. First, he wanted his exit to seem heroic in order to offset the potential criticism of the escape, even though it had been ordered in President Roosevelt's name. Second, the order commanding him to leave specified him alone (immediately amended, without his asking, to add his wife and son). As he wanted to take about fifteen members of his staff with him, and the commander of any submarine might have balked at that (and over whom he had no authority)—the PT boats were the only alternative.

14. A. B. Feuer, ed., *Bilibid Diary: The Secret Notebooks of Commander Thomas Hayes* (Archon Press, 1987). In the entry for July 22, 1942, Dr. Hayes commented that their Japanese captors were surprised at the emaciated condition of the American POWs, given the large stocks of food found on Corregidor.

15. Manchester, *American Caesar,* pp. 208–12.

16. The numbers are not in dispute, but many historians argue that the conditions were especially favorable. They point out that by the time MacArthur was fighting in the Philippines his casualty rate increased to a level commensurate with other theaters.

17. King was visiting Nimitz on Oahu just before the meeting, probably to make himself available for the show-down; but he was not invited. It's not likely that he was ordered to return to the states, but there was no reason for staying around.

18. The breaking point came when Sutherland brought his Australian mistress with him on campaign, against MacArthur's explicit order forbidding camp followers. Sutherland stayed on as MacArthur's chief of staff. However, from that point forward the relationship was strained.

19. When General Taylor was appointed Chief of Staff of the Army in 1955, he went to pay a call on MacArthur, whom he had last seen thirty-three years before (at his graduation from West Point). MacArthur greeted him, "Max, it's good to see you again!" Taylor then admitted, "Whereupon the new Chief of Staff became another fascinated victim of the famous MacArthur charm which few escaped—with the possible exception of President Truman."

20. MacArthur, *Reminiscences,* p. 277.

21. Homma's wife appealed personally to MacArthur to no avail; but MacArthur did change the method of execution from hanging to the firing squad, which was perceived by the Japanese as more honorable. It is said that during the American Revolutionary War, Major André asked the same consideration of General Washington, who advised him to withdraw his request after explaining the low state of marksmanship of the headquarters soldiers.

22. MacArthur, *Reminiscences,* p. 393. One sidelight of the relief from command was that both Truman and MacArthur were Masons. Truman had been Grand Master of Masons in Missouri in the late 1930's and had more than once said that it was his greatest honor. MacArthur was a beneficiary of the rare Masonic honor of being "raised at sight" (in the Philippines in 1936). Furthermore, both Roosevelts, Churchill, Truman, and seven (and possibly eight) of the ten principals belonged to the Masonic order: Pershing, Marshall, King, MacArthur, Arnold, Halsey, and Bradley. Eisenhower and Nimitz were not Masons. The status of Leahy is uncertain. His biographer Henry H. Adams (*Witness to Power,* p. 144) indicates that he was; but as of this writing, the author has not been able to confirm it.

23. Ward, "Douglas MacArthur," 54.

CHAPTER 8

1. He was sentenced only to a reprimand, which was effectively suspended by way of declaring the finding of the court itself as the reprimand.

2. Potter later related the complete incident at a military symposium held at the Air University, Maxwell Air Force Base, May 2 and 3, 1968. The Nimitz biography was not published until 1976, but Potter began working on the manuscript shortly after Nimitz's death in 1966.

3. When the facts became known, Halsey calmed down; but Nimitz became incensed and summarily relieved the individual responsible.

4. The act of Congress that gave the president authority to exempt five-star generals and admirals from statutory retirement for age in peacetime (he already had it in wartime) also included the authority for Spruance's permanent rank (Public Law 804; June 28, 1948). The House version of the bill included this provision only for Tooey Spaatz and Omar Bradley (mooted for Bradley by his subsequent promotion to General of the Army). The Senate added the authority to designate an admiral with qualifications that only Spruance (and the fleet admirals) met. There is no evidence that Nimitz engineered this provision; indeed, he had retired six months before. However, his earlier effort to have Spruance promoted to fleet admiral is well known.

5. The Sampson-Schley argument centered on a command by Commodore Winfield Scott Schley during which he gave the appearance of running from battle with his flagship. Apparently, this was not the case; but it was publicized as such. Schley requested a court of inquiry to clear his name, which then degenerated into a verbal brawl between the supporters of Schley and his commander, Rear Admiral William T. Sampson. Nothing was ever truly resolved, and the resulting spectacle made the Billy Mitchell court-martial seem like a model of decorum by comparison.

CHAPTER 9

1. The accident occurred on the thirteenth of the month, which thereafter made Halsey superstitious of that number. More than once he changed the starting day of an operation if it fell on the thirteenth. In one case during the early days of the war in the Pacific, his departure date was scheduled for Friday the thirteenth, and his ships had been designated task force 13. He raised so much hell that CINC-PAC headquarters let him leave on Saturday the fourteenth and redesignated the task force as 16. One suspects that the double-thirteen order was more than coincidental.

2. The accounts vary considerably, ranging from an amicable agreement that he would continue to live in New York and follow his business interests while she stayed in southern California, to the manifestation of a severe mental problem that required long-term hospitalization.

3. For example, when a ship changes direction it tends to pivot on an imaginary point about a third of the way from the bow, leaving the rear two thirds to swing wide. Halsey noticed that Roosevelt instinctively looked back repeatedly to ensure that no damage or collision occurred.

4. The original plan was to launch Doolittle's sixteen medium bombers from four hundred nautical miles out; but after being sighted, they were launched at somewhat over six hundred. This put the China coast at the extreme limit of their one-way range; and, accordingly, some of the crews were forced to ditch in the China Sea.

5. Merrill, *A Sailor's Admiral,* p. 144. In this quotation, the word *Japanese* has

been substituted for *Japs* in several instances. The interview occurred on February 20, 1945. Captain Stassen was the governor of Minnesota on a type of leave of absence. He later became the perennial presidential candidate for the Farmer-Labor party.

CHAPTER 10

1. John S. D. Eisenhower served about nineteen years of active duty in the regular army, one year shy of eligibility for retirement. Then, because he had spent so much of that time as an aide-de-camp to his father, he resigned his commission to avoid collecting that pay. However, in accepting a reserve commission he was able to rise further in rank and did become eligible for retired pay when he reached his sixtieth birthday.

2. The name Fox was Conner's real first name, not a nickname. However, there was also a Major General William D. Conner who served on Pershing's staff at the same time and who later became Superintendent of the Military Academy. The two are sometimes confused.

3. The stratagem that he used was to have Eisenhower detached to the Adjutant Generals Corps for recruiting duty and then to give one of the school quotas for that branch to him.

4. At least one writer claimed that the demonstration was Eisenhower's initiative, and that it was MacArthur who had to orally reprimand Eisenhower. There is no way to resolve this issue, but it would have been totally out of character for Eisenhower to take that kind of initiative.

5. Eisenhower, *At Ease,* p. 249. Eisenhower states that after the outburst, he started to walk out of the office; but upon reaching the door, he turned around and saw Marshall staring at him intensely, whereupon he grinned at his own outburst. Marshall smiled slightly in return, but arguably it was because Eisenhower had not only passed the test but immediately brought his temper under control.

6. Another example of a Marshall test occurred when Eisenhower first reported in. General Marshall immediately confronted him with a question to which he already had the answer, namely, the priority that would be given to the war in the Pacific vis-à-vis Europe. Eisenhower asked for a few hours to mull it over and then produced the correct answer, at least as far as Marshall was concerned.

7. The alternative of landing the bulk of the forces much further to the east was considered but was then rejected, in part, because the lines of communication would have been subject to heavy interdiction by German aircraft operating out of Sicily and southern Italy.

8. Montgomery initially had command of the British forces as well as overall command of all Allied ground forces. Thus, Bradley officially reported to Eisenhower through Montgomery while maintaining informal channels with Ike. The plan was that when the occupied area became large enough and warranted two U.S. armies, Bradley would command them as a group while Eisenhower assumed the role of ground commander, with Bradley and Montgomery reporting to him as equals.

9. Montgomery may have had an acute sense of battlefield logistics, meaning overwhelming superior firepower to ensure tactical success, but he was much less aware of what it takes to sustain an operation, especially one that pushed a salient

deep behind the general line of war. Sir Winston Churchill also had trouble under-standing logistics: he equated it with supply, and, as such, he grew enamored of Montgomery. Thus, unwittingly, he stood between the field marshal and Eisen-hower's need for unity of command.

10. The Ardennes by themselves had no strategic value and offered little tactical advantage. Eisenhower, therefore, reasoned that the Germans intended to go be-yond them and divide the Allied forces, possibly all the way to the coast. This is easy to see with hindsight, but in the heat of battle and confusion it demonstrates a clear head.

11. At the time, if a person who did not make his living from writing sold all rights in a book to a publisher, the agreement could be deemed a sale and transfer of property. It made Eisenhower a relatively wealthy man. He and Mamie had not accumulated any significant savings beforehand and had just spent most of what they did have on a new automobile.

12. Nicholas Murray Butler, "Five Evidences of an Education," *Background Readings in American Education* U.S. Department of Education (Washington, D.C.: U.S. Government Printing Office, 1965), p. 41.

13. Eisenhower, *Mandate for Change,* p. 318. Eisenhower claimed that if he could have foreseen the negative reaction to his *not* defending Marshall, he would *not* have deleted the paragraph in question. But the plain truth is that McCarthy's allegations were completely unfounded and needed to be confronted, especially by the man who owed so much to General Marshall. In short, Eisenhower sold out, at least in this one instance, to political expediency.

14. Brooks Atkinson, editor, *Selected Writings of Ralph Waldo Emerson,* Modern Library, 1940, p. 918.

CHAPTER 11

1. Bradley's first child was stillborn. Elizabeth, whom they called Lee, married Henry Shaw Beukema, class of 1944, who was the son of Colonel Herman Beu-kema, class of 1915. The younger Beukema was killed in an air accident in 1954.

2. One of the more popular books that analyzed the role of several generals in this theater was Edgar F. Puryear's *Nineteen Stars.* This book studies Marshall, Eisenhower, Patton, and MacArthur. As such, it skips the key individual between Eisenhower and Patton, implying that Bradley's role had less significance.

3. Bradley, *General's Life,* pp. 296–301.

4. About twenty years ago, the Department of the Army began to realize that army and army group headquarters were more of a hindrance than a help. Accord-ingly, the organizational doctrine was changed so that the corps would normally be the highest-level field command, reporting to the theater or theater army com-mander. This change was accompanied by so-called throughput support using the-ater-level logistical commands.

5. In *A General's Life,* Bradley gives much credit to Paul R. Hawley, the Sur-geon General (of the army), for his magnificent work with the VA hospitals. To-day the reputation of these hospitals has fallen, perhaps because they are required by law to tend to many non-service-connected chronic medical problems of indi-gent veterans without the requisite funding or the glamour of some forms of medi-cine that attract the best doctors.

6. Cedric Worth, a former Hollywood script writer and aide to Assistant Secretary of the Navy Daniel A. Kimball, concocted a "document" that financially linked Secretary of Defense Louis Johnson with Consolidated-Vultee Corporation, the manufacturer of the B-36 bomber. These unsubstantiated allegations were leaked to Representative James E. Van Zandt, who then demanded a congressional investigation. That investigation uncovered the ruse and left the navy in an untenable position.

7. Bradley, *A General's Life,* p. 511.

8. Bradley was promoted to General of the Army on September 20, 1950, about twelve weeks after the war broke out in Korea.

9. In 1945, Truman had remarked in his private diary that MacArthur was worse than the Cabots or Lodges because the latter at least coordinated their plans before telling God what to do; whereas MacArthur "tells God right off."

10. Most of *A Soldier's Story* was written by his wartime aide Major Chet Hansen, a fact acknowledged in that book.

11. Bradley, *A General's Life,* pp. 205, 210. Bradley said that General Mark Clark "seemed false somehow, too eager to impress, too hungry for the limelight, promotions, and personal publicity." General Jacob Devers was regarded as "garrulous, egotistical, shallow, intolerant, not very smart, and much too inclined to rush off half-cocked." Elsewhere, he stated that Eisenhower was a general "with rare political talents" but whose performance on the battlefield was lacking. That was true in North Africa and for the first few months of OVERLORD, but Bradley owed much of his rise to fame to Eisenhower (and he does praise him elsewhere in the book). In addition, Bradley's comments on Patton tend to be scathing or neutral at best, but then, so were Patton's comments on Bradley in his own diaries.

The author wrote to General James A. Van Fleet, who was the last surviving member of the West Point class of 1915, on this matter. He replied briefly (June 15, 1992) that he had never *heard* General Bradley make such remarks (although he had reviewed the book in manuscript form). It should also be noted that the part of Bradley's book containing these remarks was not compiled until after Bradley died and, thus, he had no opportunity to expunge them even if he had made them during his discussions with Mr. Blair.

Interestingly, Harry Truman made several unfounded allegations in his old age. For example, as reported in *Plain Speaking* (pp. 339–40), he claimed that Eisenhower planned to divorce his wife and marry Kay Summersby but that he was stopped only by General Marshall's threat to ruin his career if he did. Bradley, while making a point of criticizing Eisenhower's relationship with Summersby, states that he did not believe Truman's allegation. Moreover, no other historian has been able to substantiate it. The point is that when one grows old and disabled, it is quite possible for an individual with integrity to believe and say bitter things that have little or no basis in fact.

CHAPTER 12

1. Ladd, *Commandoes and Rangers,* p. 288.

2. Mitchell's award was originally a special gold medal bestowed in the name of Congress. In time, both Congress and the Department of Defense came to

regard it as a Medal of Honor and listed it as such in their respective official records, albeit more by osmosis than by any formal redesignation. None of the other special gold medals awarded by Congress, including those given to other military figures, have ever been so transformed.

3. Hart, *Strategy*, p. 19.

4. Towed to Pearl Harbor, the *Yorktown* underwent the fastest major repair in naval history. Fourteen hundred men rotated working on her for ninety-six continuous hours, enabling this ship to participate in the battle of Midway.

5. Greenfield, *Command Decisions*, pp. 365–82.

6. The idea behind the operation was to sail into Istanbul (then Constantinople) and scare Turkey into backing off from her relationship with Germany, which would then cause Germany to quit France: in all, a convoluted domino theory.

7. Clausewitz, *On War*, p. 572. *Army Field Manual 100–5* put the case this way: "Unless it is strategically decisive, every operation will sooner or later reach a point where the strength of the attacker no longer significantly exceeds that of the defender, and beyond which continued offensive operations therefore risk overextension, counterattack, and defeat. In operational theory, this point is called the culminating point. The art of attack at all levels is to achieve decisive objectives *before* the culminating point is reached. Conversely, the art of defense is to hasten the culmination of the attack, recognize its advent, and be prepared to go over the offense when it arrives" (p. 182).

CHAPTER 13

1. The prime minister, like every member of Parliament, is elected from a district. Each party then elects its own leader. The prime minister is the leader so elected from the party in power.

2. King and Whitehill, *Fleet Admiral King*, pp. 235–36.

3. Franklin Research Institute, *Art and Requirements of Command*, vols. 2, 3, and 4.

4. Irving, *War Between the Generals*, pp. 185, 191, 240, 313, 346, 353, 387–88, 392, 404, 406–7, 412. Jean Gordon committed suicide (in New York) two weeks after Patton died in an automobile accident (December 1945). According to Irving, Patton frequently talked about this affair with Major General Everett S. Hughes, his West Point classmate, who served on Eisenhower's staff. (General Hughes graduated from West Point with the class of 1908, Patton's original class. Patton was turned back to the class of 1909 after failing mathematics.) Apparently, a number of general officers, not just Patton, had their mistresses brought over to Europe as Red Cross "donut girls." Irving drew his information directly from Hughes' diary, which is in the Manuscript Division of the Library of Congress. Most authors writing about Patton either do not say anything about this matter or gingerly waltz around it, saying such things as "Jean and he were very close" or "Beatrice [Patton's wife] wrote and told him that Jean was coming over for a visit," and so forth. In reality, Beatrice was furious and Patton himself admitted that he caught hell when he got back to the states for a brief visit shortly after the war (in July 1945).

5. Manchester, *American Caesar*, p. 716.

6. Nimitz made it quite clear to King on a number of occasions that should he die, Spruance was to be his successor. Additionally, Nimitz intentionally kept

Spruance away from the surrender ceremony aboard the *Missouri*. The high command was concerned that the Japanese might unleash a *kamikaze* attack, and, thus, renew the war against the United States without its senior military leadership. If this were to happen, the admiral wanted to ensure that his most capable subordinate would be spared.

7. Patton, *War as I Knew It*, p. 346.

8. "Equality? None for Me, Thanks." *Mensa Bulletin* (November 1991): pp. 4–5.

9. Eisenhower, *At Ease*, p. 388. This was part of his Guildhall address in London, June 12, 1945. The quotation corrects a minor syntax error by shifting the expression "in his memories" from the middle to the end of the sentence in which it appeared. See also Eisenhower's comments in *Crusade in Europe*, especially p. 314.

CHAPTER 14

1. At the time of Pearl Harbor, King supposedly said, "When the big crises arise, they send for the sons of bitches." At the end of the war, he was asked if this were true. His reply was negative; but he added that he would have said it if he had thought of it at the time.

2. Halsey came to the defense of his classmate Husband Kimmel and maintained that view for the rest of his life. He felt that Kimmel had done his best under the circumstances. For it was Kimmel who sent Halsey to seek out a potential Japanese attacking force, thereby saving the carriers from destruction.

3. Cohen and Gooch, *Military Misfortunes*, pp. 59–94. See also King and Whitehill, *Fleet Admiral King*, pp. 445–476; and Keegan, *Price of Admiralty*, pp. 213–65. Early in the war, German "wolf packs" wreaked havoc on some convoys; but within two years Germany was losing more submarines than the merchant ships that its submarines were sinking.

4. The direct-invasion plan, scheduled for 1943, was code-named ROUNDUP. There was also a plan to conduct the invasion in 1942, code-named SLEDGEHAMMER; but this was a contingency plan to be used only if Hitler's regime started to crumble.

5. The fifteen-mile distance does not include the Cherbourg peninsula itself, which would increase that figure to about twenty-two miles. The breakout at St. Lo did not occur until July 31, exactly eight weeks after the Normandy landings. And it must be remembered that seventy-five percent of the German army was deployed on the Eastern front, and at least another five or ten percent in Italy.

6. Recall that General Marshall tried to reverse Roosevelt's empathy for Churchill's preference by throwing his weight behind Admiral King's desire to change the first priority to the Pacific theater. By this point, Roosevelt had developed such immense respect for the general that he would not confront him directly over this informal mutiny. Rather, he simply asked for detailed plans, which he knew Marshall could not produce in the time remaining. Roosevelt had a very, very great mind, one that may not be fully appreciated until many generations have passed.

7. Halsey and Bryan, *Admiral Halsey's Story*, p. 216.

8. Japan's overture to the Soviet Union to act as a mediator in a negotiated settlement stipulated that Japan be allowed to keep some of its conquered territories. The United States flatly rejected that proposition for the obvious reason.

9. The mountainous spine of the Korean peninsula eliminated the potential for a good east-west defensive line in general, but certain sections were less disadvantageous than others for this purpose.

10. Gunther, *Riddle of MacArthur*, pp. 222–23.

CHAPTER 15

1. The role of the service chiefs in wartime now concentrates on wholesale administration, training, and supply. The critical decisions are more or less in the hands of joint commands staffed by representatives of all the services.

2. General Bradley dedicated *A General's Life* to his second wife, Kitty Buhler, and said that she had on one occasion saved his life (by CPR). Hence, this second marriage, commenced at age seventy-three, seems to have been idyllic for the two of them. However, relationships of the second Mrs. Bradley with those who worked with the general, as he became increasingly invalided, were on occasion less than idyllic.

3. One possible explanation of King's caustic personality and arrogance is alcohol. He was the hardest drinker among the ten principals, although he limited his intake during World War II to beer and wine. Moreover, this idea finds correlation among the others. Halsey was also a heavy drinker to the point of saying that he did not trust another officer (with certain exceptions) who did *not* drink, although he voluntarily went on the wagon during his year at flight school. Also, when he was promoted to fleet admiral, one of his first remarks was that he hoped the extra stripe on his sleeve did not interfere with his drinking arm. Further, his heavy drinking may have exacerbated his wife's mental condition.

On the army side, Pershing initially was a heavy drinker, and had become an insufferable martinet by the time he was assigned as a tactical officer at West Point. Apparently, he learned from the experience; although twenty years later he could still be caustic enough to at least once evoke the rage of his aide Colonel Marshall. Arnold was also a heavy drinker during the early part of his career, and several of his enemies (including Roosevelt's aide "Pa" Watson) used that reputation in an attempt to get rid him in the years just before World War II. The long-term consequence was that Arnold often turned caustic toward his subordinates and grew very insensitive to his wife and children (although he never ceased trying to make amends). Arnold's daughter, Lois, also drank heavily; and at least one of King's daughters became an alcoholic. By contrast, Leahy, Marshall, Nimitz, Eisenhower, and Bradley neither consumed much alcohol nor exhibited any serious character flaws, although two of them had well-known tempers.

This leaves MacArthur, who had serious character flaws but did not drink much. On the other hand, he was rarely caustic. Rather, his problems stemmed from an egotism that was clearly in evidence by the time he was a cadet. Put another way, he drank from the nectar of the gods, reading too much Homer and not enough Thucydides.

CHAPTER 16

1. Churchill, *Memoirs*, p. 1.

2. Thucydides, *History of the Peloponnesian War*, p. 403.

SOURCES

BOOKS

Acheson, Dean. *Present at the Creation: My Years in the State Department.* New York: W. W. Norton, 1969.

Adams, Henry H. *Witness to Power: The Life of Fleet Admiral William D. Leahy.* Annapolis: Naval Institute Press, 1985.

Albion, R. G. *Makers of Naval Policy, 1798–1947.* Annapolis: Naval Institute Press, 1980.

Ambrose, Stephen E. *The Supreme Commander: The War Years of General Dwight D. Eisenhower.* Garden City, N.Y.: Doubleday, 1969.

Arnold, H. H. *Global Mission.* New York: Harper & Brothers, 1949.

Asprey, Robert B. *War in the Shadows: The Guerrilla in History.* 2 vols. Garden City, N.Y.: Doubleday, 1975.

Bernstein, Barton J., and Allen J. Matusow, eds. *The Truman Administration: A Documentary History.* New York: Harper & Row, 1966.

Bland, Larry I., ed. *The Papers of George Catlett Marshall,* Vol. 1, *The Soldierly Spirit, December 1880–June 1939.* Baltimore: Johns Hopkins University Press, 1981.

Bradley, Omar N., and Clay Blair. *A General's Life.* New York: Simon and Schuster, 1983.

Bradley, Omar N. *A Soldier's Story of the Allied Campaigns from Tunis to the Elbe.* New York: Henry Holt, 1951.

Brodie, Bernard. *War and Politics.* New York: Macmillan, 1973.

Buchanan, A. Russell. *The United States and World War II.* 2 Vols. New York: Harper & Row, 1964.

Buell, Thomas B. *Master of SeaPower: A Biography of Fleet Admiral Ernest J. King.* Boston: Little, Brown, 1980.

———. *The Quiet Warrior: A Biography of Admiral Raymond A. Spruance.* Annapolis: Naval Institute Press, 1987.

Burns, James MacGregor. *Roosevelt: The Soldier of Freedom.* New York: Harcourt, Brace Jovanovich, 1970.

Butcher, Harry C. *My Three Years with Eisenhower*. New York: Simon and Schuster, 1946.

Catton, Bruce. *The War Lords of Washington*. New York: Harcourt Brace, 1948.

Churchill, Winston S. *Memoirs of the Second World War*. Boston: Houghton Mifflin, 1959.

Clausewitz, Carl von. *On War*. Edited and translated by Michael Howard and Peter Paret. Princeton: Princeton University Press, 1976.

Coffey, Thomas M. *Hap: The Story of the U.S. Air Force and the Man Who Built It*. New York: Viking, 1982.

Cohen, Eliot A., and John Gooch. *Military Misfortunes: The Anatomy of Failure in War*. New York: Free Press, 1990.

Dixon, Norman. *On the Psychology of Military Incompetence*. New York: Basic Books, 1976.

Drea, Edward J. *MacArthur's ULTRA: Code Breaking and the War Against Japan, 1942–1945*. Lawrence: University Press of Kansas, 1992.

Durant, Will, and Ariel Durant. *The Lessons of History*. New York: Simon and Schuster, 1968.

Eisenhower, Dwight D. *At Ease: Stories I Tell Friends*. Garden City, N.Y.: Doubleday, 1967.

———. *Crusade in Europe*. Garden City, N.Y.: Doubleday, 1948.

———. *Mandate for Change, 1953–1956*. Garden City, N.Y.: Doubleday, 1963.

Goldhurst, Richard. *Pipe Clay and Drill. John J. Pershing: The Classic American Soldier*. New York: Crowell, 1977.

Gosnell, Harold F. *Truman's Crises: A Political Biography of Harry S. Truman*. Westport, Conn.: Greenwood Press, 1980.

Greenfield, Kent Roberts, ed. *Command Decisions*. Washington, D.C.: U.S. Government Printing Office, 1959.

Gunther, John. *The Riddle of MacArthur*. New York: Harper & Brothers, 1950.

Hall, George M. *Geopolitics and the Decline of Empire*. Jefferson, N.C.: McFarland, 1990.

Halsey, William F., Jr., and Joseph Bryan III. *Admiral Halsey's Story*. Washington, D.C.: Zenger, 1980.

Hart, B. H. Liddell. *History of the Second World War*. New York: G. P. Putnam's, 1970.

———. *Strategy*. 2 ed., rev. New York: Praeger, 1968.

Hartmann, Frederick H. *The Relations of Nations*, 6 ed. New York: Macmillan, 1983.

Howarth, Stephen. *To Shining Sea: A History of the United States Navy, 1775–1991*. New York: Random House, 1991.

The Iliad of Homer. Vol. 4 of Great Books of the Western World. 1 ed. Chicago: Encyclopaedia Britannica, 1952.

Irving, David. *The War between the Generals*. London: Allen Lane, 1981.

James, D. Clayton. *The Years of MacArthur*. Vol. 1, *1880–1941*, and Vol. 2, *1941–1945*. Boston: Houghton Mifflin, 1970–75.

Kecskemeti, Paul. *Strategic Surrender: The Politics and Victory and Defeat*, Palo Alto: Stanford University Press, 1958.

Keegan, John. *The Mask of Command*. New York: Viking, 1987.

———. *The Price of Admiralty*. New York: Viking, 1988.

Kennedy, Paul. *The Rise and Fall of the Great Powers*. New York: Random House, 1987.

King, Ernest J., and Walter Muir Whitehill. *Fleet Admiral King: A Naval Record*. New York: W. W. Norton, 1952.

Kohn, George C. *Dictionary of Wars*. New York: Facts on File, 1986.

Ladd, James. *Commandoes and Rangers of World War II*. New York: St. Martin's, 1978.

Laffin, John. *Links of Leadership: Thirty Centuries of Command*. London: George Harrap, 1967.

Leahy, William D. *I Was There*. New York: McGraw-Hill, 1950.

Leopold, Richard W. *The Growth of American Foreign Policy*. New York: Knopf, 1962.

Loewenheim, Francis L., et al., eds. *Roosevelt and Churchill: Their Secret Wartime Correspondence*. New York: Saturday Review Press, 1975.

Love, Robert William, Jr. *The Chiefs of Naval Operation*. Annapolis: Naval Institute Press, 1980.

Lyon, Peter. *Eisenhower: Portrait of the Hero*. Boston: Little, Brown, 1974.

Mahan, Alfred T. *The Influence of Sea Power Upon History, 1660–1783*. Boston: Little, Brown, 1890.

MacArthur, Douglas. *Reminiscences*. New York: McGraw-Hill, 1964.

Manchester, William. *American Caesar: Douglas MacArthur, 1880–1964*. Boston: Little, Brown, 1978.

Marshall, Katherine Tupper. *Together: Annals of an Army Wife*. New York: Tupper and Love, 1946.

Matloff, Maurice, and Edwin M. Snell. *The War Department: Strategic Planning for Coalition Warfare, 1941–1942*. Washington, D.C.: Office of the Chief of Military History, Department of the Army, 1953.

Medal of Honor Recipients, 1863–1973. Washington, D.C.: U.S. Government Printing Office, 1973.

Memoirs by Harry S. Truman: Year of Decisions. Garden City, N.Y.: Doubleday, 1955.

Memoirs by Harry S. Truman: Years of Trial and Hope. Garden City, N.Y.: Doubleday, 1956.

Merrill, James M. *A Sailor's Admiral: A Biography of William F. Halsey*. New York: Thomas Y. Crowell, 1976.

Miller, Merle. *Plain Speaking: An Oral Biography of Harry S. Truman*. New York: Berkley, 1973.

Milward, Alan S. *Economy and Society, 1939–1945*. Berkeley: University of California Press, 1979.

Morison, Samuel Eliot. *The Two Ocean War: A Short History of the United States Navy in the Second World War*. Boston: Little, Brown, 1963.

Palmer, Frederick. *John J. Pershing: General of the Armies*. Harrisburg, Penn.: The Military Service Publishing Company, 1948.

Patton, George S., Jr. *War as I Knew It*. New York: Houghton Mifflin, 1947.

Perry, Mark. *Four Stars*. Boston: Houghton Mifflin, 1989.

Pershing, John J. *My Experiences in the World War*. 2 Vols. New York: Stokes, 1931.

Pogue, Forrest C. *Education of a General*. New York: Viking, 1963.
———. *George C. Marshall: Ordeal and Hope*. New York: Viking, 1965.
———. *George C. Marshall: Organizer of Victory, 1943–1945*. New York: Viking, 1973.
———. *George C. Marshall: Statesman, 1945–1959*. New York: Viking, 1987.
Potter, E. B. *Bull Halsey*. Annapolis: Naval Institute Press, 1985.
———. *Nimitz*. Annapolis: Naval Institute Press, 1976.
Puryear, Edgar F., Jr. *Nineteen Stars*. Washington, D.C.: Coiner, 1971.
Register of Graduates and Former Cadets, 1990: Dwight D. Eisenhower Centennial Edition. Edited by Paul W. Child, Jr. West Point: Association of Graduates, 1990.
Reynolds, Clark G. *Famous American Admirals*. New York: Van Nostrand Reinhold, 1978.
Smith, W. Bedell. *Eisenhower's Six Great Decisions: Europe, 1944–1945*. New York: Longmans, Green, 1956.
Smythe, Donald. *Guerrilla Warrior: The Early Life of John J. Pershing*. New York: Scribner's, 1973.
Stoessinger, John G. *Why Nations Go to War*. New York: St. Martin's, 1974.
Summers, Harry G., Jr. *On Strategy: The Vietnam War in Context*. Carlisle Barracks, Penn.: Strategic Studies Institute, 1981.
Summary of Selected Military Campaigns. West Point: U.S. Military Academy, 1958.
Thucydides. *The History of the Peloponnesian War*. Vol. 6 of *Great Books of the Western World*. 1 Ed. Chicago: Encyclopaedia Britannica, 1952.
Toland, John. *The Rising Sun*. New York: Random House, 1970.
Tuchman, Barbara W. *The Guns of August*. New York: Macmillan, 1962.
———. *The March of Folly: From Troy to Vietnam*. London: Michael Joseph, 1984.
U.S. Army Field Manual 100–5: Operations. Washington, D.C.: U.S. Government Printing Office, 1986.
Vandiver, Frederick E. *Black Jack: The Life and Times of John J. Pershing*. College Station: Texas A & M University Press, 1977.
War Reports of General of the Army George C. Marshall, General of the Army H. H. Arnold, and Fleet Admiral Ernest J. King. Philadelphia: Lippincott, 1947.
Weigley, Russell F. *Eisenhower's Lieutenants: The Campaign of France and Germany*. 2 Vols. Bloomington: Indiana University Press, 1981.
The Works of Theodore Roosevelt. Vol. 18, *American Problems*. New York: Scribner's, 1925.

ACTS OF CONGRESS

General Statutes, Chapter 48, March 3, 1799.
General Statutes, Chapter 232, July 25, 1866.
General Statutes, Chapter 378, March 2, 1899.
Public Law 45, September 3, 1919.
Public Law 482, December 14, 1944.
Public Law 333, March 23, 1946.
Public Law 804, June 28, 1948.
Private Law 957, September 18, 1950.

ARTICLES AND PAPERS

Andidora, Ronald. "The Autumn of 1944: Boldness Is Not Enough." *Parameters* (December 1987): 71–80.

Ambrose, Stephen E. "Eisenhower's Generalship." *Parameters* (June 1990): 2–12.

Blumenson, Martin. "America's World War II Leaders in Europe: Some Thoughts." *Parameters* (December 1989): 2–13.

———. "Eisenhower Then and Now: Fireside Reflections." *Parameters* (Summer 1991): 22–34.

Bradley, Omar. "Leadership." Reprinted in *To Get the Job Done: Readings in Leadership and Management,* U.S. Naval Institute, pp. 97–101.

Brement, Marshall. "Civilian-Military Relations in the Context of National Security Policymaking." *Naval War College Review* (Winter 1988): 27–32.

Calvert, Robert, Jr. "Drum, Drum: I Wish He Would Stop Beating His Own Drum." *Army* (September 1989): 56–60.

Cameron, Williams, E. "The Four 'Iron Laws' of Naval Protection of Merchant Shipping." *Naval War College Review* (May–June 1986): 35–50.

Clarke, Bruce, and John G. Hill. *Art and Requirements of Command.* Vol. 2, *Generalship Study.* Technical Report 1-191, prepared for the Office of the Director of Special Studies, Office of the Chief of Staff, Department of the Army, April 1967.

Clarke, Bruce C. "Leadership—Commandership—Generalship—Followership." *Armor* (September–October 1963): 16–19.

Freeman, Douglas. "Leadership." *Naval War College Review* (March–April 1979): 3–10.

Gatchel, Theodore L. "Can a Battle Be Lost in the Mind of a Commander?" *Naval War College Review* (January–February 1985): 96–99.

Hall, George M. "Culminating Points." *Military Review* (July 1989): 79–86.

———. "Military Operations: Catchall, Catch-22." *Army* (November 1989): 16–23.

Heskett, James L. "Logistics—Essential to Strategy." *Harvard Business Review* (November–December, 1977): 85–96.

Hyde, Arthur P. S. "Douglas MacArthur." *Assembly* (October 1942): 3.

Kingseed, Cole C. "Eisenhower's Prewar Anonymity: Myth or Reality?" *Parameters* (Autumn 1991): 87–98.

Levinson, Harry. "The Abrasive Personality." *Harvard Business Review* (May–June 1978): 86–94.

Mahan, Lyle Evans. "My Parents, Rear Admiral and Mrs. Alfred Thayer Mahan." *Naval War College Review* (Autumn 1990): 81–97.

Nicholson, Robert J. "West Point's First Captains." *Assembly* (Winter 1970): 2–5.

Palmer, Michael A. "Lord Nelson: Master of Command." *Naval War College Review* (Winter 1988): 105–16.

Pardew, James W., Jr. "The Iraqi Army's Defeat in Kuwait." *Parameters* (Winter 1991–92): 17–23.

Potter, E. B. "The Command Personality: Some American Naval Officers of World War II." Paper presented at the Second Military History Symposium, *Command and Commanders in Modern Warfare,* U.S. Air Force Academy, May 2–3, 1968.

Sackton, Frank J. "The Gentle Conqueror: MacArthur in Japan." *Army* (September 1990): 62–72.

Shortal, John F. "MacArthur's Fireman: Robert L. Eichelberger." *Parameters* (Autumn 1986): 58–67.

Skinner, Wickhan, and W. Earl Sasser. "Managers with Impact: Versatile and Inconsistent." *Harvard Business Review* (November–December, 1977): 140–48.

Slim, Sir William. "Higher Command in War." Address at the U.S. Army Command & General Staff College, April 8, 1952.

Smith, Richard K. "Not a Success, but a Triumph: Eighty Years since Kitty Hawk." *Naval War College Review* (November–December 1983): 4–20.

Stimson, Henry L. "The Decision To Use the Atomic Bomb." *Harper's Magazine* (February 1947): 97–107.

Ward, Geoffrey C. "Douglas MacArthur: An American Soldier." *National Geographic Magazine* (March 1992): 54–83.

Zais, Mitchell M. "Strategic Vision and Strength of Will: Imperatives for Theater Command." *Parameters* (Winter 1985): 59–63.

Zaleznik, Abraham. "Managers and Leaders: Are They Different." *Harvard Business Review* (May–June 1977): 67–78.

———. "Power and Politics in Organizational Life." *Harvard Business Review* (May–June 1970): 47–60.

INDEX

The suffix "f" indicates a reference to a caption or figure. The suffix "n" followed by a number indicates a reference to an endnote. When the same page has two endnotes with the same number, the chapter number precedes the note number in parentheses.

About the Author

GEORGE M. HALL graduated from West Point in 1958 and served five years in the Corps of Engineers. He left the service to teach, returning to active duty from 1977–1982. He is a graduate of the Air War College, the Naval War College, and the Army War College; he earned his doctorate at American University. He is a frequent contributor to professional journals of all three services, and presently teaches at Pima Community College in Tucson, Arizona.